CHILDREN'S FRIENDSHIP TRAINING

Fred Frankel, Ph.D., and Robert Myatt, Ph.D.

Routledge
Taylor & Francis Group
New York   London

Routledge is an imprint of the
Taylor & Francis Group, an informa business

Routledge
Taylor & Francis Group
270 Madison Avenue
New York, NY 10016

Routledge
Taylor & Francis Group
2 Park Square
Milton Park, Abingdon
Oxon OX14 4RN

© 2003 by Taylor & Francis Group, LLC
Routledge is an imprint of Taylor & Francis Group

Printed in the United States of America on acid-free paper
10 9 8 7 6 5 4 3 2
International Standard Book Number-13: 978-1-58391-308-6 (Softcover)

Library of Congress Cataloging-in-Publication Data

Frankel, Fred.
    Children's friendship training / Fred Frankel and Robert Myatt.
    p.   cm.
    Includes bibliographical references and index
    ISBN 1-58391-308-4 (pbk. : alk. paper)
    1. Behavior therapy for children. 2. Social skills in children—Study and teaching. 3. Friendship in children.
    I. Myatt, Robert. II. Title.
    RJ505.B4 .F736   2002
    618.92'89142—dc21   2002009812

**Visit the Taylor & Francis Web site at
http://www.taylorandfrancis.com**

**and the Routledge Web site at
http://www.routledge.com**

Contents

PART I
BACKGROUND

8/14 (1)

8/21 (2)

8/28 (3)

Foreword

peer network

The intervention described in this volume was developed in a clinical setting with patients who were paying for treatment and hoping that their children would benefit. Our previously published studies reported the results of diagnostically homogeneous groups of children having attention deficit/hyperactivity disorder (ADHD) with or without comorbid oppositional defiant disorder (ODD) or subjects who qualified for no research diagnosis. In actuality, we have presented this treatment to over 800 children since 1991. Only a small proportion of these children fell neatly into research categories and could be reported in research journals.

We have adopted a process-oriented perspective of social competence (Taylor & Asher, 1984) in which we select important social interaction processes and address the specific components that contribute to successful social transactions. Our goal is to give children the skills to have mutually satisfying social interactions with peers, which lead to higher regard within the peer group and the development of satisfying best friendships. The program described in this book addresses the friendless child's relationships with peers in four crucial areas:

1. Abating the effects of the child's reputation within his current peer group (cf. Bierman, 1989) by reducing intrusive and inappropriate behaviors.
2. Diminishing the importance of the rejecting peer group for the child by giving him or her skills to expand his or her peer network.
3. Instructing parents and children as to how to work together to promote more successful *play dates*. (We define play date as an appointment made between two children to play in the home of one of them). It was hypothesized that this would allow the development of best friendships despite a nonfunctional peer network. Best friendships might promote continued acquisition of social skills (cf. Hartup, 1983).
4. Supporting the child's efforts to "lay low" in a rejecting peer group where he or she has a bad reputation. The results of Nangle, Erdley, and Gold (1996) suggests it is relatively easy to decrease a bad reputation but harder to increase liking by peers. Avoiding continuing provocation from peers was the goal in improving the child's competence at nonaggressive responses to teasing and to conflicts with children and adults.

2003

process oriented perspective of social competence
social interaction processes → address specific components

Preface

This book is about building bridges: bridges between what clinical professionals know about interventions for social skills and what developmental psychologists know about children's friendships; bridges between research on effective treatment for the child without friends and professionals interested in effectively helping these children; bridges between parents who are worried about their children's friendships and don't know what to do and professionals who want to use parents more effectively in the treatment; bridges between what children learn about making and keeping friends in treatment and what they see socially competent children doing at school; bridges between what parents learn through social skills training and how they can apply it to help their child make sustainable friendships in their neighborhoods.

I first realized something was missing in the social skills groups I offered, when I saw my wife networking with other parents to make play dates for my then 6-year-old child. I had read nothing about this in the social skills training literature. Together, Bob Myatt and I worked out a way for us to teach parents to do this while teaching their children to effectively use this. Although adults operate primarily by the golden rule, children also operate by what I call the prime directive of childhood: Play with others who are fun to play with. Our job was to make children more fun to play with.

—F. F.

*　*　*

My first exposure to the power and limitations of social skills training took place in my role as a research assistant at a VA hospital in 1981. I was able to see the many practical benefits that a comprehensive social skills training program provided to a very challenging clinical population—chronic schizophrenic veterans. However, the experience also underscored the shortcomings of this type of program and the need for constant revision, development, and enhancement of the intervention. Through the years, I have had the opportunity to provide social skills training to teenagers who have become involved in the criminal justice system, depressed/suicidal adolescents who have been psychiatrically hospitalized, children on an inpatient psychiatric ward, and shy/withdrawn children in an elementary school setting.

While completing my dissertation, I saw fourth- and fifth-grade children who were experiencing high levels of clinical depression and beginning to develop suicidal ideation related to their social deficits and social isolation. During my psychology training at the UCLA Neuropsychiatric Institute, I had the opportunity to begin what has turned out to be a 14-year partnership and journey with Fred Frankel, Ph.D., to develop a comprehensive social skills training program for children. Throughout the years, we have sought feedback from the children, their parents and teachers, the psychology interns, social work trainees, and child psychiatry fellows we have trained, and professional colleagues who have referred their young clients to us. This book represents a compilation and distillation of all that we have learned. We hope that it will be helpful to other clinicians who recognize the importance of providing friendship training to their clients.

—R. M.

Purpose and Organization of This Manual

A Self-Contained Guide for the Clinician

The purpose of this book is to provide a complete, self-contained guide for the clinician who wants to model a social skills program after our approach. It is hard for many clinicians to change gears and learn new techniques. Although we have designed the program as an integrated entity, clinicians may prefer to try it piecemeal. We don't feel this will ruin the intervention but will rather add spice to what a clinician is more comfortable doing. We have enjoyed leading the parent and the child sessions and are confident that other clinicians will find this rewarding.

Training Socially Valid Behaviors

An intervention has *social validity* when it targets behaviors that discriminate children having peer difficulties from children who do not. Social validity has been an important influence in the development of our training modules. Few components used in social skills training studies have been assessed for social validity (Budd, 1985). Evidence suggests that focus on socially valid behaviors enhances the likelihood that children will be better accepted by peers after training. For instance, cooperation with peers and peer support skills (e.g., active listening skills) have been shown to differentiate accepted from rejected children (see Chap. 9.2, for a more com-

plete discussion of categories of peer acceptance and peer sociometrics). Studies that trained these skills demonstrated improved peer sociometric ratings (Bierman & Furman, 1984; Gresham & Nagle, 1980; Hepler & Rose, 1988; Oden & Asher, 1977; Tiffen & Spence, 1986). Another example is Oden and Asher (1977), who focused on coaching children to have fun and make sure the game partner had fun as well. The children chosen were initially the least popular within their class, as derived from peer sociometric ratings. At follow-up, researchers found lasting improvement in peer acceptance.

Training socially valid behaviors may help in three ways. First, children may be better able to focus on key behaviors to observe in their social milieu. Second, they are more likely to observe better accepted children perform these behaviors with desirable social outcomes. Third, they are more likely to have successful outcomes when they perform these behaviors (if performed in situations in which they have no prior negative reputation to interfere with the outcome). The approach taken in this volume is to present the evidence establishing the social validity of behaviors targeted for each intervention session and then to describe ways we have found successful in getting children to employ them outside of the treatment situation.

Maintaining Treatment Integrity

Treatment integrity is defined as the correspondence between session plans and the way treatment is actually delivered. *Clinician drift* is a phenomenon that decreases treatment integrity. Clinician drift is defined as the tendency of a clinician to change features of an intervention each time it is presented. We have been able to maintain treatment integrity and avoid clinician drift by maintaining an outline of each treatment module and collecting pre and post data on each patient (when parents have consented). The percentage of patients showing improvement is provided to our clinicians after each treatment group is completed. Clinicians know that if this percentage falls below 90% of parent report or 70% of teacher report, they are asked to examine any features they may have changed. In this way, we have held ourselves accountable to maintain adequate levels of positive treatment response.

We believe that a treatment manual, such as the present volume, is the best way to ensure faithful delivery of empirically validated treatments (Wilson, 1996). Manuals may benefit both novice and experienced clinicians (Chambless, 1996; Eifert, Schulte, Zvolensky, Lejuez, & Lau, 1997). Detailed manuals have been found to produce greater positive intervention effects (Weisz & Weisz, 1990).

Organization of This Manual

This book is divided into three major sections. Part I presents the rationale for the present treatment. Part II presents methods to help the clinician compose groups. Section III devotes a chapter to each treatment session in the order the sessions are given. The empirical foundation of each module is briefly summarized. This is to allow parent session leaders to be sufficiently versed in the theory to provide guidance to parents and to speak extemporaneously to the parent groups on the rare occasion in which the material does not fill the entire parent session. The description of methods also includes clinical examples of the "average cases" as well as the instructive exceptions (Hibbs, Clarke, Hectman, et al., 1997). The important points are outlined in the parent and child session outlines for quick reference by group leaders during each session. Our field-tested parent handouts are also included. These are meant to be self-contained, abbreviated descriptions to which parents can refer quickly between sessions. The clinician should thoroughly review the contents of Sections II and III before beginning the first treatment groups and use the Parent and Child Session Plans while delivering treatment.

We have trained six other child group leaders and seven different parent group leaders and have replicated improvement levels. This suggests that the effects extend beyond a *founder's effect,* in which only the original developers see a high level of improvement. Your experiences will hopefully continue to confirm this.

Related Resources

A parent self-help book based on these modules (Frankel, 1996) is also available as a supplement, not a replacement, for parent participation. It can also be used as an extended program brochure, a means to give parents some immediate help while they are waiting for the start of the next treatment group, or a referral for parents having children too young to benefit from the intervention.

BACKGROUND

P A R T I

CHAPTER

1

Reasons to Treat Peer Relationship Problems

Operating within an outpatient child psychiatry clinical training program, we are constantly struck by the relatively little attention paid by many clinicians to the peer relationships of their patients. Children in therapy are twice as likely to have peer problems than children not in therapy (Malik & Furman, 1993; Rutter & Garmezy, 1983). Peer problems have been only peripherally included in diagnostic schema. Often, when the presenting psychopathology has been treated, the peer problem doesn't go away and yet is usually not addressed by further treatment. It is estimated that as many as 10% of children without any known risk factors have problems making and keeping friendships (Asher, 1990). In a 1-year follow-up study of 10-year-olds, Bukowski, Hoza, and Newcomb (1991, cited in Hartup, 1996) found that having friends had subsequent positive effects on self-esteem. Peer problems in childhood have effects on functioning in later life. In their 12-year follow-up study, Bagwell, Newcomb, and Bukowski (1998) found that peer rejection and lack of at least one best friend in childhood contributed equally to psychopathology of young adults.

We define a *quality friendship* as "a mutual relationship formed with affection and commitment between two individuals who consider themselves as equals."[1] Maintaining quality friendships is perhaps the single most salient measure of a child's successful adjustment. In order to have quality friendships, children must suspend egoism, treat the friend as an equal, and deal effectively with conflict (Hartup, 1996). Friends share a "climate of agreement" much greater than that among nonfriends (Gottman, 1983; Hartup & Laursen, 1993). Children's problem solving is generally better when done with friends as compared with nonfriends (Azmitia & Montgomery, 1993). Friendships may moderate the negative impact of divorce (Wasserstein & La Greca, 1996). Friendships are the context for learning social skills, learning about and feeling good about oneself, and providing resources for support (Hartup, 1993). According to Malik and Furman (1993), "peers are not only playmates but also confidantes, allies and sources of support in times of stress" (p. 1303).

---

[1]The best definition of friendship we have encountered. Unfortunately, the original author for this has been lost to us.

PART I
CHAPTER
2

Assessment of Outcomes

It is difficult to evaluate the research literature on social skills training without first examining the measures used to demonstrate outcome. A frequent misconception among parents and therapists about formal outcome assessment within a clinical context is that assessment is always associated with some kind of research. Although rarely done, formal outcome assessment should play an integral part in clinical practice for the following reasons:

1. We and others have noted that even the best clinicians are subject to clinician drift over time. Perhaps because creative clinicians get tired of delivering the same intervention repeatedly, they are constantly injecting new features. They may consider these new features acceptable variations on a standard treatment. We have also noticed that our clinicians can successfully present an approach 40 or 50 times but are thrown when it doesn't work quite as well just once. They may then modify their time-worn procedure without consideration of how successfully it usually has worked. We have detected these variations when outcome on teacher measures for a particular group drops (parent measures seem to be less sensitive to procedural variations).
2. We have attempted treatment upgrades on three occasions. On one attempt, we noticed that teacher outcome substantially worsened

when compared to the previous groups. We reverted back to our original approach and recaptured previous levels of positive teacher outcome.
3. Posttreatment teacher calls are completed usually within 3 weeks after the last treatment session. We have found that about 30% of parents will call for this feedback. When parents call for this posttreatment feedback, we use the occasion to encourage parents to maintain treatment gains.

Types of Outcome Assessment

There are six types of outcome assessment procedures used by researchers and clinicians: peer assessment, informal "clinical" indexes, ratings from the child patients, behavioral ratings, teacher reports, and parent ratings.

Informal clinical indexes of improvement, such as unstructured parent feedback, clinician ratings of child behavior changes in session, and the clinician's impressions global impression of change, have very little validity for the assessment of changes in peer acceptance of the rejected child: Parents are usually glad they brought their child to the groups and children almost always have a good time (or they leave and aren't around for the posttest). When effective behavioral control techniques are used within the

4

group, the children are better behaved. It is the generalization of these changes to the child's social environment that is of paramount importance.

As a training and clinical tool, we ask the child group leaders to rate improvement and then compare these ratings with formal parent and teacher measures. The correlation is close to 0. For instance, our clinicians will typically rate a child who disrupts the group or challenges the leader as unimproved. Yet parent and teacher ratings often show some benefit of treatment (this finding has served as impetus for our clinicians to persist with these children). The following subsections briefly review the types of formalized assessments that have been used to measure improvement in social skills training programs.

Assessment Using Peers Without Social Problems

Peer assessment entails having members of a peer group evaluate each other. According to Gresham and Stuart (1992), peer ratings are the most frequently employed types of peer-referenced assessment in research studies. Many researchers consider this form of assessment as the most valid because peers frequently observe each other and operate from a child's frame of reference (Daniels-Beirness, 1989). As Landau and Moore (1991) pointed out, children are more aware of interpersonal interactions of their peers than are teachers and parents.

Peer assessments are too cumbersome to use in typical clinical outpatient settings. For example, our outpatient program draws from more than 200 different schools. Visiting each school and setting up peer ratings for each patient would be a logistic nightmare. Peer assessments are presented here in order to help the reader to better understand and evaluate research studies and categories of peer acceptance (see Chap. 9) that are derived from them. Two types of peer assessment are ratings and nominations.

In a *peer nomination* procedure, a classroom of elementary school children are asked to list the other children in their class they would like to play with the most and the least (Dodge, Coie, Pettit, & Price, 1990). Peer status is tabulated for each child using *social preference* (number liked

nominations – number disliked nominations) and *social impact* scores (total number of nominations; Asher & Hymel, 1981; Coie & Dodge, 1983). Gresham and Stuart (1992) found that liked least nominations showed the most stability with test–retest correlations of .60. Extensive research (e.g., Coie & Dodge, 1983; Coie & Kupersmidt, 1983; Dodge, 1983) has indicated the stability of status and predictability of negative outcomes. There has been some concern that the negative nomination procedure might subsequently lead to more negative behavior toward low-status children (Asher & Hymel, 1981), although two studies have failed to show negative effects (Bell-Dolan, Foster, & Sikora, 1989; Bell-Dolan, Foster, & Christopher, 1992).

A *peer rating* procedure requires each child to rate each other child in his or her group using predefined criteria. A simple example is the "roster and rating" sociometric procedure (Singleton & Asher, 1977). Children are given rosters of all same-sex classmates and are asked to rate how much they like each one on a 5-point Likert scale with endpoint anchors of *like a lot* and *dislike a lot*. Other examples are, "How much does _____ get picked on?" and "How much does _____ cooperate?" (endpoint anchors would be *not at all* and *very much*). Average rating is tabulated for each child.

Rating procedures are more apt than nomination procedures to pick up children who have low visibility but are enjoyed as playmates (Asher & Hymel, 1981). The average rating received from classmates (or from same-sex classmates) is highly stable over time even with young children (Asher, Singleton, Tinsley, & Hymel, 1979), is sensitive to the effects of intervention (Ladd, 1981; Oden & Asher, 1977), but is also sensitive to variations in the wording of the criterion (Oden & Asher, 1977; Singleton & Asher, 1977). Another important advantage of the rating-scale method is that children are not required to list anyone as disliked. Due to the advantages and disadvantages of each type of peer assessment, we have used both in our 5-year National Institute for Mental Health (NIMH)-funded study (Frankel & Erhardt, 2001). Individual interviews take about 8 minutes per student and most children seem to enjoy doing them.

Ratings from Child Patients

Ratings from child patients are easily obtained, but show the least correlations with other assessments and may be susceptible to social desirability response set (Ledingham, Younger, Schwartzman, & Bergeron, 1982). Children's actual behavior may not correspond to their responses to queries about what they would do in hypothetical situations (Bearison & Gass, 1979; Damon, 1977). An example of this was a study by Grenell, Glass, and Katz (1987). They asked 15 boys diagnosed with attention deficit/hyperactivity disorder (ADHD) and 15 comparison boys what they thought they should do in 16 hypothetical situations. Adult judges rated their responses on friendliness, impulse control, assertiveness, and effectiveness in relationship enhancement. Raters also observed and rated them in free play, a cooperative puzzle task (where one boy was the worker and another was the helper), and a persuasion task (where they tried to persuade their partner to play their choice of game). Correlations of ratings of the responses to hypothetical situations with observed prosocial behavior were low (absolute value of correlations ranged from .37 to .43) although statistically significant.

Another example is the Preschool Interpersonal Problem Solving measure (PIPS; Spivack & Shure, 1974). The psychometric properties are adequate, although there are no normative data. Similar to the ratings of Grenell et al. (1987), the number and quality of solutions generated to various hypothetical situations are scored. However the content areas of the PIPS has been criticized as not representative of social problems encountered by preschoolers (Brochin & Wasik, 1992) and not adequately covering the domain of peer issues (Getz, Goldman, & Corsini, 1984). Others have suggested enhancements in responses to teasing (Feldman & Dodge, 1987) and management of conflict with other children (Brochin & Wasik, 1992).

Asking child patients to list who likes them seems also to be of limited value. Children without friends can usually list "friends" when asked (Hartup, 1996). Sociometrically rejected children were the least accurate in their judgments of who liked them, when compared to average and neglected status children (see Chap. 9, for more on these sociometric categories; MacDonald &

Cohen, 1995). On the other hand, asking child patients to rate peer behaviors yields more valid results. Whalen and Henker (1985) reported similarities between their summer camp cohorts of 24 children diagnosed with ADHD and 24 non-ADHD peers: Both cohorts rated their peers' negative behaviors similarly. Correlations between the cohorts ranged from .80 for "causes trouble" to .85 for "noisy." Correlations with teacher ratings were comparable for the cohort diagnosed with ADHD (.69) and those that were not (.65). Hinshaw and Melnick (1995) reported systematic distortions: Boys diagnosed with ADHD were less likely to give positive nominations to non-ADHD peers than the non-ADHD peers were. Behavioral ratings may therefore be useful outcome measures in contexts where children with peer problems are mixed together with peers without social problems.

Although we have avoided the use of ratings from child patients, assessment of self-esteem has been an exception, because the child is uniquely qualified to be asked about perceptions of self-competence. We have used the Piers-Harris Self Concept Scale (PHS).[2] The PHS is an 80-item yes–no self-report measure that takes about 20 minutes for a child to complete. Among instruments commonly used to measure self-esteem, the PHS has been regarded as the most psychometrically sound. The coverage of the relevant domain is adequate (Ross, 1992), and the factor structure of specific self-esteem scales is well-known (Hughes, 1984; Jeske, 1985). The PHS manual provides factor scores on six scales measuring specific self-esteem (Piers, 1984) and a Global score that is a weighted composite of items from the specific self-esteem factors. Among children scoring in the low range of PHS self-esteem at baseline (only about 20% of children enrolled in our groups), we have noticed that about 80% show some improvement on posttreatment assessment.

Behavioral Ratings

Behavioral ratings of negative peer behaviors by adult observers may provide a objective measure of an important aspect of peer relations. An example is a study by Pelham and Bender (1982).

[2]The domain of this assessment is very similar to the Harter scales (Harter, 1982), which may yield similar results.

They formed play groups of one child diagnosed with ADHD and four non-ADHD peers. The children played together for 36 minutes of arts and crafts (which involved sharing the same materials) and free play. Results showed that children diagnosed with ADHD were rated by observers as spending significantly more time in conversation and asking questions, and engaging in 2 to 10 times more negative behavior (e.g., loud repeated yelling, hitting, noncompliance, interrupting another's activity) than comparison children. Hinshaw and Melnick (1995) compared 101 boys diagnosed with ADHD with 80 non-ADHD peers during their participation in a summer camp. Observers rated several categories of behavior in free-play situations. Results showed that boys diagnosed with ADHD had significantly more rule violations, defiance, and disruptive behaviors than the non-ADHD cohort, regardless of the levels of aggression rated by teachers.

In contrast, behavioral ratings of prosocial events, such as, frequency of peer contact and percentage of time interacting with peers, have long been discredited as valid measures of peer adjustment (cf. Gottman, 1977). Correlations between these behavioral ratings and peer ratings have been low. Rate of peer interaction without consideration of quality of interaction is not related to measures of peer acceptance (Asher, Markell, & Hymel, 1981). For example, rejected children may "bug" others more in unsuccessful attempts at entry, whereas liked children may be successful on the first or second attempt (or take no for an answer, cf. Chap. 12). Behavioral measures of attempts at peer entry might therefore favor the rejected child. Valid behavioral measurement of treatment success may entail focus on "critical events" that occur too rarely to be observed under usual procedures (Bierman, Smoot, & Aumiller, 1993).

We have not employed behavioral observations in judging outcome to our interventions, due to severe limitations on their usefulness. Training observers and data reduction involve an extensive time commitment, with only limited reward within an outpatient clinical setting.

Teacher Reports

Teacher reports of peer relationships correspond more closely than any other informant to peer ratings (Glow & Glow, 1980). Hinshaw and Melnick (1995) found that asking teachers and parents to rate their child's popularity on a Likert scale from 1 (*extremely popular*) to 5 (*not at all*) correlated at .62 with each other and .43 with peer preference ratings. Teachers may be able to make finer differentiation than peers, but may not be able to observe important social contexts (i.e., how children behave without adults present) and may be biased by what they see in the classroom (Bierman et al., 1993). Teacher reports must be supplemented with standardized assessments using parents in order to tap into best friendships.

One of the most commonly used teacher report scales is the Pupil Evaluation Inventory (PEI; Pekarik, Prinz, Liebert, Weintraub, & Neil, 1976). It consists of 35 items, each rated as "describes child" or "does not describe child" by the child's teacher. The scales take about 5 minutes to complete. Withdrawal, Likability, and Aggression subscales were derived through factor analysis of peer ratings (Pekarik et al., 1976). Correlations between peer and teacher ratings exceeded .54 on all scales (Johnston, Pelham, & Murphy, 1985; Ledingham et al., 1982). Teacher and peer assessments in first grade have been shown to be equally good predictors of antisocial behavior 7 years later (Tremblay, LeBlanc, & Schwartzman, 1988). La Greca (1981) and Ledingham and Younger (1985) reported that Aggression and Withdrawal scale scores provided an accurate basis for classifying peer acceptance in children when compared with peer ratings of preferred playmates.

We have used the PEI for the past 14 years. The assessment takes about 5 minutes (once the teacher and investigator are through playing "telephone tag"). Most teachers are happy to comply, although some would rather have an open-ended format rather than the yes–no format of responses. The instrument is treatment sensitive, with about 50% to 70% of teachers reporting improvement (outcome interacts with diagnosis and medication status of the children; cf. Frankel, in press; Frankel & Myatt, 2002).

Parent Ratings

By its nature, the best friendship network cannot be observed by the teacher or most peers, but parents must be relied on for this assessment (Frankel, Myatt, Cantwell & Feinberg, 1997b). A widely used parent questionnaire is the Social Skills Rating System (SSRS; Gresham & Elliott, 1990). It consists of 48 items rated as either "never," "sometimes," or "very often." The parent form should be administered to the mother. The instrument has been divided into two major scales. The Social Skills scale (38 items) inquires about social situations with peers and parents. The Problem Behavior scale (18 items) concentrates on behavioral problems. Correlations with teacher ($r = .36$) and peer versions ($r = .12$) of the instrument are low but statistically significant.

Due to the lack of measures available to assess play interactions in the home, we developed the Quality of Play Questionnaire (QPQ; Frankel, 2002b). It is a measure completed by the parent in which the quality of the last play date and the frequency of play dates are assessed. The Conflict factor-based scale was refined through factor analysis of data collected for 112 nonclinic and 48 clinic-referred children (75 boys and 85 girls). A cut point of 3.5 on the Conflict scale resulted in correct classification of 66.7% of the clinic group and 72.3% of the nonclinic group. A cut point of 2.5 for number of play dates at other children's houses resulted in correct classification of 66.7% of the clinic group and 60.7% of the nonclinic group. A cut point of 2.5 for number of play dates at the index child's house resulted in correct classification of 66.7% of the clinic group and 59.8% of the nonclinic group.

We have been using the SSRS Social Skills scale to measure outcome for the past 14 years. We have found that about 90% of parents report some improvement on this scale as a result of our intervention (Frankel, Cantwell, & Myatt, 1996). Comparisons with wait-list control subjects have been highly significant (Frankel et al., 1997b). We have recently begun to use the QPQ to assess outcome. Pre and post data were available for nine children who were in the problematic range of functioning at baseline. Seven of the nine children fell within the nonclinic range at posttest.

Types of Children's Social Skills Treatment

Most children's social skills treatment takes the form of small groups of children meeting within a school setting, without the involvement of their parents (Beelman, Pfingsten, & Lösel, 1994; Erwin, 1994). Unimodal programs were more effective for 3- to 8-year-olds, while multimodal programs more effective for 9- to 15-year-olds. Beelman et al. (1994) reported that parent and teacher reports showed the least improvement of all types of outcome measures. The typical degree of generalization of treatment gains to children's actual environment from these groups has been small (Kavale, Mathur, Forness, Rutherford, & Quinn, 1996). Perhaps due to these limited gains or the difficulty in implementing this type of treatment, clinicians and researchers have sought alternative treatments. This chapter briefly reviews these alternatives.

Individual Treatment to Enhance Friendships

Malik and Furman (1993, p. 1316), in commenting on group versus individual approaches to social skills enhancement, concluded, "Although inclusion of peers makes this approach much less practical for individual practitioners, we have found little evidence that training sessions with adults will generalize to interactions with peers." In a test of this contention, Bierman and Furman (1984) found that small-group training of conversational skills was more effective in changing peer ratings than individual coaching. Many friendless children prefer the company of adults rather than other children. It is difficult to see how individual treatment with an adult therapist would make a friendless child more comfortable with other children.

One interesting variant of individual treatment for social skill problems was a small study done by Kehle, Clark, Jenson, and Wampold (1986). They videotaped four behavior-disordered, hyperactive males, aged 10 to 23 years. The subjects were shown an 11-minute videotape with their disruptive behaviors edited out. Three subjects decreased disruption through 6 weeks of follow-up, whereas one subject who viewed the unedited tape of his behavior increased disruption. While appearing to be promising, this technique has only obtained limited replication in one other small sample of subjects (Possell, Kehle, Mcloughlin, & Bray, 1999). No evidence was presented that these individuals were better accepted by their peers.

Peer Pairing

Peer pairing is another technique used to improve the social status of rejected children. Pairing unpopular children with more popular peers alone was not as effective as peer pairing with concomitant social skills training (Bierman, 1986a). For example, developmentally disabled children were paired with more popular nonretarded children. Once the pairing stopped, social relationships were not maintained (Chennault, 1967; Lilly, 1971; Rucker & Vincenzo, 1970).

Two studies used competent peers both as instructors in sessions and as prompters within the classroom situation. Middleton and Cartledge (1995) used two or three socially competent peers as models during instruction with each of five highly aggressive first- and second-grade African American males. The peers also gave prompts to each target child in the classroom. Although hitting and arguing were reduced to 16.8% of baseline, there were no effects on acceptance by other peers. Prinz, Blechman, and Dumas (1994) paired groups of four aggressive children with four socially competent children (total *n* was 48 aggressive and 52 competent children) during a median of 22 sessions of 50 minutes each. Each session employed role playing, in which the socially competent child first demonstrated the correct example. Although aggressive behavior decreased in comparison with an attention control group, changes in peer rankings failed to materialize.

Peer pairing has been proposed as an effective alternative on several grounds. First, it may make a friendless child more comfortable around peers. Second, socially competent peers can model appropriate behavior in a way that is more salient to the friendless child. These suppositions seem reasonable in the light of the results obtained. In contrast, other suppositions have not been supported. There is little evidence that the friendless child will become friends or that the peer tutor might facilitate friendships within his or her friendship circle. Anecdotal accounts suggest that the tutor rarely wants to mix socially with his or her pupil outside of the tutoring situation.

Parent Involvement in Social Skills Acquisition

According to Ladd, LeSieur, and Profilet (1993), parents may directly influence young children's peer relations in four ways: First, they integrate their child into social environments outside the home. Second, they help their child select playmates and arrange play dates. Third, they supervise interactions with peers; fourth, they help their child solve interpersonal problems. Despite the major role of parents in their child's friendships, parents have been notably absent from contributing to social skills training programs (Budd, 1985; Ladd & Asher, 1985; La Greca, 1993; Sheridan, Dee, Morgan, McCormick, & Walker, 1996). It is reasonable to expect that parental involvement would enhance treatment generalization (Frankel, 1996; Ladd, Profilet & Hart, 1992; Lollis & Ross, 1987, cited in Ladd, 1992).

Collateral Parent Management Training

One way of integrating parents into their children's social skills training has been to train parents to better manage the conduct problems of their children in the home (collateral parent management training). This approach comes from a research tradition that focuses primarily on the reduction of aggressive behavior as opposed to the enhancement of friendships. The rationale for application of this approach to friendship problems is that rejected children are usually aggressive (Dishion, 1990) and their aggression is a key cause of peer rejection. Bierman and Smoot (1991), using a standard method of classifying rejected children, found that only about one-third of boys with poor peer relations fit this model. Other authors (Bierman, 1986b; French, 1988) find that about half of all rejected children exhibit conduct problems at school. They note that conduct problems at school (but not at home) correlate significantly with peer acceptance in the classroom.

Thus, collateral parent management training may be successful in addressing social problems in a segment of children who are rejected by peers. Home-based reward programs have been successful in eliminating aggressive behaviors in school (cf. Barth, 1979, for a review; Kazdin, Esveldt-Dawson, French, & Unis, 1987). However, for many rejected children, collateral parent management training may not address key issues in establishing friendships, for instance, the ability of children to play together harmoniously (Powell, Salzberg, Rukle, Levy, & Itzkowitz, 1983).

Parents as Promoters of Negative Peer Interactions

Not only have parents been missing from the corrective experiences of social skill training, but there is evidence that some parents may directly or indirectly promote behaviors that result in peer rejection. Putallaz (1987) found that mothers who were highly aversive to their children tended to be more highly aversive with other mothers in a laboratory setting. These mothers were not only training their children to be aggressive, but were less likely to be helpful in securing play dates because of their own demeanor. Mothers of rejected children were less likely to appropriately monitor play experiences (Ladd et al., 1992; Pettit, Bates, Dodge, & Meece, 1999) than mothers of popular children and had less social competence themselves (Prinstein & LaGreca, 1999). Mothers of rejected children may fail to teach their child conflict management skills and rules of behavior (Kennedy, 1992) and also may unwittingly allow their child to maintain coercive control of play (Ladd, 1992).

Several researchers have found processes in mothers of rejected children that parallel the social errors of their children. Dodge, Schlundt, Schocken, and Delugach (1983) found that mothers of rejected children were more likely to dominate a group of children at play and ignore ongoing activity than mothers of popular children. Russell and Finnie (1990) found that mothers of rejected preschool children would coerce an ongoing play group to integrate their children rather than help their children observe ways to fit in. Perhaps the view that parents may lack

social skills themselves and are thus less able to teach them to their children has inhibited development of social skills programs involving parents (Budd, 1985; Cousins & Weiss, 1993).

Teaching Parents to Better Manage Children's Friendships

Several landmark studies refute the contention that parents of friendless children are unable to help in delivery of treatment components to their children. Shure and Spivak (1978) trained parents to be surrogate teachers of a prepackaged social problem-solving program. The focus of the program was decreasing aggression in children rather than increasing peer acceptance and friendships. This was a very ambitious program that intensively trained parents. It demonstrated that parents could be counted on to institute detailed programs. Results clearly indicated improved problem solving in the children.

Cousins and Weiss (1993) implemented a treatment combining training children in social skills with training parents in management skills relevant to peer relationships. They advocated teaching parents to organize the child's social agenda and having the parents debrief the child after social contacts. Pfiffner and McBurnett (1997) demonstrated that social skills training benefits readily generalized to the home when parents were trained to promote this generalization. Sheridan et al. (1996) taught parents supportive listening skills, helping their child solve social problems, setting social goals, and helping their children transfer skills to the home environment. Parent and teacher reports suggested general improvement for most boys.

We have found that most parents of friendless children possess adequate skills in most areas of social functioning, with the exception of a few localized "blind spots." With a little information from us, parents can help each other to improve the way they manage their children's peer relations. The techniques described in this volume were readily used by most parents of children enrolled in our program.

Common Diagnosis of Children Obtaining Training

Children entering into our friendship classes are heterogeneous. For many children, social concerns are part of a larger constellation of maladjustment. Most commonly, children will carry diagnoses of either ADHD, oppositional defiant disorder (ODD), or an autism spectrum disorder (ASD). We have observed that between 40% and 60% of children in any particular friendship class will have ADHD and perhaps 20% will have ASD. The remaining children may have generalized anxiety disorder or social phobia or do not satisfy criteria for any psychopathology. We find it beneficial to mix these different types of children, because the skills they bring to sessions may complement each other. Children with ADHD represent a more normalized peer group for high-functioning children with ASD. Their enthusiasm may be contagious to more cautious children. The children with ASD that we select for treatment are a good stabilizing influence. They highly value and help promote focus on each activity. Our goal for all children in these groups is to integrate them into a mainstream, well-behaved peer group. The next sections review the three most common disorders present among children in social skills training and social deficits commonly attributed to them.

Attention Deficit/Hyperactivity Disorder (ADHD)

Children with ADHD are at substantial risk for poor social relationships with peers (Barkley, 1990; Frederick & Olmi, 1994; Pelham & Bender, 1982; Pope, Bierman, & Mumma, 1989; Teeter, 1991; Whalen & Henker, 1985). Estimates of children with ADHD who are rejected by peers run as high as 60% (Carlson, Lahey, Frame, Walker, & Hynd, 1987; Zentall, 1989). Some studies suggest that children with ADHD are more likely to be rejected by peers than children with other disruptive behavior disorders (Carlson et al., 1987; Landau & Moore, 1991; Pope et al., 1989).

In addition to having low social status among their peer groups, ADHD children may also fail to develop a best friend (George & Hartmann, 1996; Ray, Cohen, Secrist, & Duncan, 1997). Children with ADHD have less knowledge of how to maintain established friendships when compared to normal peers (cf. Landau & Moore, 1991). Pelham and Bender (1982) reported that peer dysfunction remained after Ritalin improved academic performance of children with ADHD. The available evidence suggests that medication may help decrease negative behaviors (Pelham et al., 1987), but no clear evidence exists that medication alone will improve social skill or change social goals (Melnick & Hinshaw, 1996).

Research to date has begun to identify areas of social deficiencies in samples of children diagnosed with ADHD. Child interviews have shown that children diagnosed with ADHD tended to dislike peers for the same reasons as non-ADHD children (Whalen & Henker, 1985). However, they differed from non-ADHD children as to whom they nominated as most liked (Hinshaw & Melnick, 1995). Child interviews about hypothetical social situations have revealed that children diagnosed with ADHD think about less friendly and effective, more assertive and impulsive solutions to social problems than do their non-ADHD peers (Grenell et al., 1987). Similarly, they tend to attribute hostile intent and expect future aggression, but are prone to gather less information before making their conclusions (Milich & Dodge, 1984). Observation studies have shown that children diagnosed with ADHD have a high quantity of social output, especially negative behavior (Pelham & Bender, 1982). Children with ADHD have been found to be less likely to change their behavior to fit the social situation (Landau & Milich, 1988). In addition, studies investigating social problem solving have found deficits in encoding social cues associated with the diagnosis of ADHD (Matthys, Cuperus, & Van Engeland, 1999), but selection of aggressive responses and confidence in performing them seemed more associated with ODD than ADHD.

Oppositional Defiant Disorder (ODD)

ADHD is often comorbid with ODD with comorbidity rates ranging between 42% and 93% (Biederman, Munir, & Knee, 1987; Jensen, Martin, & Cantwell, 1997). Partly due to this high rate of comorbidity, little is known about the unique social deficits associated with ODD. In analogue game situations, children with ODD and ADHD were more aggressive in response to provocation by imagined competitors than

children with ODD alone (Atkins & Stoff, 1993). Using a factorial design, Frankel and Feinberg (2002) were able to tease out the additive contributions of diagnoses of ADHD and ODD to social dysfunction. Subjects diagnosed with ODD were rated by parents as showing more disrespectful behavior toward adults. Diagnoses of ADHD and ODD were each associated with parent ratings of decreased resistance to provocation from peers. Teacher ratings indicated that subjects with ADHD showed more disruptive behavior but subjects diagnosed with ODD were more hostile toward peers. Much research remains to be done to identify social deficits associated with ODD.

Autism Spectrum Disorders (ASD)

Children with ASD are at substantial risk for social problems with peers. Bauminger and Kasari (2000) reported that 7- to 14-year-olds with ASD felt more lonely and had poorer quality friendships (in terms of companionship, security, and help) than same-aged typically developing control children. A review of the last 10 years of literature on ASD suggests the following:

1. Although there are many studies on cognitive and linguistic problems in ASD, there are no studies of specific deficits in making and sustaining friendships.
2. There are few interventions that are aimed at improving peer relations among children with ASD (cf. Marriage, Gordon, & Brand, 1995).
3. These interventions have not been formally tested in terms of their immediate or long-term results in improving peer acceptance or the development and quality of best friends.

Two examples of studies illustrate points 2 and 3. Mesibov (1984) described group treatment of social skills for highly verbal autistic adolescents attempting to improve communication, positive peer interaction, and self-esteem. Outcome data were only qualitative in nature but suggestive of benefits. *Theory of mind* is a general social cognitive strategy, measured by telling stories to a child after which they are asked to infer what others must be thinking or to predict other's actions. Ozonoff and Miller (1995) utilized a program that applied trained theory of mind to nine autistic children. Although theory of mind measures improved after treatment, no concomitant improvement in friendships was found. Relationships between theory of mind and ability to develop and sustain friendships have not been examined directly.

Research on the UCLA Children's Friendship Program

The intervention described in this volume has taken 14 years to reach its current form. This chapter reviews the changes over the years as well as factors we have discovered which limit treatment response. The original 12-session treatment program (Frankel, Myatt, & Cantwell, 1995) consisted of child didactic, socialization homework, and free-play coaching modules, but only the beginning steps of parent involvement: Informational presentations were made to parents for the first two sessions. Parents were encouraged to wait in a meeting room and socialize with each other until the last 15 minutes of Sessions 3 through 11. During these last 15 minutes, a brief review was made of the contents of the child session and parents were given a handout covering guidelines for the child's socialization homework assignment. Potential problems with compliance were briefly discussed.

Results suggested generalization had occurred outside the treatment situation. We compared 36 boys receiving treatment with 17 boys on the wait list for the same length of time. Significantly greater mean improvement for the Social Skills scale score of the parent-reported SSRS (Gresham & Elliott, 1990) was obtained for boys receiving treatment. Child diagnosis of ADHD did not have a significant impact on parent outcome measures. This was a surprise, be-

cause we thought that boys diagnosed with ADHD might have more difficulty in following the rules of etiquette and therefore would not show improvement at home.

Changes in school also occurred. Mean improvement on the teacher-reported PEI Withdrawal and Aggression scales (Pekarik et al., 1976) was statistically significant for boys without ODD (n = 17 in the treatment group). Again, we were surprised that the presence of ADHD (n = 27 in the treatment group) did not have a significant impact on teacher outcome measures.

We were able to develop models for predicting teacher-reported outcome on the Withdrawal, Likability, and Aggression scales of the PEI (Frankel, Myatt, Cantwell, & Fineberg, 1997a). Fifty-two subjects were divided into treatment responders and nonresponders using a double median split procedure (eliminating subjects improving at the median of each outcome measure). Parent Achenbach Child Behavior Checklist (CBCL; Achenbach, 1991) ratings and *DSM–III–R* diagnoses for boys completing our original intervention were submitted to multiple logistic regression analysis (cf. Afifi & Clark, 1984; Frankel & Simmons, 1992). We confirmed that the *DSM–III–R* diagnosis of ODD predicted poorer response to treatment on the teacher-rated withdrawal measure (69.94% accuracy). A majority of nonresponding subjects who were predicted to be responders for either Aggression or Withdrawal scales came from only 2 of the 12 treatment replications (randomization tests, p values < .05). Parents in these treatment replications chose not to stay and socialize during the unstructured time, but did attend the last segment of each session as required.

Our program was subsequently enhanced so as to make the intervention more effective for subjects with ODD who failed to respond to treatment. Parent attendance became required for the entire session. We developed eight more parent modules and accompanying handouts, which gave the parents the "script" that the children received for key social situations and enabled parents to remind children of this script before execution of homework assignments. Parents reported completed socialization homework assignments in detail at the beginning of each session. Our hypothesis was that this would mitigate the effects of ODD on outcome by improving child compliance with socialization homework.

Four treatment replications, totaling 16 boys and 5 girls, completed the Enhanced program (Frankel et al., 1996). These results were compared with the outcome obtained on the original program with 26 additional treated subjects (total n = 50 boys and 12 girls, Original program). A reliability of change score [RC = (pretreatment – posttreatment)/SE$_{ds}$, where SE$_{ds}$ is the standard error of the difference scores for each measure] was calculated for each subject in the pathological range on each measure at baseline. An RC > 2 was designated as reliable. Results revealed significantly more teachers reported reliable change in PEI Aggression and Likability after the Enhanced versus Original program. RCs after the Enhanced program were substantially above Wait List (22 boys and 4 girls) levels on all measures except for PEI Withdrawal.

A study of the Enhanced program (Frankel et al., 1997b) compared 35 children with ADHD, who began stimulant medication prior to the start of the study, and 14 children without ADHD who also received social skills treatment, with respective wait-list control groups (12 children each group). Subjects in both diagnostic groups showed comparable benefits over their wait-list controls on both parent and teacher ratings. Chil-

dren with ODD were not different from those without ODD on most outcome measures. Effect sizes ranged from 0.93 to 1.34.

Our approach focuses on social etiquette or rules of behavior enforced by the peer group. It is a simple way for children with ASD to understand social context. We have identified 17 patients diagnosed with ASD who have taken part in our friendship classes over the last 3 years. Although this number seems small, it is larger than nearly all of the previously published research on social skills training in children with ASD.

Outcome measures were the SSRS (completed by the parent), the PHS (completed by the child), and the PEI (administered by telephone to the child's teachers). Results revealed significant improvements in Assertiveness and Problem behaviors, but not Self-control. Inspection of individual children revealed that 9 of 17 children (52.9%) showed improvement on each of the two scales initially in the problematic range and 14 of 17 children (82.3%) improved on at least one of these scales.

Pre- and posttreatment data for PEI scales were available for seven children. Inspection of individual patients revealed that five of seven children (71.4%) showed improvement on at least one of these scales. The PHS was collected on 12 patients. Eight patients initially scored in the "low self-esteem" range on the PHS. All eight patients showed improvement in a positive direction on posttesting. Five of the eight showed improvement that exceeded the test–retest reliability (range of improvement was 14–42 points increase in total self-esteem scores).

Two studies assessed possible synergistic effects between pretreatment prescriptions for medication and treatment response to our program. The first study focused on subjects who were diagnosed with ADHD with or without ODD but with no other comorbid disorder (Frankel, 2002c). Mean age was 8.5 years. Seventeen subjects satisfied criteria for ADHD alone, and 31 met criteria for with ADHD and ODD. Medication status was broken into three groups: Unmedicated (n = 11), Stimulant only (n = 27), and Other medication (n = 21). The most commonly prescribed other medications were Zoloft (n = 8), Depekote (n = 5), Prozac (n = 5), and

Clonodine (*n* = 3), either alone (*n* = 10) or in combination with one or two other medications (*n* = 18). Examination of individual scores revealed that 74% of subjects in the Stimulant only group (17/24) displayed improvement, versus 37.5% (6/16) of Unmedicated group and 25% (5/20) of Other medication group. Of the five subjects who improved in the Other medication group, four were prescribed stimulants in combination with other medications.

The second study focused on the medication status of twenty-five 6- to 13-year-old children with ASD (Frankel & Myatt, 2002). Thirteen subjects were prescribed medication by community physicians prior to and unrelated to their participation in the program (3 subjects were prescribed Ritalin, 2 Adderall, 1 Dexedrine, 1 Depekote, 1 Prozac, 1 Lithium, 1 Lithium and Mellaril, 1 Zoloft and Ritalin, 1 Depekote and Resperidone, and 1 Zoloft, Resperidol, and Depekote), whereas 12 were unmedicated. Results revealed significantly greater mean improvement in the Unmedicated group for SSRS Self-control subscale and PEI Likability and Aggression scales.

Clearly, subjects with ADHD medicated with stimulants and unmedicated subjects with ASD showed greater benefits after children's friendship training. It is currently unclear whether medication status produces changes in treatment response or indicates more treatment-resistant subjects.

PART

II

PREPARING FOR TREATMENT

In Parts II and III, we present each step in preparation for treatment and session delivery as a chapter. Each chapter is divided into two major portions: "Treatment Rationale" presents the basis for the development of the step or session. "How to Conduct the Session" gives a narrative description of the steps to implement the intervention. In order to promote group leader spontaneity, parent and child session plans appear in outline form. "Clinical Examples" and "Potential Problems" are inserted at points in the description of intervention in which they typically occur in order to provide group leaders with greater benefits from our experience.

sports played during school recess on playgrounds: handball four square tetherball basketball jump rope

Screening

Treatment Rationale

In order to conduct groups that are maximally beneficial to the variety of children needing friendship training, it is necessary to screen children who would benefit from the skills being taught and group children together who will be comfortable in being together in the same class. Screening begins with the parent phone call to the therapist. The initial phone call can establish whether the child meets more obvious criteria and can inform the parent about the program and how to present the initial visit to the child. Parents of children who do not meet obvious criteria can be referred to other resources.

6.1 Screening Criteria for Social Functioning

The most frequent reasons for not meeting screening criteria are children who are too old (eighth grade or higher) or too young (kindergarten or lower), functioning at too low a social level for the classes, or inappropriately referred (e.g., they need "social skills training" to listen to their parents or teachers better). This intervention assumes children have certain prerequisite skills. Criteria for social functioning are that the child:

1. Knows how to play simple board games independently and has the concept of winning and losing in the context of a board game.
2. Has played simple sports that are likely to be played by children during school recess on playgrounds (e.g., handball, Four Square, tetherball, basketball, jump rope).
3. Can potentially maintain a shared focus in conversation with another member of the class (is able to switch topics from a primary interest and has sufficient communication ability).
4. Has no more than slight delay in age-appropriate social interests (conversation, toys, games, and activities).
5. Can be managed in an outpatient setting (i.e., behavior can be controlled with reward and/ or brief time out).
6. Doesn't exhibit "offensive" behaviors (e.g., public masturbation or nose picking in a fifth grader). Without first eliminating these behaviors, a child is unlikely to be accepted by peers, regardless of progress in the class.
7. Has completed most of first grade. We don't start first graders in our groups until May or June. This is because we have found first graders to be too intimidated by the didactic segment. On the other hand we have had 6½-year-old second graders who were very comfortable in this situation and indistinguishable from other second graders.

critical mass

6.2 Grouping Children Who Would Be Comfortable Together

Each specific class of children needs to be limited in their range of sociodevelopmental level. We like to keep each group of children within one grade of each other for small total group size (less than eight children) or within two grade levels for a group of 10 children. There are two reasons to limit the range of developmental levels within one group:

1. The children will have difficulty interacting with each other within the sessions and may show more resistance to interacting with group members who are at substantially lower developmental levels than they are. It is appropriate for children to be selective in this regard.
2. Parents may be uncomfortable about this divergence, fearing that the intake professional feels their child is more severely disabled than they can accept. Parents may also worry that their child may learn deviant behaviors from group members who are at significantly lower developmental levels.

Gender issues are problematic, as referral rates for boys are about four to five times that for girls. We don't recommend putting one girl in with nine boys. Since same-sex friendships are encouraged (see Chap. 18), three girls within one grade of each other is an ideal minimum (we have rarely had more in one group). If we can only get two together in a group, then we consult with the parents of both girls to see if they are willing to risk having their girl be alone with the boys for a session when the other girl is absent. If a girl is comfortable playing with boys, then parents generally don't mind.

6.3 Formation of the First Few Groups

The most difficult part of the process is the formation of the first few groups. Referral sources haven't been alerted to the groups or what they can provide, and no "track record" has been established (in either the capacity to form adequate groups or the ability to benefit children). In order to start a group, parents of children with comparable characteristics must be enrolled within about a 2-month period of each other. Any longer than this and parents will usually not want to wait or will lose confidence that you can provide the intervention that has been described to them. You should not compromise on these criteria in order to get the initial groups under way; just try to get at least six in a group. This is the "critical mass" or the minimal number of participants that feels like a "group" to both participants and group leaders. Other compromises could risk the "word-of-mouth" reputation of your fledgling clinical enterprise. Seven or eight participants is a safer number to start, as absences will be less likely to take the group below critical mass. Recommended maximum group size is 10, as this allows parents adequate time for discussion within a 1-hour session. If the session length is 90 minutes, then 12 is a comfortable maximum size.

How to Conduct Telephone Screening

The first contact with a professional is usually through a telephone call by the parent. Most have been referred by either a teacher, a mental health professional, or another parent whose child was previously in our class. Effective screening, beginning with the initial phone call, insures that the eventual group experience will be compatible with the child's problems and the parent's expectations. In order to justify social skills training it is necessary for children to have friendship problems, which includes peer rejection or neglect, lack of closer friendships, or other negative behavioral concomitants. Sometimes children are rejected by peers for reasons other than poor social skills, such as appearance or ethnic group (Bierman, 1986a). These are not modifiable by the interventions described in this book. Children have differing degrees of preferences to do activities with others (Evers-Pasquale, 1978). Children who seem to genuinely enjoy playing alone and do not appear to show any signs of loneliness may not benefit from interventions teaching them how to make friends.

Mothers are the most reliable informants,

since they are most likely to supervise the play dates (i.e., if play dates are being supervised by either parent). It is strongly suggested that the telephone intake be done with mom in order to engage her in treatment. The telephone screening form in Table 1 may be helpful to assess if children meet the criteria just reviewed.

Although some parents would like to do so, it is counterproductive to get children to admit that they have peer problems. Parents should be advised to tell their child that there is a class that teaches children how to make and keep friends and that they will be talking to someone about this class. Discussion with the child about how much the child needs this class should be discouraged.

Clinical Example of a Typical Telephone Screening Call

Screener: What grade is your child in?

Mom: Third grade.

Screener: What problems does your child have in making or keeping friends?[1]

Mom: He doesn't have any problems making friends, but once they get to know him, they don't want to play with him anymore.

Screener: Are there any children that he regularly hangs around with at school?

Mom: There are only one or two.

Screener: Do children seek out your child at school or does your child generally seek out others to play?[2]

Mom: Yes, there is one child, but I don't like him because he gets in trouble a lot.[3]

Screener: How often would you say that your child has play dates?[4]

Mom: Once in a while he'll have a play date.

Screener: Are the play dates generally harmonious or are there frequent disagreements?[5]

Mom: Occasional disagreements. But once children come over, they don't want to come back again.

Screener: What types of games does your child like to play with other children?

Mom: He likes videogames.

Screener: Does he know how to play any board games?

Mom: Yes. He plays checkers, Clue, and Sorry.

Screener: Does he play any sports?

Mom: He's not much of a sports person.

Screener: Does he know how to play any sport—for instance, handball or soccer?

Mom: Yes. He knows how to play handball but he says the other kids don't let him play.

If this interview establishes social problems in one or more areas, and the child has play interests that are commensurate with his or her grade, then a program description should be provided.

[Sample program description] Screener: We offer a 12-week program. We cover how to have a two-way conversation, how to make a good first impression, how to join others at play, how to be a good sport, how to resist teasing, and how to be a good host on a play date. Are those things you think your child needs?

[Variant] Screener: It sounds like your child already has some of the basic social skills that we teach in the initial group sessions. The area he has most trouble with seems to be the play dates. Each of the sessions in our program builds cumulatively upon the previous week's lesson. Participation in all of the program sessions will help your son or daughter to build a total repertoire of skills that will likely increase his or her chances of having more frequent and better quality play dates. Would that be of interest to you?

---

[1]This will detect children who need behavioral programs for other reasons, such as compliance with parents or teachers.

[2]This probe is repeated in the child mental status exam. Gresham (1982) found that peer status is better predicted by the approach of others rather than overall rates of peer interaction. This is because rejected children may be tolerated by others whereas well-like children may be sought out by them.

[3]This is a pattern in rejected and neglected children. Children that seek them out tend to be rejected and have behavioral problems.

[4]Less than once a week is probably too few.

[5]By second grade, children should have mostly harmonious play dates. By fourth grade, disagreements should almost never happen.

TABLE 6.1 Telephone Screening Form

Children's Friendship Training

Telephone Screening Form

Today's Date: ___/___/___

Person taking information: _____

Child Name: _____   Male ☐   Female ☐

DOB:___/___/___   Age: _____   Grade: __

Date Packet Sent: ___/___/___

Referrant: _____

Therapist ☐   School ☐   Friend ☐   Professional ☐

Family Information

Family Type: 2-Parent ☐   Single-Parent ☐

Who will come: Bio mom ☐   Bio Dad ☐   Step Mom ☐   Step Dad ☐

Parent(s) Name(s): _____

Address: _____

Home Phone: (____)____-_____   Work Phone: (____)_____-_____

Diagnosis:_____   Medications: _____

Sibs: _____

Insurance: _____

Child Problems (check all that apply):

Aggressive to peers ☐   Classroom behavior problems ☐   Teased ☐

No friends at school ☐   no one seeks him/her out at school ☐

No play dates ☐   Infrequent play dates (< 2 per month) ☐

Play date quality:

Generally harmonius ☐   Occasional disagreements ☐   Bossy/frequent disagreements ☐

Comments:

_____

_____

_____

_____

Play skills:

Knows how to play basic board games ☐   Knows how to play school recess games ☐

Wants to have friends ☐

[If the mom says yes to the last question in either variant, then go on]. Screener: We will mail you a packet of questionnaires to fill out (see Part 7.2). It should take you about 30 minutes to complete. Fill it out and send it back. When we receive it from you, we will schedule you and your child for an intake appointment. The purpose of this appointment is for us to meet your child and determine if this is the right treatment for him and if he will fit in with the other children we have at this time. Do you have any questions?

Mom: Yes. What do I tell my child about the class?

Screener: Tell your child that there is a class that teaches kids how to make and keep friends and that he will be talking to someone who runs that class about things that he likes to play. It is not necessary to get your child to admit that he needs the class.

Potential Problems

Desperate for Any Group

The mother of a moderately developmentally disabled second grader attempted to conceal this from the telephone interviewer. Eventual probes established that the child was in a special class, was academically 3 years behind agemates, tended to have friends who were in preschool, and couldn't play simple board games (even Candyland).

Denying More Serious Psychopathology

One mom offered only interpretations of her son's aloofness and descriptions that gave far more credit for social cognition than warranted. The initial mental status examination revealed strong signs of severe autism.

PART II
CHAPTER
7

Intake

The intervention described in this volume may at first appear to be an unrestricted "class" to some parents (like gardening or flower arranging) or group therapy to other parents. But the process and content of the intake appointment clarify it as the beginning of a syllabus-driven treatment group.

Treatment Rationale

7.1 Goals of the Intake

Broadly speaking, intake appointments are used to get information and then give information. For the information received:

1. Meeting with the child may establish the child's social–developmental level so that compatibility with the group currently being assembled can be assessed.
2. Interview with the parent can confirm the need for treatment and clear up any parent misunderstandings or misgivings.
3. The child can complete needed baseline measures (e.g., self-esteem questionnaire) that can't be mailed with the packet.
4. The parents can be administered a structured diagnostic interview to establish child diagnosis both for treatment and for insurance billing purposes.

The information given by the clinician to the parent can establish a viable treatment contract with the parent and determine any preconditions to treatment (e.g., buy more board games, continue medication during treatment, enroll child in camp for better access to peers in the summer). The clinician can prepare the child for treatment by providing a description of the first session.

7.2 Packets

We recommend that a packet of questionnaires and forms be mailed to the parents, completed by them, and received by the clinician before scheduling the intake appointment. This saves time in the session and provides the clinician with a brief introduction to the patient's issues and diagnosis. Our packets contain the following:

1. A brief biographical form (see Table 7.1).
2. Consent to release the home phone number to others in the group (presented to all participants as a group roster in Session 1). This is necessary for the telephone homework assignments to be done. This is only released to others if the child is accepted into the class.
3. A medical screening form, which consists of information about important health conditions (e.g., allergies) and a brief developmen-

TABLE 7.1 Biographical Form

Children's Friendship Training

BIOGRAPHICAL FORM

Please answer *all* items. ALL INFORMATION PROVIDED WILL REMAIN IN STRICTEST PROFESSIONAL CONFIDENCE.

MOTHER: LAST NAME _____ , FIRST NAME _____ , M.I. ____

FATHER: LAST NAME _____ , FIRST NAME _____ , M.I. ____

Home Address _____ City _____ Zip _____

Home Telephone ( )_____ Work Telephone ( )_____

Today's Date _____ Your Birth Date _____

---

1. Child's Sex: Male _____ Female _____

2. Racial Background:

   White _____   Hispanic _____

   Black _____   Asian _____

   Other (specify)_____

3. Religion:

   None _____   Jewish _____

   Catholic _____   Protestant _____

   Other (specify)_____

4. Current Marital Status:

   Unmarried _____ Separated _____

   Married _____ Widowed _____

   Divorced _____

   Living with common law spouse _____

5. Children: Please write in the name, sex, and birth date of each of your children. If adopted, put age at time of adoption.

   Name   Sex   Birthdate

   _____ ___ _____

   _____ ___ _____

   _____ ___ _____

6. Does your child have any problems with his/her behavior and/or academic adjustment in school?
   Yes ____ No ____

   Specify_____

7. Is your child in a special class of any kind?
   Yes _____ No _____

   Specify_____

8a. Occupation: Please write in the kind of work you <u>most usually do.</u> Please use a "job title" indicating what you do (not merely where you work).

   _____

8b. Number of hours per week employed _____

9. Occupation of spouse/partner (even if separated/divorced).

   _____

10. Education: Highest grade or level achieved and degrees held?

    Yourself _____

    Spouse/Partner _____

11. Referral Information:
    Who referred you to the Children's Friendship Program?
    Self? _____ Friend? _____

    Or if Professional:

    Name: _____

    Degree: _____

    Phone: ( ) _____

tal history (helpful in screening for developmental disabilities).

4. Pretest on the SSRS, QPQ, and consent to obtain the PEI from the child's teacher.
5. The SNAP (Swanson, 1992) to screen for the presence of ADHD and ODD.
6. The ASSQ (Ehlers, Gillberg, & Wing, 1999) to screen for autism spectrum disorder.

This packet takes about 30 minutes for parents to complete. Using the packet does not demonstrably increase dropouts, serves as an indication of the parent's commitment, and gives the intake professional useful information to guide the intake interview.

How to Conduct the Intake Interviews

The intake proceeds as follows: First the parent is interviewed alone for 5 minutes to confirm the presenting problems discussed over the telephone. This may be especially helpful if the mom made the call and the dad is now also present for the intake interview. Asking dad to give additional information helps to get both parents to accept the treatment contract. Next, the child mental status exam is administered in an individual interview with the child (parents are in the waiting room). After the child returns to the waiting room, the parents are given the results of the mental status exam. A parent structured diagnostic interview is next. If the child meets criteria for the class, the parents are informed of the match, the class is described, and any potential problems that might interfere with treatment response are addressed. The parents are given the details of the specific class, such as start and end dates and session times. At this point, the interviewer should secure a commitment from the parents (especially mothers) to attend all of the sessions.

In order to get mothers to participate, it is often necessary to allow them to bring siblings of the patient to the class. Siblings stay with the parents in the parent meeting room. If parents need to bring siblings, they are told to bring activities to keep them busy (such as things to color, something to read, small travel games, or home-

work) so that the parents can concentrate on the material being presented. Siblings have not generally posed a problem when this is followed.

The Child Mental Status Exam

The goal is to assess the child within narrow domains relevant to friendship training. Along with the usual goals of the mental status exam, this structured interview provides information that will enable the interviewer to make a reasonable estimate of the child's communication and play skills (tapping a domain that is of optimal use to the children's friendship program). The interviewer can become proficient in getting this information after a relatively short (10–15 minutes) interview. This may begin to occur after 10 to 20 children have been interviewed using the suggested probes in the Child Mental Status Examination Template (Table 7.2).

Medication Issues

As reviewed in Section I, Chapter 5, ADHD children prescribed only stimulants have double the chance of improved teacher reports on posttesting than either unmedicated ADHD children or ADHD children prescribed other psychotropic medications (Frankel, in press). Children with ASD who are unmedicated do better than those prescribed psychotropic medication (Frankel & Myatt, 2002). These data are not conclusive, as it is possible that prescription patterns are confounded with initial severity of psychopathology. Regardless of the reasons for these observations, it is prudent to suggest that children with ADHD who are normally medicated with stimulants remain so during instruction and during interactions with peers (play dates and other homework assignments arising from the group).

Clinical Example of Describing the Class to the Parent

Screener: Let me tell you about the children's friendship class. It's going to start next week at 5:45. There will be about 10 children in the class. It is run as a class with a syllabus for each session. You are required to attend each

TABLE 7.2 Child Mental Examination Template.

Children's Friendship Training

Mental Status Examination Template

Child Name _____

1. Did your parents tell you why you're here today?
   ☐ gave correct answer   ☐ didn't know, incorrect
2. We have a class that teaches kids how to make and keep friends. Is that something you might be interested in?
   ☐ yes   ☐ no   ☐ don't know
3. I'd like to find out about the things you like to play. Do they have a time at your school when you are free to pick whatever you want to play?
   ☐ yes   ☐ no (skip to question #10)
4. What do you usually do at recess?
   ☐ play with other kids   ☐ alone
5. Are there kids that you usually hang around with?
   ☐ yes   ☐ no (skip to question#10)
6. What are their first names?
   ☐ provides up to 5 first names   ☐ provides no first names or tries to name everyone in class
7. Are they the same age older or younger than you?
   ☐ same age   ☐ not same age
8. How do you meet at recess?
   ☐ we decide together   ☐ I find where they are
9. What kind of games do you usually play
   ☐ just talk/sit & watch others   ☐ outdoor sport, specify_____
10. What kinds of games do you like to play outside your house?
    ☐ skate/ride bike or skooter   ☐ climbing\chasing\hide & seek   ☐ sport, specify_____
11. Have you been on any teams (have child specify which teams)?
    ☐ no   ☐ yes, specify_____
12. What kinds of games do you like to play inside your house (don't accept arts/crafts, reading, or TV)?
    ☐ electronic games   ☐ board games
13. What board games do you have in your house that you like to play?
    ☐ board games named by child_____   ☐ none
14. Is there anyone who comes over to your house just to play with you?
    ☐ yes   ☐ no (end interview)
15. When was the last time someone was over?
    within last   ☐ week   ☐ month   ☐ longer than 1 month
16. What was the child's name?
    ☐ gave name, specify_____   ☐ couldn't remember
17. What did you do together (prompt for complete answer)?
    ☐ mixed different activities   ☐ exclusively electronic games and/or TV
18. Reported interest in a class that teaches kids how to make and keep friends:
    ☐ not interested, has plenty of friends
    ☐ undecided about class
    ☐ stated interest in the class

Global Impressions:
Oriented x3?   ☐ yes   ☐ no
Mood and affect appropriate to the situation   ☐ yes   ☐ no
Established rapport with the examiner?   ☐ readily   ☐ eventually   ☐ never
Cognitive abilities: ☐ below average   ☐ average   ☐ above average
Social maturity: ☐ 1–2 years below age level   ☐ age level   ☐ above age level

Characteristics of note: _____

session. The parents are in one room and the kids are in another. Each session, the kids are told something about making friends, they practice it, and they play for a while. They are coached in the skill during their play. They are given a homework assignment. The first homework assignment is to call another member of the class and find out something nice that happened to them that day. Parents are to work out the day and time of the call and see that their child gets to the phone at the appointed time. The homework gets a little more complex each session. Do you have any questions?

Clinical Example of How to Prepare the Child

Screener [at the end of the mental status examination]: That's all the questions I have for you. Do you have any questions for me?

Child: No.

Screener: Let me tell you about the class. It's going to start next week at 5:45. There will be about 10 children in the class, including you. It will be in the building across the street. Your parents will come in with you and meet in one room. Then Dr. Bob will take all the children to another room and tell you something about making and keeping friends. Then you will go out to the outside play area where you'll play "Capture the flag." Do you know how to play that game?

Child: Yes.

Screener: Good! At the end, Dr. Bob will give the kids a homework assignment. It will be to call another member of the class and find out something nice that happened to them that day. Your parents will work out the day and time of the call. How's that sound?

Child: OK.

Potential Problems

Parental Ambivalence

The mother of a fifth-grade girl initially reported her daughter had no friends at school and no play dates. After delaying return of the packet and putting off the intake appointment, she said her daughter was beginning to mix more easily with other children in group situations. The interviewer asked her if she wanted to continue with the class for her daughter in the light of what she felt about her daughter's current peer relationships. She said she didn't know, but that her daughter was still complaining of not having friends and was feeling lonely at home.

The mental status exam revealed she usually played with several children during school recess, but these children would never seek her out. The last play date she reported was 2 months prior to the intake. When the interviewer asked the child if she was interested in the class, she emphatically said "yes." The interviewer shared this with the child's mother, together with the results of the PHS. Her profile was in the low self-esteem range on popularity. Her mother decided to go ahead, saying that she wished to make her daughter happier.

Child Doesn't Want to Attend

A third-grade boy emphatically stated during the mental status exam that he had plenty of friends and wasn't interested in taking the class. During the parent interview, his mother reported that she was aware of his resistance. The interviewer said that the boy might benefit from the class despite his reluctance, but this would depend on two things: (a) her resolve that this was the appropriate intervention for her son and (b) the ability for her and the interviewer to devise a reward system that would motivate the boy to attend and cooperate. The mother said she firmly believed that the class would help her son. The interviewer suggested that she give him a small reward after coming and cooperating for each of the first two sessions. The mom agreed and gave her son $1 toward a music CD after each of the first two sessions. Although her son said he did not like coming, he continued to come and cooperate throughout the 12 weeks.

Alternating Parents

The mother of a fourth-grade girl had one other child at home. Without discussing this with the intake interviewer, she and her husband agreed to alternate coming to the sessions, so that one parent could take care of the sibling. Group leaders noticed that whenever dad was responsible for the homework, it didn't get done.

We now ensure the same parent is committed to come consistently to each parent session. When parents suggest that they might find this difficult, we suggest bringing the siblings to sit in the parent meeting room.

Overscheduled Children

A single working mom of a fourth-grade boy had her children in numerous activities throughout the week: an after-school program every day until 6 p.m., followed by homework, meals, baths, and bedtime. On the weekends, it was soccer team, karate, and "family time." When it came time to schedule a play date, child and mother agreed that there was no time in their existing schedule.

Currently, we inform the parent that the child will have to have one or two play dates per week toward the end of the class (and after the class is over). The interviewer has the parent ensure adequate time for play dates before the child is accepted into the class.

Divorced Parents Sharing Joint Custody

The divorced mother and father of a sixth-grade boy rotated full custody every 2 weeks, living apart by a 45-minute car ride. Both were invested in their child's improvement of friendships. The intake interviewer reviewed with them how they were going to ensure that their son's friendships would maintain continuity, despite the custody arrangement. Both parents agreed to attend all classes. During the intervention, the boy made friends at his mother's house and the father encouraged his son to make phone calls to these friends. He offered to pick up and drop off any children having play dates at his house.

Forcing Continued Failure

The mother of a seventh-grade girl insisted that her daughter obtain the phone numbers of girls from school, despite the fact that her daughter had a bad reputation among them. The inter-

viewer urged the mother to stop her efforts for the time being, because she might be trying too hard and this might result in further alienation of the other girls. The interviewer suggested that after the daughter learned the prerequisite skills, she would be in a better position to acquire school friends. Even then, it might take a while for the daughter's reputation to die down.

Precocious Daughter

The mother of a sixth-grade girl said she didn't have any same-sex friends. However, she boasted, "People think that my daughter is much older than her age." Mental status interview revealed that the girl was dressed in tight "short-shorts" and bathing-suit top, with full makeup, and began discussing who her "new boyfriend" was. This type of dress and conversation may cause many of the other girls discomfort and make a girl vulnerable to sexual exploitation by older male peers. The interviewer discussed these concerns with the girl's mother, and the mother agreed to set limits on the daughter's dress and makeup.

Parent Encouragement of Inappropriate Attire

One second-grade boy appeared at intake dressed in rubber rain boots that were not age or weather appropriate. When asked about this, the parent replied, "He just looks so cute in his boots—just like Christopher Robin from Winnie-the-Pooh!" The intake interviewer informed the parent that her son needed every advantage in order to improve his peer relationships and that his "cute" attire was likely to be an impediment to friendship making. His mother agreed to have him dress in a manner more consistent with the other boys in his class.

Advertising Child's Diagnosis

Parents brought in a third-grade boy who was diagnosed as having Asperger's disorder. At the intake appointment it was clear that the boy was functioning high enough to be able to benefit from the children's friendship program and to be able to develop friendships with typically developing peers. He was wearing a T-shirt with the main logo of the local autism society on it.

Parents were advised against disclosing their child's diagnosis until they got to know the new parents and children much better. The goal of this program is to integrate children into the mainstream. It was also suggested that the child not wear clothes that indicated he was a representative of a particular diagnosis. The parents readily accepted these suggestions, stating that this was exactly what they were looking for.

Inappropriate Behavior Involving Adults

An 8-year-old second grader in a parochial school was teased and rejected at school. His teacher reported to the parents that he was not being included in any of his peer's games. The intake interviewer helped his teacher identify two behaviors that significantly impaired his acceptance by peers: (a) He tattled on other children and (b) he laughed inappropriately (too long and when nothing was really funny).

A daily report card (cf. Barkley, 1991) was set up in which the teacher checked off whether or not each of these behaviors occurred in the morning and afternoon. Parents reminded the boy before dropping him off each day to work on inhibiting these behaviors and gave him a reward at the end of the week for 7 or more out of 10 possible good reports from the teacher. After 3 weeks, neither behavior was occurring. He began children's friendship training, which finished during the summer. Mom was able to set up play dates with schoolmates. He continued to have two successful play dates per week well past the end of the program. When school started in the

fall, he was regularly included into a particular group of five boys (with whom he had play dates).

Decreasing Obsessions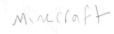

A 7-year-old first grader with Asperger's disorder was obsessed with trains and would not talk about anything else, if he were allowed to talk about trains. He was told by the group leader that he would not be allowed to talk about trains when in session or doing homework for the class. His mother gladly agreed. Throughout the class, these rules were enforced and his obsession with trains greatly decreased.

Played Together Before the Group Started

A second-grade boy and girl were referred to the group at the same time by their teacher. They had played together on occasion. In this case, as with all other children in the class, the parents were told at intake that they must agree that the children not play together until after Session 12 of the class. The parents were advised to tell their children that this is one of the rules of the class. The reasons for this were as follows:

The children may not actually want to play together. This allows them a graceful way to avoid an uncomfortable situation.

When the children hear each other's reports of playing with other children on play dates (starting in Session 8), it will minimize any hurtful impact. Rather than thinking "she's having a play date without me," they might think "we're not allowed to play together."

During the program, we encourage the development of same-sex friendships.

PART II

CHAPTER

8

Program Infrastructure

Treatment Rationale

This intervention requires extensive planning before the first session starts. This chapter will help the clinician ensure that physical layout and staff talent is commensurate with this task. An invariant framework for sessions is described. Having a constant framework is helpful for patients so that they can anticipate key therapeutic features in order to better focus on content.

8.1 Physical Facilities

There are three locations to secure before beginning the class: indoor locations for parent and child classes, and an outdoor location (play deck) for some of the child games. Parent and child rooms and the outside play area should be as close as possible to each other for quick transport of children during each session.

Parent Room: The parent room should have a large table and enough space for all parents to be seated together at the same time. It is helpful to create a classroom atmosphere for the parent sessions.

Child Room: The child room should have a blackboard or marker board, tables, and chairs for children to sit in. There must be "floor room" for

sessions focusing on play dates or as an alternative area during periods of inclement weather.

Play Deck: The outside play area used to teach skills for outside games should resemble a schoolyard as much as possible. It should have sports equipment such as a basketball hoop, soccer goal net, and tetherball pole, and should be fully fenced in for safety.

8.2 Therapist Characteristics

Hibbs et al. (1997) suggested that the following types of therapists might be suited better for an intervention that involves a manual: those more comfortable with psychoeducational approaches (e.g., parent training), and "crossover" professionals (e.g., teachers, school counselors, or primary health care paraprofessionals). The child group leader must be comfortable as a teacher of young children. Classroom behavioral techniques—ease in praising children, correcting children when they are incorrect, and setting limits when they seek negative attention—are requirements for an effective child group leader.

We have trained group leaders at various educational levels. Child group leaders have been social work, psychology, and psychiatry trainees and UCLA undergraduate students. Parent group leaders have been clinical social workers, social work trainees, and clinical psychology trainees.

This has worked well, with new group leaders yielding outcome data consistent with our seasoned veterans.

How to Organize the Sessions

We have had to work with 1-hour sessions and have indicated times based on this total session length. Parent sessions can be completed within an hour (limiting group size to 10 children). It is important for parent and child classes to end in synchrony. The parent class should end as the children are coming back from the child group. Child misbehavior most often happens when children are waiting outside the parent room for the parent class to end.

Parent Sessions

The parent session mission is to teach skills, correct parent errors, and help effect the solution of specific impediments to homework compliance. Table 8.1 presents general guidelines for working with parents. Allowing parents to get off track or adopt counterproductive positions will detract from the clarity of teaching and frustrate other parents who want to get on with the mission of the group. Thus, group leaders must be ready to cut parents off when they don't follow instructions.

The standard session agenda facilitates staying on track. Each parent session (except for Sessions 1 and 12) is broken down into four segments:

Initial Gathering (5 minutes): Parents and children gather and the group leaders inspect the toys that the children have brought in before the children leave the room for their session.

Homework Review (25 minutes): Each parent reports the results of the previously assigned homework. This holds the parent accountable for homework compliance and also instructs the whole group on how to overcome problems. Discussion includes anticipation of possible problems on the next homework assignment.

Parent Handout/Homework Assignment (20 minutes): A handout is presented and reviewed. The purpose is to inform parents of their roles in the peer acceptance of their children, ensure that parents take their assigned roles in the homework, and ensure that parents provide support for the principles the children are being taught.

End-of-Session Reunification (10 minutes): The parents and children are reunited. The date and time and other party to the homework assignment are negotiated between each parent and child before they leave the session.

TABLE 8.1 Summary Guidelines for Working With Parents

Do

1. Stick to the session plan.
2. Interrupt parents when they take the group off track.
3. Hold parents responsible for their parts of the homework assignment.
4. Review the specifics of newly assigned completed homework.
5. Ask first for homework successes and have the parents who had them report first. This serves three purposes: (1) It fills the session with positive examples of homework compliance. (2) It encourages parents who haven't completed the homework to try it next week. (3) It doesn't allow much time for excuses for why the homework couldn't be done.
6. Help parents with any problem solving necessary to attempt the next homework assignment.
7. Review handouts by reading and commenting (suggestions will be in the therapist guides). Reading the handout ensures that parents attend to all parts of the handout.

Don't

1. Never make side conversations with a parent (you are distracting them from the purpose of the intervention and leaving out other parents in the group).
2. Avoid posing general and "feeling" questions to the group.
3. Avoid discussing what will happen in future sessions (unless it is in the therapist guide to the session handout)—parents need to focus on what is needed each week.

The handling of homework assignments is the key to generalization: (a) homework reports come early in the parent session, (b) there is explicit review of the homework, and (c) the assignments are easier at first, and gradually become more difficult. High compliance rates for the easier assignments, together with pressure from the group, set the expectation for homework compliance.

Parents have occasionally attempted to evade help for uncompleted homework. It is usually helpful to ask for homework successes first, because most parents will complete the homework. This tactic has the effect of casting homework noncompliance as the exception rather than the rule. Sometimes a parent will give several excuses for homework noncompliance, hoping to get support for this from either other participants or the group leader. The group leader should respond by ignoring excuses and helping the parent work out a plan for homework completion for the next session.

Potential Problems

"Snowing" the Group Leader

When the group was asked for homework successes, a parent said she didn't do homework but had her child do something else (not covered in class). She then complimented the group leader by saying how much better her child was as a result of the group. The group leader interrupted the parent and said, "I need to hear from someone who did the assignment right now." Not listening to excuses and interrupting a parent may make the parent momentarily upset, but will be silently welcomed by parents who are on track and will increase the probability of compliance with homework from the noncompliant parent in the future.

Attempting to Commandeer the Agenda

The mother of a fifth-grade boy asked, "My child is getting into fights at school—can't you talk about that now?" The group leader stated that this was not the purpose of the parent group and that there was an agenda for this session. He advised that if she wanted individual help, he could refer her to a counselor at the end of the session. The parent accepted this redirection.

Chronic Lateness

A second-grade girl and her mother consistently arrived 15 minutes late each session. On the third such instance, the group leader took the mother aside (at the very end of the session) and told her, "I notice that your daughter has been coming late. Today she missed the homework review and part of the instruction. She learns quickly. But if she doesn't hear whole lessons, she won't learn them. Is there anything you can do to get her here earlier?" The mom apologized and said she had to wait for the babysitter to arrive for her other three children. She would try to have the babysitter come earlier.

Child Sessions

Children learn more from doing something than from talking about it. In our sessions, the talking parts serve to reinforce homework compliance and alert the children to the rules to be learned. The play portion keeps them interested and concretizes the rules for them.

Table 8.2 presents guidelines for working with children. Coaches and group leaders act as consultants rather than playmates, watching and dispensing token and verbal reinforcement, and providing consequences for misbehavior (Ladd & Golter, 1988). They avoid playing and conversing with children. Rejected children tend to seek out adults rather than other children. This should not be encouraged because it helps them avoid difficult social situations and deprives them of social learning opportunities.

The child session begins as the children are led out of the parent room after the initial gathering and into the child room. It ends when the children reenter the parent room for the end-of-session reunification. Each child session (except for the first and last) is broken down into three segments:

Homework Review (10 minutes): Children report on the results of the homework assignment given in the previous session. Motivation for children to do the homework comes from parent insis-

TABLE 8.2 Summary Guidelines for Working With Children

Do
1. Establish a teacher-pupil relationship with the children.
2. Keep homework review and didactic segments short and on track.
3. Allow as much time as possible for the real play segment.
4. Use *specific praise* (stating exactly what the child has done correctly).
5. Enforce appropriate body boundaries (discourage "fast friends" and "horseplay").
6. Enforce the rules of the group.

Don't
1. Never join in the children's play (we are teaching them how to play with other children, not adults).
2. Never carry on conversations with an individual child (e.g., on the way to the deck activity after didactic). Always direct children to speak only to other children.
3. Don't call on children who shout out the answer during the didactic presentation (interrupting and calling out should not be rewarded).
4. Never support incorrect statements by children (e.g., "not having enough time" to do their homework as assigned).

Rules for Using a Socratic Method
The Socratic method actively involves the children in producing rules for behavior and explaining their importance. This approach is recommended for most sessions that introduce new rules (Rules of a Good Sport, Rules of a Good Host, Rules of a Good Winner):

1. The group leader keeps in mind the *template* for the session plan. Rules don't have to be reviewed in the order given, but rather as the children come up with them.
2. If a child says something that can be changed a little to fit into one of the rules, accept it and praise the child.
3. Restate the rule as in the session plan and ask the group, "Why is it a good idea to follow that rule?"
4. If a child says something incorrect, make an unelaborated response such as "No, that is not a rule for . . ." and then ask another child for correct rules.
5. Do not engage in a "debate" with the child regarding his or her rationale.

tence on it, combined with hearing the other children's successes and getting a star (see Table 6) for attempting it.

Didactic (20 minutes): The didactic presentation may help children to attend to key situations in their social world and lay the groundwork for subsequent practice in session and at home.

Real Play (20 minutes): This is the segment of the session the children like the most. They get to play either in the child room or in the outside play area, depending on the module being presented.

Homework review and didactic segments mimic a classroom setting. The group leaders only recognize children who raise their hand. Children's responses during these segments require specific feedback so that they can identify things they do correctly and eliminate counterproductive behaviors. Correcting errors might make a child uncomfortable at the moment but

will make clear to the child and the other group members that the response was incorrect. It is advisable to keep the homework review and didactic segments as brief as possible (covering all of the material in the session plan) so that the real play segment will last as long as possible.

Verbal instruction can be effective in orienting children to the skill being taught, especially if a Socratic method is used (see Table 10.8, in chapter 10). However, didactic presentation is not sufficient to change child behaviors. Children consolidate knowledge more readily through coaching in the real play segment. But remember, most of the important practice will be done under the supervision of parents during the homework assignments.

A Note on Sports Proficiency

Some of the children in our groups are in dire need of instruction on the basic rules and strategies of sports play. Many have been rejected for

TABLE 8.3 Behavior Control Techniques, Child Sessions 1–12

Delivering Stars During the Didactic Portion

1. Stars should be given consistently across sessions—a star for bringing in the correct toy, a star for each part of the homework completion, extra credit stars for astute contributions during the didactic.
2. The tactic of counting individual stars toward everyone's party eliminates jealousy and competition among the children over who has the most stars, because everybody benefits from everybody else's contribution of stars.
3. It is important to give a star only for completion of the assigned homework and to not give more stars for extra homework attempts or completions. This may encourage children to "make up" homework reports to get additional stars.

Introducing Prompts and Time Outs

1. The topic of "time outs" is discussed during the first session. When a child is disruptive for the first time, tell the child, "This is your first prompt. On the next prompt, you will be sent out of the room for a 1-minute time out."
2. If a child persists, give the time out, stating, "Now it's time for you to take a time out for 1-minute. I'll time it and let you back in the room after it is over." Take the child just outside of the room leaving the door ajar so he or she can hear what is going on. During the real play segment, the time out area is off to the side of the play area.
3. Time the one-minute interval and neutrally tell the child to come back in the room without any further explanation.

Behaviors requiring prompts:

- Continued disruption.
- Rolling eyes.
- Inappropriate sexual comments.
- Putting feet up on the table.
- Taking out a book and starting to read.
- Belittling the program or peers.

Behaviors requiring immediate time out:

- Name calling.
- Verbal or physical aggression.

so long that they haven't kept up with what other agemates know about the games. Shy children may be hesitant to join in play even after they are invited into a game. Limiting the length of the treatment to 12 weeks does not allow instruction on both how to play certain games and good sportsmanship. Clearly we feel good sportsmanship is more important as children can usually find others who are proficient at their level of play (a life task for boys and men who want to enjoy the company of others).

If the intervention is expanded to 18 weeks, there will be adequate time to coach in different games. In this case, we would recommend coaching first the games that are played spontaneously by children on schoolyards at recess. This would

include handball, Chinese jumprope, and basketball (small group rather than full team).

Behavioral Control Techniques

The reward program and level of stimulation of the session are more important than the format of negative consequences. Rewards take two forms: (a) stars during the didactic segments and (b) tokens during deck activities (Sessions 6, 10–11). During the homework review and didactic segments of each session, children are given stars on the blackboard for quietly listening in the seat, raising hands before talking, class participation, and homework compliance. Rewards to the whole group are occasionally delivered (see Table 8.3 for more on delivering stars, prompts, and time outs, and Table 13.1, in Chapter 13, for delivering tokens).

Potential Problems

Resistant Child Number 1: Supplementing Stars With Greater Rewards

Despite a fourth-grade boy's refusal to participate in the program, his mother was initially able to prevail. However, by Session 3, he became increasingly disruptive during the didactic segment of the class, threatening and intimidating peers and refusing to take time outs.

He was placed on a modified "star program" in which he earned up to 10 stars (the stars usually given out in a session) for appropriate behavior, good contributions to class, and using the social components he was taught. Five bonus stars were awarded for completing homework assignments (his mother was consulted during the initial gathering of each session prior to awarding this). A star was subtracted for each offense that earned a time out (threatening others or noncompliance with the group leader). Refusing to take time out would result in losing another star. At the end of each session, his mother was handed a sheet completed by the group leader listing stars and time outs. Earning at least 10 stars was rewarded with a meal at a local fast food restaurant after session. Earning 70 total stars would earn him a CD player.

On almost all sessions he earned all stars, with few negative behaviors, limited disruption of the lesson, and ready compliance with the group leader. He showed remarkable improvement in his relations with peers: He became quite gentle in group games, praising others, ensuring that they enjoyed the game, politely making requests, and easily accepting his requests being turned down.

Resistant Child Number 2: Separate Contract With Resistant Child

Across three sessions, the mother of a sixth-grade boy had increasing difficulty getting him to come.

She asked the group leader to "tell him why he needs to come." The leader stated that he would be glad to talk to the boy, but previous experience had indicated that "telling children why they needed to come" probably wouldn't be helpful. The session was scheduled just before the group, so it would be easier for the mom to get him to come to the class that day.

During the individual session, the boy said that the things we were teaching made him feel "stupid," he didn't like coming, and he didn't want to be friends with the others in the group. The group leader told him that he appeared to be pretty smart, but that whenever we teach a class we have to say things that some children may already know, just to make sure all of the children in the class know them. We weren't concerned if he didn't like the group—because there are other things he doesn't like that are still beneficial for him, like going to the dentist. We were more concerned that he be able to use some of the things we talk about to help him at home and at school. The boy was told to check back with the group leader after Session 7. The boy said that if he was able to use something from the class, he would change his mind. The interviewer praised the boy, saying, "I'm glad you are keeping an open mind." The boy was also told that he didn't have to like the other children in the class. His behavior toward others had been very good (particularly considering he didn't like them), and he should continue this. The boy presented no further problems in the group.

Body Boundaries

Rejected children may have one of three problems with body boundaries. Girls may start "pairing" by Session 3 (but the pairs are not stable from session to session). You may see one girl putting her arm on another girl's shoulder while walking to the childrens room. This is inappropriate for two reasons. First, it can be overpowering for other girls who might not be comfortable addressing it. Second, it is obvious to other girls present that they are being left out. Excluding others at this early stage of getting acquainted is not a productive behavior. Instead, children need to keep their options open so that they find others with whom they are compatible.

Boys may be roughly horsing around with each other, as if they were very best friends. Asperger's children may be attempting to hug or kiss other children whether or not it is welcome (sometimes with the encouragement of their parents). In all cases, these behaviors should be stopped by the group leader, first with a short informal group discussion and then later with prompts and time outs.

Clinical Example of Group Discussion About Body Boundaries

GL [to the group after two children are seen violating body boundaries]: Is it okay to touch someone when you hardly know them?

Several children: No!

GL. That's right. You don't begin to touch someone until you know him or her for a while and you both are good friends. Right now no one knows each other well enough to be good friends.

PART

III

SESSION CONTENT

Table iii.1 presents an overview of all child and parent modules. The first session establishes the ground rules for both parents and children, gives some rudimentary phone skills to the children, and has parents begin to "network" with each other and supervise the child's phone call. Children are taught to gather information about the play interests of other children. At first they practice with another group member (homework assigned for Sessions 2–6) and eventually with a child who could be a potential playmate (homework assigned for Sessions 4–12). Parents are taught active listening skills (Session 2) in order to enhance their ability to supervise their child, and they begin to look for neighborhood resources for their child to meet new friends (assignment for Sessions 4 and 5). Children are taught how to attempt to "slip in" to a game being played by other children and to accept being turned down in their attempt. These skills culminate in the "slipping in" assignment due on Sessions 6–9, in which parents take their child to a local park to join others at play. These skills are buttressed in Child Sessions 5 and 6 with the rules of a good sport, which govern children's behavior after they join others at play.

The focus shifts to inside games and the play date, starting in Session 7. Children learn the rules of a good host and parents learn how to monitor and enforce these rules over the course of weekly play dates with a new child each week (homework assigned for Sessions 8–12). Resisting teasing and dealing with adult complaints about the child are addressed in Parent and Child Sessions 8 and 9.

Finally the focus shifts back to outside games as children are introduced to skills necessary in competitive games (the rules of a good winner). Parents are presented with two educative handouts, dealing with boy–girl differences in socialization (Session 10) and decreasing physical fights (Session 11). Graduation takes place at the end of Session 12, after posttreatment assessment.

The "How to Conduct the Session" portion of each chapter in this section is organized separately by parent and child sessions. This is so that group leaders can bring this volume to sessions, open to the session outline and use the outline, to guide the session. Numbers indicate the sequence of steps that group leaders should follow for each segment of the sessions. Chapters 9–16 in this section each contain group leader guides to parent handouts (and/or parent assignments) so that group leaders can add material for clarification.

TABLE III.1 Overview of Parent and Child Sessions

Session	Parent Handout	Parent Homework Assigned	Child Didactic	Real Play
1	Goals and limits	In-group call (2–6) Outside toy (2–6)	Session rules Topics of conversation	Winning unimportant (Capture the flag)
2	Two-way conversations; Active listening	Monitor two-way conversations (3–7)	Places and times to make friends; two-way conversations	Preliminary group entry (Wolf pack)
3	Resources for friends	Outside group call (4–12); look for neighborhood play area (4, 5)	Slipping in	Slipping in (Prisoner)
4	Slipping in		Level of disclosure Being turned down	Group entry; being turned down (Soccer)
5	Slipping in	Slipping in (6–9)	Rules of a good sport	Slipping in (Magic Johnson Basketball)
6	Inside games	Inside toy (7–9)	Rules of a good sport Ending games	Good sportsmanship (children pick game)
7	Play dates	Play dates (8–12)	Rules of a good host	Good host rules (inside game)
8	Resisting teasing	Practice making fun of the tease (9, 10)	Making fun of the tease	Good host rules (inside game)
9	Adult complaints about child	Outside competitive toy (10, 11)	"Unjust" adult accusations	Good host rules Unjust accusations (children pick outside games)
10	Boy–girl differences		Rules of a good winner	Rules of a good winner (children pick outside games)
11	Decreasing physical fights	Graduation party	Ways to stay out of a fight	Rules of a good winner (children pick outside games)
12	Post assessment	Where to go from here	Post-assessment	Graduation party

Note. Numbers in parentheses indicate sessions on which the assignment is due (reported during the following sessions).

We have inserted typical *clinical examples* of how things work well and *potential problems* we have encountered at the end of the steps of each segment, so that group leaders will not have to "wade through" these examples while delivering session material. Footnotes serve as memory prompts and clarification.

Every session has parent handouts and/or homework assignment sheets that are distributed to parents to take home as reminders. We have kept these handouts simple and give them out only one at a time (not the whole set at once) so that parents will be more apt to look at them when they need to be reminded. Child group leaders have one additional type of handout: Rules for games are provided each time a game is introduced during the real play segment. Parent handouts and parent assignment sheets are at the end of each parent session plan. Table iii.2 is a materials list, covering all sessions.

TABLE III.2 Materials List for All Sessions

Children's Friendship Training

Materials list

Parent Sessions:

1. Accordion file
2. Attendance sheet (each name to be checked off when the child and parent come)
3. Blank name tags
4. Broad-point markers (parents and children write names on name tags)
5. Current handouts
6. Telephone rosters (with child name, parent names, and home phone number where they can be reached for calls by other group members)
7. Current child and parent session outlines

Child Sessions:

1. A file box
2. Reward tracking sheet (to record totals of stars and tokens awarded to each child)
3. About 70 tokens
4. Erasers and chalk for writing stars and important points on the blackboard.

Session 1:

1. Planned absence sheets (the child name is at the top and the dates of each session are listed for check-off by parents indicating they will not be able to come).

Party (Session 12):

1. Diplomas should be printed on fancy paper with each child's name and signed by the group leaders.
2. Party decorations, plates, and cups should be on hand.
3. A separate table should be set up in the children's room on which to place the food and drinks.
4. A VCR and monitor with a supply of screened, age-appropriate tapes should be set up in the children's room. The children will vote for the videotape that they would most like to see.

PART III

CHAPTER

9

Introductory Session/Setting the Stage

Treatment Rationale

Many parents enter treatment with misconceptions about the causes of their child's friendship problems, the mechanisms for improving their child's peer relations, and their role in the process. The primary treatment hypothesis is that adequate information will focus parents on homework compliance, which is the major vehicle for therapeutic change.

Children may not know what to expect from this class. This may result in either apprehension or misbehavior. Setting and enforcing behavioral guidelines for children will clarify their expectations and promote the children's opportunity to learn.

9.1 Importance of Parent Knowledge

According to Mize, Pettit, and Brown (1995), parents who raise children who are well-liked by peers believe that social skills are important and modifiable and that parents help to socialize their children through specific types of supervision. These parents not only act differently, but they have beliefs and knowledge different from those of parents of children who are rejected by peers. DeAenlle (1979, cited in Parke, MacDonald, & Bhavnagri, 1988) presented parents with hypothetical vignettes of social problem situations

their child might reasonably get into. Parents were asked what advice they might give to their child about each. Parents of well-liked children were able to give more specific answers than parents of least-liked children. It is therefore necessary to change parental knowledge about their children's friendships. A review of categories of peer acceptance is a good start.

9.2 Definition and Categories of Peer Acceptance

Acceptance is defined as how well liked a child is within his or her peer group. Peer nomination procedures were reviewed in Chapter 2. A common classification system breaks the social status continuum into five categories (Dodge et al., 1990): *average,* who obtain about the class average in positive social preference scores (number liked nominations outnumber number disliked nominations) and social impact scores; *popular,* who are substantially above average in positive social preference and social impact scores; *rejected,* who are substantially above average in negative social preference scores; *neglected,* who are substantially below average in social impact scores; and *controversial* who are above average on social impact and who receive both liked and disliked nominations. Proportions of children in these categories vary between 37% and 52% for average, 14% to 21% for popular, 12% to 19% for rejected, 13% to 23% for neglected, and 2% to 9% for controversial (Bukowski & Newcomb, 1985; Coie, Dodge, & Copoletti, 1982; Crick & Grotpeter, 1995; Wentzel & Asher, 1995).

Research on Categories of Peer Acceptance

9.3 Context and Stability of Sociometric Categories

With the exception of the controversial category, several researchers have found these categories to be relatively stable for up to 2 years (Howes, 1990; Parke et al., 1997). Coie and Dodge (1983) and Harrist, Zaia, Bates, Dodge, and Pettit (1997) found that rejected status was more stable across 4 years than either neglected or controversial status. Consistent with this, Gresham and Stuart (1992) found that liked least ratings showed the most stability, with test-retest correlations of .60. Coie and Kupersmidt (1983) demonstrated cross-situational stability: When getting to know new peers, children quickly reestablish the social status they had with familiar peers.

Even though there are stability problems with some categories of peer acceptance, these categories are a useful shorthand rubric to describe different children who enroll in social skills programs. The following sections describe characteristics associated with each category.

9.4 Popular

In a meta-analysis, Newcomb, Bukowski, and Pattee (1993) have shown that psychometrically popular children show less aggression, disruption, loneliness, and withdrawal and more problem-solving skills, positive social interactions, and friendship skills when compared to average accepted children. Results differ when children are administered peer sociometric techniques versus when they are simply asked who is popular (labeled as popular). According to the results of Parkhurst and Hopmeyer (1998), seventh and eighth graders nominated as most liked were not necessarily high on perceived popularity. Sociometrically popular children

were characterized by peers as kind and trustworthy, whereas children labeled as popular were characterized as dominant, aggressive, or "stuck-up."

9.5 Neglected Versus Withdrawn

There is much confusion among researchers between children who are sociometrically neglected (by peers) versus those who are classified (by adults) as withdrawn through behavioral observations and teacher ratings. Some authors report overlap (e.g., Newcomb et al., 1993). Perhaps the most definitive study to date was Harrist et al. (1997), who identified 26% of kindergartners as socially withdrawn, based on behavioral observations of free-play behavior. In collecting peer ratings on all children, they noted that most sociometrically neglected children (70%) were not classified as withdrawn. Cluster analysis of withdrawn children revealed three groupings. The most problematic grouping were children in the active-isolate cluster, who showed a strong tendency (59%) to be rejected, whereas most children (60–77%) in the other clusters were either average or popular.

Bell-Dolan et al. (1995) reported that withdrawn-rejected elementary school girls had more internalizing problems (self-report and teacher report) than neglected girls (whether withdrawn or not). Many children with serious psychopathology, such as autism, Asperger's syndrome, major depression, and anxious children would probably be classified as withdrawn-rejected.

Sociometrically neglected children seem to have a better prognosis than behaviorally withdrawn children. Bell-Dolan et al. (1995) found that neglected girls did not evidence any significant adjustment problems. Others find that neglected children may have quite positive academic profiles. When compared with average status children, sociometrically neglected sixth and seventh graders reported higher levels of motivation and were described by teachers as more self-regulated learners and more compliant (Wentzel & Asher, 1995). Neglected children seem to make a fresh start in new groups and may not remain neglected (Coie & Dodge, 1983; Coie & Kupersmidt, 1983). Perhaps some neglected children do not mind playing with others but would rather play alone. These children may have high rates of solitary constructive play but are rated by teachers as having adequate social competence (Rubin, 1982).

In conclusion, behavioral withdrawal, as with behavioral observations in general, doesn't correlate strongly with peer sociometrics. The combination of rejection and withdrawal seems to indicate potentially serious social problems. Withdrawn-rejected children are not withdrawn by their own choice (Rubin, Stewart, & Coplan, 1995). Care should be taken in initial telephone contacts with parents to assess if behavioral withdrawal noted by teachers and parents is really a personal preference in a child with adequate functioning in academic areas, respect for others, and good quality close friendships. Children with a personal preference for solitary play may not require social skills training if there are no indicators of loneliness or peer dislike.

9.6 Rejected

Between 12% and 19% of school-aged children are rejected by their classmates (Burleson, 1985; Kupersmidt, Griesler, DeRosier, Patterson, & Davis, 1995). Rejected children report more loneliness than children do from any other psychometric category (Asher & Wheeler, 1985). Rejected status can be a relatively enduring peer response (Coie & Dodge, 1983; Coie & Kupersmidt, 1983; Tremblay et al., 1988). Children rejected by their peers in the classroom became similarly rejected in a play group with unfamiliar peers by the end of the first 45-minute session (Dodge et al., 1990). Rejected status has been shown to be predictive of a child's later social problems (Hymel, Rubin, Rowden, & LeMare, 1990; Michelson, Foster, & Ritchey, 1977; Tremblay et al., 1988), delinquency (Roff, Sells, & Golden, 1972), and adult maladjustment (Cowen, Pederson, Babigan, Izzo, & Trost, 1973). The study by Cowen and associates showed that rejected status in third grade was a better predictor of life adjustment than a battery that included self-report, school records, and intellectual performance.

Rejected children have been shown to be more socially inappropriate, aggressive, and disruptive than their peers are (Newcomb et al.,

1993; Oden, 1986). However, this may be misleading, because rejected boys and girls differ considerably and even rejected boys are heterogeneous with respect to other important behavioral characteristics.

Important subgroupings of rejected boys are those with and without aggression. Bierman et al. (1993) employed multiple teacher and peer measures. Almost 80% of males they classified as aggressive-rejected showed a consistent profile that included verbal aggression and rule violations (see Chap. 19 for a more detailed review of aggressive-rejected children). Teachers' Conners' Inattention Scales tended to be elevated, suggesting the influence of ADHD. Nonaggressive-rejected boys could be discriminated from the other groups by peer report as having peculiar, immature habits, behavior, or appearance, although only 40% showed a common profile (Bierman et al., 1993). The results of Wentzel and Asher (1995) suggest that aggressive-rejected children tend to have problematic academic profiles whereas nonaggressive-rejected children do not.

According to Kupersmidt, DeRosier, and Patterson (1995), girls have rates of rejection comparable to those of boys (12% vs. 15% in their sample of 1,271 second through fifth graders). Physical aggression does not characterize most rejected girls, although physically aggressive girls are more likely to be rejected than physically aggressive boys (Stormshak et al., 1999), probably because physical aggression is relatively unusual in girls. Lack of research leaves the profile of rejected girls as somewhat of a mystery.

9.7 Controversial

Controversial children receive "liked most" ratings from some children and "disliked most" ratings from others, thus receiving high social impact scores and average social preference scores on peer assessments (Coie et al., 1982). Dodge (1983) and Newcomb et al. (1993) reported them to be more sociable than popular and average accepted children, but they tend to make hostile statements and play aggressively. Controversial sixth and seventh graders were described by teachers as less likely to follow rules or learn independently and more likely to start fights than average accepted children (Wentzel & Asher, 1995). Controversial children have more friends than rejected children, largely because friendship is more related to positive rather than negative nominations from peers (Bukowski, Pizzamiglio, Newcomb, & Hoza, 1996).

Johnstone, Frame, and Bouman (1992) compared controversial, rejected-aggressive, and popular elementary school boys on physical attractiveness, athletic ability, and academic ability, using peer and teacher ratings. They found that in many respects, controversial boys had more resources than rejected-aggressive boys did. They were rated by peers as equivalent to the popular boys in athletic abilities, similar to rejected-aggressive boys in academic abilities, and falling between the two groups in physical attractiveness.

Crick and Grotpeter (1995) noted that controversial children employ relational aggression more than other peer status groups. They measured relational aggression by soliciting peer nominations of children in the class who: (a) exclude others from their group out of anger, (b) tell children they will stop liking them unless they do what they say, and (c) ignore people when mad at them. In order for relational aggression to be effective, the perpetrator has to be liked by some peers, thus explaining the greater prevalence among sociometrically controversial children. The study also found many similarities between relational aggression among girls and physical aggression among boys (Crick, 1995, 1996; Crick & Grotpeter, 1995, 1996).

Results are contradictory with regard to the stability of controversial status. Parke et al. (1997) reported sex differences in developmental trajectories of children classified as controversial in kindergarten through second grade: Most controversial first-grade boys were rated as rejected in second grade, whereas most controversial first-grade girls were rated as average in second grade. Newcomb and Bukowski (1984) found only 41% of fifth-grade boys and girls classified as controversial remained so for 1 month, and none remained so for the 2-year study period. However, one long-term follow-up study found that the controversial category had predictive power for girls. Underwood, Kupersmidt, and Coie (1996), following 226 girls, found that controversial fourth-grade girls were more likely to become pregnant in their teens. Perhaps this category is more significant for older girls.

9.8 Implications From Research and Clinical Practice

Children referred for outpatient treatment for friendship problems are heterogeneous with respect to presentation. The vast majority of children will be boys who would fall in the sociometrically rejected category. They will typically present with either verbal or physical aggression or varying degrees of peculiarities. The peer status of these children is unlikely to change without intervention. In contrast, neglected and withdrawn children are extremely variable in their need for intervention. It is likely that evidence of psychopathology (anxiety, depression, shyness, autism spectrum disorder) is a better clue as to the stability of their peer problems and the need for intervention and thus the need for a diagnostic workup. Some children may have less need for peer interaction and may be quite content to play alone for much of their time even though they have adequate social skills. It is likely that intervention is not necessary for these children.

Regardless of the presentation of the child, many parents feel that rejected children either will "grow out of it" or will be accepted in a new peer group. Some parents may blame their child's present peer group, rather than focusing on the behavioral causes for their child's rejection. We have found that it is instructive for parents to be familiar with some of the research just described (and for group leaders to be familiar with all of the described research, in case parents have questions).

Despite having the same observed prevalence of peer problems, girls are referred for social skills training at a much lower rate than boys are. This may result from girls' peer groups being more tolerant of social ineptness than the peer groups of boys, or girls' peer problems being subtler, as in the use of relational aggression rather than overt physical aggression. Girls are also more likely to drop out before treatment begins. We recently found evidence (Frankel, 2002a) that mothers of girls who have social problems may themselves have more social problems than mothers of boys with social problems. This may be a factor in etiology and dropout rates.

How to Conduct the Session

Until Now

Your dealings with parents have focused on social deficits. Parents are worried about how the group will affect their child. Some parents fear contagion of bad behavior between other group participants and their child, and others are hoping their child will not fail in this group. Regardless of how concerted the attempts are to prepare parents for participation in this group, the group is likely to be different than what they have experienced before. Some parents might expect that this is similar to a school classroom where they can take the teacher aside and try to get special consideration for their children, perhaps influencing the curriculum. Other parents might expect that the class will deal with feelings rather than teach skills. However, most parents should quickly become comfortable within the structure provided by the class.

In This Session

The purpose of this session is to guide participant expectations to a fruitful path for the next 12 sessions. This is accomplished by conveying reasonable expectations for treatment to the parents and children and a clear understanding of the methods and goals of the program. The parents will invariably need more specific instruction on this than the children will. One crucial goal of this session (which sets the tone for all the subsequent sessions) is to discourage any complaints or negative talk parents may have about how hard their children are to manage or how socially inept their children are. The expectation should also be set that parents examine the part that they can play to improve their child's peer relationships. Group leaders should earn the confidence of parents by demonstrating that the procedures being taught have proven success, and that the leaders will not allow deviation from the planned curriculum.

Children should come to expect that although there is work to be done, they will have a good time, that nothing in the class will be too hard for them, that the leaders (rather than disruptive children) are in control of the group, and that they will learn about relationships with other children. Group leaders should not encourage participants to develop friendships with each other, as this will detract from the group focus, which is to develop skills to form new friendships in their own schools and neighborhoods.

Parent Session Plan 1

Initial Gathering

The main focus of the initial gathering of parents and children in this session is to hold participants, inevitably arriving at staggered times, so that they all start instruction together. It is not beneficial to have parents spend too much time talking to each other informally before there has been an opportunity to set a positive tone for the session. The reason for this is that some parents will want to begin "swapping" negative experiences about their child as a way of handling their own nervousness and to gain support. Other parents may want to be in special favor with the group leaders. Keep parents busy so that they don't engage in this behavior until they learn that the group will have a positive focus and no one will be treated differently.

1. Before parents arrive, make sure chairs are arranged in "horseshoe" shape around a table (group leader sits in the open end of the horseshoe). Have telephone roster and planned absence sheets on the table.
2. Say hello to participants as they arrive but avoid getting into extended conversations, saying that you will start when everyone arrives.
3. Have each parent and child fill out a name tag in large print and have them put it in a visible place on their chests. Group leaders should wear name tags as well. Children should *not* use name tags humorously (i.e., writing made-up nicknames instead of their name).
4. As participants are arriving, take attendance. Don't wait longer than 10 minutes after the scheduled start of the session to get under way.
5. The sessions formally begin when the children line up and are led out of the room.
6. Collect planned absence sheets. Check for holidays or other occasions in which many class members may miss a session.
7. Check accuracy of telephone rosters with par-

ents. Make corrections as they are needed. Caution parents on limits of confidentiality in a group situation. They should not share anything about someone else in the group that will identify them.

Potential Problems

Arriving Late and Flustered

Some parents may arrive late and be flustered at the adversity they came upon in getting to the first session. Group leaders won't have time to comfort parents. It sets a good precedent that "the class must go on" (not to mention that it is good social skill for parents not to disrupt a working group with their own woes).

Parent Cross-Talk

Some parents will get into an interesting (to them) conversation that continues after the group leader starts. Don't let this continue. The group leader should interrupt the cross-talk and make sure he or she has everyone's attention.

Planning to Miss Substantial Numbers of Sessions

During the intake session, parents of an 8-year-old boy were enthusiastic about the class and committed to the 12 sessions. However, when the first session started, they indicated the last four sessions as planned absences. The group leader noticed this and took the parents aside, saying quietly to them that their son would miss a major part of the program. When the group leader suggested they hold back starting until they could commit to all sessions, the parents assured him that they would come. Subsequently, they only missed one of the last four sessions.

Child Writes Silly Name on Name Tag

A third-grade boy smilingly wrote a nickname he clearly had just made up on his name tag, in an apparent attempt to establish himself as a "class clown." The group leader asked his parent if that was the name he actually went by. When the parent said "no," the group leader had the

parent help him write his actual name on the tag.

Initial Introductions

[After the children leave to start the child session, brief parent introductions provide beneficial initial structure to the group].

1. Have the parents say their child's name, their name, their child's grade and age, and what they like best about their child. If they say negative things (speak about their child's diagnosis, etc.), refocus them to say just what was asked.[1]
2. Briefly summarize (no more than a few words) what each parent likes best about their child after he or she says it. When all parents have finished, summarize the age range of the group and state this as the reason they are grouped together.
3. Talk about the program: It's been given to over 800 children, starting in 1989; 90% of parents report some benefits; 70% of teachers report improvement; 80% of children with low self-esteem have higher measured self-esteem after the group is over.
4. Give the rationale for collecting pre and post data: to give parent feedback on the degree of improvement; to monitor quality control of the class; to assess changes in the program.
5. Briefly summarize how children in popular/accepted, neglected, and rejected categories are assessed (liked most and liked least nominations from a roster).
6. Say that children who are labeled by peers as popular are not necessarily most liked. Children who are most liked are viewed as kind and trustworthy, whereas children labeled as popular are viewed as dominant or "stuck up." Children who remain withdrawn at Grade 2 and who were withdrawn in either kindergarten or first grade are at particular risk for self-esteem and friendship problems. Children who are rejected by peers tend to remain so in the absence of treatment. They are rejected because of their behavior: They are no fun to play with and frequently have a negative repu-

---

[1] We find this structure changes the tone of the sessions from complaining about children to emphasizing strengths. There is no discussion or emphasis on diagnostic or behavioral criteria—these aren't "bad" children.

tation among their peers. When these children have best friends, the friendship tends to be of a poorer quality.

7. Say that research shows that withdrawn and rejected children differ from accepted/popular children in how they approach some key situations. Group leaders will be teaching children how to behave in each of these key situations.

8. If a child is rejected, he or she may have a negative reputation in school. Other children will hold onto this for a few months, even if a child doesn't do anything to injure his or her reputation. Group leaders will be telling parents how to deal with this as sessions progress.

Parent Handouts

The group leader guide below contains all information on the parent handout and parent assignment (in regular type) and comments for group leaders to add [*in italics and brackets*]. The goals and limitations handout is self-contained. Read each point, pausing once in a while to ask for questions. During the presentation of the handout, parents begin to react in a manner characteristic of their participation throughout all sessions. Two typical patterns are as follows.

Quiet Assimilation of Concepts

Parents listen attentively, but generally do not raise any questions when material is presented. The more intellectual parents may ask questions (sometimes quite esoteric). Surprisingly, these parents don't usually ask questions about their own child. Pursuing questions about research or generating discussion among parents at this point will not be productive for the parents.

Active Working Group

Parents ask relevant questions that clearly indicate they are thinking about how to accomplish the assignment. A few parents will attempt to anticipate and understand all of the details. They will ask for clarification as you review each part of the assignment. Some group leaders prefer this type of group—they present as more actively engaged—whereas others may view this group as more challenging. We have not observed outcome

to be different for the two types of groups (although we haven't tested this empirically) and don't believe that group leaders need be concerned about this difference.

Group Leader Guide to Parent Handout—Session 1: Goals and Limitations

Goals of the Children's Friendship Class
1. To help your child make and keep friends.
2. To help you more effectively support your child's efforts at finding suitable friends.
3. To help you more effectively support your child's ability to make new acquaintances and develop close friendships.

Methods
1. Your child will be asked to bring in games that he or she might want to play with friends. We will coach him or her in their appropriate use.
2. At each session, brief instruction will be given to your child on how to handle a difficult social situation.
3. Your child will be encouraged to rehearse the skill being taught and will be coached during this practice.
4. Your child will be given homework assignments every week in order to try out skills in situations that are likely to help. [*Mention the homework sheet you will go over after this handout, which will have more specifics on the homework assignment for next session.*]
5. We have developed a series of preplanned sessions. Our research shows that most children need all of these sessions in the order we give them.
6. The purpose of the parent group is to give you suggestions as to how best to support your child's homework efforts. **This will be a "how do I get my child to do the homework class," not a "parent support group."** [*Mention that many parents find this group boring at first because the handouts are read aloud. This is to ensure that parents absorb vital information.*]

Limitations of the Class: What *Not* to Expect
1. That *all* your child's problems will be solved as a result of participation in this class. [*Ask if any parents were thinking this before starting the class (a meager attempt at humor).*]

2. That your child's attitude and friendships will change immediately.

3. That your child's social skills will improve without *regular, prompt attendance and attempts to do homework assignments.* [*Give the following account: If a child is 10 minutes late, he or she misses the homework review; 20 minutes late and he or she misses the teaching part of the session and enters the play portion of the session bewildered. Also, missing more than three sessions dramatically decreases the chance of the child's friendships improving. Mention that there is no opportunity to provide "makeup" discussions of material that was presented during their missed sessions. Parents must get this on the next session from other parents' reports of homework completion.*]

4. That your child's social skills will improve without your active encouragement and support for his or her efforts to do assignments on his/her own. [*Mention that parents make sure what is taught in session gets used at home and in school. If parents don't attempt to get their child to do homework, the chance of the child's friendships improving decreases dramatically. Advise the parents that we won't be giving parents feedback on how their child did in sessions after the group is over. This is unimportant. Instead, the parents will be giving us feedback on how the child used the skills at home each week.*]

5. That we will change our session plans. These sessions have been shown to help most children the way they are presented.

6. That your child will make lasting friendships from this class. The purpose of this class is to try out new things first before trying them out at school and at home.

Parents are cautioned not to follow through on play dates that children may want to make with other children in this class until after the 12 sessions are over. [*Mention that this includes any social contact between families currently in the class together. No family dinners or playing together outside immediately after a session is over. The children may want to do it. Tell parents it's our policy that this doesn't happen until after Session 12, even if children knew and played with each other before the group started.*]

Potential Problem

Out-of-Session Social Contacts Among Group Members

We initially *suggested against* (rather than prohibited, as is now the case) play dates or other social contact between group members. Well before play dates were introduced in sessions (and without consulting us), parents of two boys in the group arranged a play date. As is typical of the errors parents make, the host's mom went off shopping and left both boys with a non-English-speaking maid. The boys played in the pool and during an argument, one boy held the other boy's head under water for a long period of time. When they came into the next session, the boys were angry with each other and wouldn't talk to each other. The parents were also enraged over the play-date incident. They blamed each other. They expected us to take class time to resolve the issue (time that would not have been spent teaching the whole class items on the agenda). The boys and parents continued to be angry through the remaining sessions. Social contact outside the class is seen as counterproductive for the following additional reasons:

1. It may make children and parents who are geographically inaccessible feel "left out."
2. It may put unnecessary pressure on children to be friends with each other even if they don't like each other.
3. It may add an atmosphere of competition among class members to see who can be friends first.
4. Children who share the same psychopathology generally make very poor friends which each other: Children with ADHD behave much worse in pairs than individually; children with ASD may "feed" into each other's oddities and make them more pronounced.

Review of Homework Handout

This assignment sets the mechanics of the phone call in place: Parents of the pair of children assigned to call each other are to work out the date and time of the call before leaving the session (a rudimentary networking skill that some parents need to learn). Some parents will expect their child to have a perfect phone call on the very first time. Group leaders are to attempt to avert this by setting the expectation that children will often have a brief uneventful phone call and will generally be clumsy about it. Parents should be reassured that the finer points of these interactions will evolve throughout subsequent sessions.

Group Leader Guide to Parent Assignment—Due on Sessions 2–6

GOALS
1. To provide an opportunity for your child to practice conversational skills learned in class.
2. To assist your child in the appropriate social use of games he or she has within play groups.

At the end of every session: Your child has been assigned a phone call with a class member. Get together with the other child and his or her parents and set day and time for the call. [*Tell parents this will happen before they leave the session.*]
At the time of the call:

1. It is your job to get your child to the phone at the time you arranged with the other child's parent. It is your child's job to use what she/he has learned during the call.
2. Set rules for acceptable behavior on telephone.
   a. The child must be ready to make or receive the call.
   b. The child must understand what he is expected to do on the telephone—assure this by asking your child to recite what is to happen and how she or he is to treat the other child (no silly stuff on phone, just say hello and ask about the other child's day).
   c. Just prior to the call, agree with your child on the length of the call, if necessary.
3. Make sure there are no distractions and no others in the room. If your child is the one to call then see that the call is made; if waiting for a call that is delayed, have your child make the call after 20 minutes of waiting.
4. Others are *not* to listen in while your child is on the phone. However, leave the room slowly enough to ensure that your child is taking the assignment seriously. Parents are to continue to listen in on the call until it is completed.

We will ask you to report on it the following week.

[*Tell parents, "Your mission will be accomplished this week if the children simply connect and have a five-minute phone call, in which they behave appropriately. The expectations for these phone calls will increase each week." Ask if any parent anticipates a problem with their child talking too long on the phone. If yes, then have them tell their child that the phone call should not be longer than 15 minutes (or any length the parent considers as reasonable). Ask if any parent has any type of call blocking, answering service, or uses an answering machine to screen calls that would prevent the calling child from getting through.*]
Before each friendship class:
Have your child select a toy to bring in next time that he or she can play well and that he or she **w**ould be likely to play with when meeting other children at playgrounds etc. This must be a toy with which at least two children can play, that almost everyone will know how to play. We will be using this to help him or her learn how to play more appropriately with other children in group situations. *Good toys:* basketball, soccerball, Nerfball, Frisbee, handball, tennis ball.

Children are not to bring any of the following types of toys:
Dangerous/aggressive toys: martial arts toys, Super Soakers, water balloons.
Solitary/parallel play: books, skateboards, toy guns.
Too good a toy: expensive toy that will upset the child if lost or damaged.

Children are *not* to bring in *anything else* to share with the class—no candy, artwork, or other toys.

[*Have each parent to think of a toy and tell you what it is. This is done in case their child can't think of any toy to bring at the end-of-session reunification.*]

Potential Problems

Child Reaches the Answering Machine or Service
This has become an increasing problem in this day of telephone technology. The additional

layer of bureaucracy that potential friends have to go through is either off-putting to some children or showy to others. To avoid this, the group leader should have parents ensure that the number on the telephone roster is one that directly reaches the child.

Child Cannot Get Through Because of Caller ID Blocking

One child trying to make his homework call kept getting a busy signal. After 10 minutes of sorting out the problem in the next session, it was clear that the caller ID function of the receiving family's phone was blocking the ability of the calling child to complete the call. This warranted disabling this feature at the time the next in-group call was scheduled. One wonders how difficult this would be for potential friends who are faced with a similar complication.

Child Session Plan 1

On the Way to the Child Session Room

Praise children for following rules on the way to the child session room: Walk together, quietly; no running; no bouncing balls indoors; and no touching others. As they seat themselves, write their names in one column on the board with room for stars to be added throughout the session.

Didactic

Children need to expect that they will have fun (the "prime directive" of children) while also learning vital skills. However, out of necessity, the focus for the first session should be on setting rules and maintaining order. Review Table 6 for behavior control techniques.

1. Announce the rules of session:
   Do: Raise your hand.
   Don't: Try to make friends when any teacher is talking—children don't like to hang around with someone who is disrespectful of adults.
   Don't: Try to be silly before you know someone—they might think you're making fun of them.

2. Say that stars are given for good sportsmanship, doing homework and good answers to the group leader's questions. Announce that earning stars as a group will contribute to a better party for Session 12.
3. Ask, "If Mary earns an extra-credit star, is she helping herself or the group?" Answer: "Both. Extra credit helps the whole group by improving our party."
4. Say that the party will be during Session 12 when they will have treats, pizza, drinks, watch a videotape of their choosing, and "graduate."
5. Tell the children they will spend about half the time of each session in this room, until all of the group discussion is done. The rest of the time will be spent playing.
6. Review the elements of good communication
   Do: speak loud enough to be heard and maintain appropriate physical distance.
   Don't: Brag about yourself, act silly, or tell things that are too personal.
7. The group leader models incorrect voice volume (whispering and shouting) and inappropriate body boundaries (getting too close or too far away) and asks children what the other person would think if someone does this.
8. Teach the elements of good communication by having children turn to the child next to them and introduce themselves: "Tell the person sitting next to you your name, age and where you go to school." [2]
9. Praise what was done correctly or instruct the child to, for example, "turn up the volume," as necessary. Correct children who violate the "Don'ts."

Homework Assignment

The homework assignment is made before the children sample the real play activity. Group members alternate between being "the caller" and "the receiver" over successive weeks on these phone calls so that they have the opportunity to practice both sets of skills.

1. Assign each child another (same-sex) child in the group to call. Tell them that their job for

[2] Introductions come after the group rules are set because some children will violate group rules during this part of the session.

this week is to find out what the other child did that day and report back to group next week.

2. Tell children that next week they will "Bring their thing"—an outside toy to be used to get acquainted with new children. Go over guidelines: An outside game that can be shared by two or more children. No violent games (guns) or provocative games (water pistols, Nerf guns) or solitary activities (books). Don't bring a cherished toy because it may be lost or damaged. Go around the room and ask each child what he or she will bring for next time.

Potential Problems

Trying to Make a Negative Impression During Introductions

When it was his turn to introduce himself, a fourth-grade boy said, "It's a waste of time to introduce myself. People won't want to get to know me. Nobody likes me." The group leader asked, "Are you sure everybody in your school is thinking this?" The boy replied, "Well three kids I know of and I'm not sure about the rest." The group leader said, "Let's practice for the rest" and the boy complied.

Too Much Self-Disclosure

One 11-year-old boy replied during introductions, "I'm the one that got kicked out of school, I'm the kid that gets into fights." The group leader replied, "When you're first getting to know each other, you don't want to tell too much about yourself. Just keep it simple and say things about yourself that other people would like to hear."

Unknowingly Critical of Others

One 9-year-old boy with Asperger's disorder pointed out whenever another child did things wrong. The group leader told him that it was his job to figure out only what *he* was doing incorrectly. After being given a time out for persisting with this behavior, he stopped pointing out other children's mistakes and became more focused on his own behaviors.

Negative Response to In-Group Call Assignment

Boys typically are afraid they won't have anything to talk about. Sometimes they attempt to dodge the assignment by saying that the child they are assigned to call is "geeky" or "weird." The group leader puts an end to this with the reply, "It's your homework, just like any homework assigned at school." Warnings, followed by timeouts, are administered to group members who make statements such as, "Oh no! I don't want to have to call him or her!"

Too Busy for Homework

In response to the homework assignment, a fifth-grade boy pulled out a "day planner" and in a loud voice announced "No can do. I'm all booked this week." When the boy's mother was advised of this, she said, "Let me see your planner." Instead of supporting the group leader's contention that there should be enough time to do the group homework, the mother stated to her son, "Boy, you are really busy this week." Mom was told that it was necessary to work out a time for this assignment and each succeeding assignment or there would be little benefit to their participation in the group.

Real Play

Usually there is only a little time to play outside during the first 1-hour session. Enough time should be allowed to take the children out to the play area, discuss the rules getting to and from the area (no running, walk in line, maintain quiet in the hallways), and play a few minutes of Capture the Flag. The primary point of this game is to begin a shift in focus that emphasizes letting everyone have fun rather than concentrating on who wins the game.

The outside area should be shown to the children and if there is time, they should have a quick game of Capture the Flag.

1. State the rules for getting to and from the play deck (no bouncing balls if in a building, walk quietly and stay together).

2. Keep in mind: Rule violations get one prompt and then a time out on the play deck (missing play time for 1 minute).
3. See "Rules for Capture the Flag."
4. Have children line up at the end of the real play segment. When they are all in line have them return to the parent room.
5. If a child is at a disadvantage (e.g., one child has two numbers to cover), praise the child and give the child a star for handling this inequity well. Note that children never get stars for scoring. When the child scores, the leader acknowledges the success, but doesn't record it as a point or keep score in any way.

Potential Problems

Odd Number of Children

If one side of Capture the Flag has more children, a child on the side with fewer children will be assigned two numbers. Note that adults are never to play with the children.

Opting Out of Play

An 8-year-old boy was accidentally pushed during the game. His reaction was to start crying and walk away. By disengaging and taking himself out of the play situation, he "loses his place" and has changed the situation from one in which he is incorporated into play to one in which he will later have to regain entry (a more difficult situation). It is often a "ticket out" of an uncomfortable situation for a child who feels awkward.

After quickly checking that there was no injury, the group leader ignored the crying and instructed him to immediately get back into the game. The boy quickly reengaged and stopped crying (probably because he became engrossed in play and forgot he was crying). The importance of the inadvertent "push" was also minimized because this is a common occurrence in any athletic play activity.

End-of-Session Reunification

The important part of this portion is the brief individual attention the group leader gives dur-

ing step 3. Being actively engaged with parent and child during this portion of the session supports the message that the homework is important. Group leaders have an early opportunity to correct parent errors before they become incorporated into patterns of resistance.

1. Announce to parents and children, "Today we worked on having a conversation with someone on the telephone. I saw a lot of good telephone behavior in this group. Let's all give the children a big round of applause for their effort."
2. The child leader reads off the in-group telephone-call assignments one by one. He tells the children to come up with an outside toy to bring next week.
3. The child leader and coaches go to each parent and child and check to make sure they have a toy in mind to bring for next session (child and parent select this toy to fit the guidelines).

Potential Problems

Impatient Parent

One mother became impatient in making the in-group call arrangement because the mother with whom she was to coordinate had two assigned calls to schedule. This can occur when there is an uneven number of group participants at that particular session and a "double-duty" phone assignment is made. She started to leave, telling her husband, "Let's leave and call her later." The group leader intervened and said the mother needed to wait and do this now.

Inappropriate Toy

A fourth-grade boy with Asperger's disorder agreed with his mother to bring a Frisbee for the next session. However, he said that his dog had chewed it and wanted to know if it would be OK to bring the Frisbee even if it was chewed up. The group leader replied to the parent that now is a good time to purchase a new Frisbee.

Children's Friendship Training

Parent Handout—Session 1

Goals and Limitations

GOALS OF THE CHILDREN'S FRIENDSHIP CLASS

1. To help your child make and keep friends.
2. To help you more effectively support your child's efforts at finding suitable friends.
3. To help you more effectively support your child's ability to make new acquaintances and develop close friendships.

METHODS

1. Your child will be asked to bring in games that he or she might want to play with friends. We will coach him or her in their appropriate use.
2. Each session, brief instruction will be given to your child on how to handle a difficult social situation.
3. Your child will be encouraged to rehearse the skill being taught and will be coached during this practice.
4. Your child will be given homework assignments every week in order to try out skills in situations that are likely to help.
5. We have developed a series of preplanned sessions. Our research shows that most children need all of these sessions in the order we give them.
6. The purpose of the parent group is to give you suggestions as to how best to support your child's homework efforts. **This will be a "how do I get my child to do the homework class," not a "parent support group."**

LIMITATIONS OF THE CLASS: WHAT *NOT* TO EXPECT

1. That *all* your child's problems will be solved as a result of participation in this class.
2. That your child's attitude and friendships will change immediately.
3. That your child's social skills will improve without *regular, prompt attendance and attempts to do homework assignments.*
4. That your child's social skills will improve without your active encouragement and support for his or her efforts to do assignments on his or her own.
5. That we will change our session plans. These sessions have been shown to help most children the way they are presented.
6. That your child will make lasting friendships from this class. The purpose of this class is to try out new things first before trying them out at school and at home.

Parents are cautioned not to follow through on play dates that children may want to make with other children in this class until after the 12 sessions are over.

Children's Friendship Training

Parent Assignment—Given on Session 1

Due on Sessions 2–6

GOALS: 1. To provide an opportunity for your child to practice conversational skills learned in class.
2. To assist your child in the appropriate social uses of games he or she has within play groups.

At the end of every session:

Your child has been assigned a phone call with a class member. Get together with the other child and his or her parents and set day and time for the call.

At the time of the call:

1. It is your job to get your child to the phone at the time you arranged with the other child's parent. It is your child's job to use what she/he has learned during the call.
2. Set rules for acceptable behavior on telephone.
   (a) The child must be ready to make or receive the call.
   (b) The child must understand what he is expected to do on the telephone—ensure this by asking your child to recite what is to happen and how she or he is to treat the other child (no silly stuff on phone, just say hello and ask about the other child's day).
   (c) Just prior to the call, agree with your child on the length of the call, if necessary.
3. Make sure there are no distractions and no others in the room. If your child is the one to call then see that the call is made; if waiting for a call that is delayed, have your child make the call after 20 minutes of waiting.
4. Others are *not* to listen in while your child is on the phone. However, leave the room slowly enough to ensure that your child is taking the assignment seriously. Parents are to continue to listen in on the call until it is completed. We will ask you to report on it the following week.

Before each friendship class:

Have your child select a toy to bring in next time that he or she can play with well and that he or she **would be likely to play with when meeting other children at playgrounds, etc.** This must be a toy with which at least two children can play, that almost everyone will know how to play. We will be using this to help him or her learn how to play more appropriately with other children in group situations.

Good toys—basketball, soccer ball, Nerfball, Frisbee, handball, tennis ball.

Children are not to bring any of the following types of toys:

Dangerous/aggressive toys—martial arts toys, Super Soakers, water balloons.

Solitary/parallel play—books, skateboards, toy guns.

Too good a toy—expensive toy that will upset the your child if lost or damaged.

Children are **not** to bring in **anything else** to share with the class—no candy, artwork or other toys.

Children's Friendship Training

Rules for Capture the Flag

Child Session 1

Gather Children

1. A blackboard eraser or other similar sized object is the "flag" and placed in the middle of the field.
2. The playing field is a square 10 m × 10 m. On each of two opposite sides, write numbers 1 through half the total number of children. Each side gets assigned the same numbers.

Assign Sides

3. Divide children into two equal teams and have each child stand on a team number. In the event of an uneven number of children, one of the children can be assigned to cover two numbers (i.e., "Jeff, you are going to be number 4 and number 5.").

Tell Game Rules

4. A point is scored when:
   • A child is able to grab the "flag" and take it back to his side without being touched by anyone from the other side; or
   • The child tags a child on the other team who has the "flag" before the other child returns to his or her side.

Start the Game

5. The group leader calls one, two, or three numbers (i.e., "Numbers 2 and 4" or "Numbers 1, 3, and 5"). Sometimes the group leader will call a number not on the field (i.e., "24" or "16") to insure the children's continued attention and to promote a fun aspect of the game.
6. To avoid the common error of a child simply grabbing the "flag" and getting immediately tagged, the group leader has the children take a turn in slow motion, so that they can see the benefit of being more "tricky" and utilizing team work.

Core Instruction

7. At the halfway point of the real play segment, switch half the children between the two teams, bringing home the concept that having fun is important, not winning or keeping score.

Debriefing at End of Game

8. After this segment is over, have the children get into a huddle for debriefing with the following questions:
   • Why wasn't I keeping score? (Answer: The score isn't the most important thing. It's more important to have a good time.)
   • Why did I switch players between both of the teams? (Answer: So kids get to play with other kids. It pays to treat the other side well because sometimes they will be on your team or it might be up to them to pick you to be on their team.)

PART III

CHAPTER

10

Conversational Skills

Treatment Rationale

The first task for anyone first meeting someone with whom they would like to be friends is to search for common-ground activities. This involves sharing the conversation and listening to others. Many rejected children may be no better at sharing conversations than they are at sharing activities and toys. They may dominate the conversation or fail to maintain its flow. The primary treatment hypothesis for this session is that teaching them how to share and to give and get useful information from a conversation, together with teaching parents how to monitor their child's conversations, will improve their ability to search for common-ground topics and activities with potential playmates.

10.1 Importance of Conversational Skills

Conversational skills that enhance intimacy may develop quite early and earlier among girls than boys (Buhrmester & Furman, 1987). As early as 6 to 7 years old, children know more about similarities and differences with their close friends than they know about acquaintances (Ladd & Emerson, 1984). Conversational skills that regulate intimacy are probably fully functional before children reach adolescence: Preadolescents do

not differ from adolescents in their ratings of intimacy of their friendships (Buhrmester, 1990; Bukowski & Hoza, 1989). Zarbatany, Hartmann, and Rankin (1990) had fifth- and sixth-grade children generate diaries of peer activities. Over 85% took place in the absence of adults. Most of their time was spent conversing directly with peers; next was "hanging out," followed by walking to school and conversing on the telephone. They found that conversations helped to enhance relationships and a sense of belonging.

10.2 Problems in Conversation

Three problems plague the conversations of friendless children: poor intimacy regulation, low rates of "social" conversation, and inadequate information query skills. Dodge et al. (1990) found low rates of social conversation to be characteristic of rejected children. Little is known about conversational styles of neglected children, except that neglected children were comparable to rejected children in feeling less companionship with their best friends (Patterson, Kupersmidt, & Greisler, 1990). Our clinical observations suggest that withdrawn children may have difficulty in maintaining the flow of conversations whereas rejected children may have problems in sharing the conversation.

60

Research on Conversational Problems

10.3 Intimacy Regulation

Effective intimacy regulation is defined as the increase in personal disclosure only with repeated contact and receptivity by the partner. Altman and Taylor (1973) developed "social penetration theory," which described stages in developing friendships among adults. Furman (1987) drew parallels between Altman and Taylor's research and the development of children's friendships. According to this theory, children regulate how intimate their exchanges are, depending on the phase of their relationships. Examples of poor intimacy regulation are when a child immediately tells others of his or her inpatient psychiatric experience or tells others he or she gets in trouble at school. Not only is this inappropriate in emphasizing negative behaviors, but it violates social norms by getting too personal too fast.

10.4 Defining Social Conversation

We define *social conversation* as an exchange of information, with positive affect, which is meant to promote closer relationships. Initially, children need to focus on information exchange of superficial aspects describing what they like and dislike. They need to avoid evaluating each other, especially in a negative light, and need to avoid telling each other what to do (Doyle, Connolly, & Rivest, 1980; Furman, 1987). This process is learned very early by many children. Unacquainted preschool children who were starting to know each other asked more questions about their partners and gave more information about themselves (Jormakka, 1976, cited in Furman, 1987). In contrast, Black and Hazen (1990) reported that rejected children didn't closely attend to the information provided in the conversation of others. Consequently, they lacked conversational responsiveness and maintenance of relevance during conversational discourse (Asher, 1983; Putallaz, 1983).

10.5 Conversational Dominance Versus Information Exchange

Several studies support our observation that rejected children dominate conversations with a peer and lack information exchange and query skills. Rejected children tended to dominate conversations with best friends when compared to popular children (Austin & Draper, 1984). This was especially characteristic of children with ADHD. Kim (1999) found that children with ADHD didn't respond to their conversational partner's questions or requests and frequently interrupted their partner. Dishion, Andrews, and Crosby (1995) found that giving directives and commands (indicative of conversational dominance) correlated negatively with relationship satisfaction and was especially evident in the conversations of aggressive boys with their friends.

Gottman, Gonso, and Rasmussen (1975) demonstrated that accepted children were better at information query skills than rejected children (we refer to these skills in our program as "two-way conversations"). Information query skills can put a child in an information-gathering mode that may heighten the child's attention to the speaker and focus the child on information he or she needs to plan and sustain interactions. Children are also likely to be favorably impressed when a peer demonstrates enough interest in them to ask appropriate personal questions.

Furman (1987) observed this process in third graders. They found that children first getting to know each other shared information about themselves and asked about their playmate. Unacquainted children voiced less disapproval and commands than acquainted children did. According to Furman, girls were better than boys in sharing information about themselves, whereas boys were more interested in playing than sharing information. Another way to view this is that girls and boys are gathering the information most relevant to how they sustain interactions. Girls at this age sustain interactions more through talking than boys do, whereas boys sustain interactions more through play than girls do (cf. Frankel, 1996). Gottman (1983) noted that children who "hit it off" to later become friends, asked more questions of their playmates, gave more information about themselves, and established common ground activities on the first three play dates.

10.6 Small Talk, Gossip, and Telling Jokes

The *peer culture* is defined as knowledge about current games and toys in vogue. Children have been able to communicate peer culture by themselves, without the help of, and sometimes in spite of, adults. In theory, the skills, knowledge, and social goals contained in the culture guide children's behavior and values (cf. Zarbatany et al., 1990). Many parents feel that this kind of conversation promotes friendship: Telling jokes, gossiping, and knowing about the latest fads are seen as skills helpful in getting to know other children better. However, because there is no information exchange of a personal nature, the mechanism promoting greater intimacy is suspect.

Parker and Seal (1996) studied these conversational tools and their effects on friendship formation and maintenance. They observed changes in friendships over a 1-month sleep-away camp experience for 216 children, ages 8 to 15. They noted five patterns of friendship maintenance throughout the camp experience, each associated with different communication patterns:

Keeping the same friends. Children evidencing this pattern were least likely to know funny jokes, kid around with others or tell others' secrets. Girls in this group were seen as honest.

Increasing the number of friends. This group was least likely to gossip, tell on others, start fights, be bossy, or show off.

Rotating friends. Boys in this group were rated highest as knowing funny jokes, which perhaps represented a superficial approach to engaging in conversations. Children in this group violated various loyalty norms: They gossiped, told on others, put others down, bossed others around, started fights, and couldn't keep secrets. Girls in this group were unlikely to be honest. Although this group was not labeled by the authors as having problems (they had adequate numbers

of friends at any given time and were able to make new friends), they were the loneliest of the four groups with friends. This was because stable friendships decrease feelings of loneliness. This group mastered superficial friendships, perhaps by replacing personal information exchange with "funny jokes" and other off-putting behaviors.

Decreasing friends. These children joked and gossiped with others, were caring, did not start fights, but showed off all the time. This seems like a mixture of supportive behaviors with immodesty and a sprinkle of disloyalty. Girls in this group were rated as honest, caring about others, and knowing funny jokes. The authors seemed to think that the decline may have been due to carefully culling friends or not wanting to start new friendships later in camp session when they knew they wouldn't last. This pattern sounds more typical of the girls, because boys do not cull friends (see Chap. 18). In the present context, showing off may be a form of conversational dominance.

Friendless children. This was the most clearly problematic group. Although it was common for many children not to have friends at some point during camp, the friendless children failed to have at least one friend at any time. These children had the highest scores in self-reported loneliness, implying their friendship status was not by choice. They were perceived by other children as easily angered, saying nonsensical things, responding poorly to being teased, untrustworthy, uncaring, and uncooperative. Many of these features have been interpreted as evidence of negative affect, criticism, and conversational dominance.

10.7 Conversational Skills Interventions and Increased Peer Acceptance

Many social skill interventions that have trained active listening skills have been successful in increasing peer acceptance among participants (Bierman & Furman, 1984; Gresham & Nagle, 1980; Hepler & Rose, 1988; Oden & Asher, 1977; Tiffen & Spence, 1986). In these studies, the children selected were the least popular within their class. At follow-up, researchers found lasting improvement in peer acceptance (Oden & Asher, 1977). Our clinical experience has been that teaching "two-way conversations" is an important tool for children to have prior to a play date. Children can establish common ground activities in telephone conversations prior to a play date ("What should we do when we get together?").

Bierman (1986a) compared children taught conversational skills with a control group. The skills were: sharing information about oneself, asking others about themselves and giving advice, and suggestions and invitations (as opposed to giving commands and making demands). The group receiving conversational skills training was significantly better in demonstrating the target skills. More important, correlational analysis showed that unpopular children who used the conversational techniques increased the probability of a positive peer response to them. Both the frequency of use of techniques and positive peer response (especially the latter) correlated significantly with improvements in peer sociometrics.

10.8 Implications From Research and Clinical Practice

Many parents complain that their child lacks attention to social cues. Nothing may more epitomize this than the inability to manage social conversations. Conversational skills are a conduit for intimacy throughout the age range of children in the program. Conversations with best friends tend to be one-sided, except in reciprocating negative statements and actions. The following conversational skills would seem important for maintaining friendships: trading information, regulating intimacy, being serious, listening and avoiding telling jokes. Knowing gossip, telling on others, putting others down, bossing others around, and starting fights need to be discouraged.

How to Conduct the Session

Until Now

Group leaders have focused on familiarizing parents and children with the session expectations. Children have been taught to follow the rules of the session, to be serious on first exchange with

a potential friend or acquaintance, and to bring toys appropriate for sustaining outside interactions. Parents have been guided to recognize and accentuate the positive in their child while also facilitating their child's homework compliance.

In This Session

There are three "firsts" in this session. It is the first time parents are held accountable for coming late to session; and the first time that the toys children brought to the sessions are screened; and the first time parents are helped with any problems they encountered in getting homework assignments done (in-group telephone calls and outside toys). New material in this session more completely utilizes the telephone call as a training vehicle: Children are taught two-way conversation skills and parents are taught to monitor phone calls to insure practice and generalization of these skills.

Parent Session Plan 2

Initial Gathering

Beginning in this session, the main focus of the initial gathering of parents and children is to screen the toys brought for the session. The purposes of this screening are first to ensure that the toys brought are conducive to the objectives of the session, and second to assess the child's toy collection in order to make sure it promotes rather than interferes with the development of friendships. Starting in this session, it is assumed that participants will arrive within 5 minutes of the scheduled start of the session. The session starts on time, regardless of whether all participants are present.

1. Before parents arrive, make sure chairs are arranged in "horseshoe" shape. Have phone list and planned absence sheets laid out on the table.
2. Check child toys as they come in and have parents hold toys that are in excluded categories.[1]

[1]*Dangerous/aggressive toys*—martial arts toys, Super Soakers, water balloons; *solitary/parallel play*—books, skateboards, toy guns; *Too good a toy*—expensive toy that will upset the child if lost or damaged.

3. Have each parent and child fill out a name tag in large print and put in a visible place on their chest.
4. Take attendance.

Potential Problems

Ventilation/Damaging the Child's Reputation

One mother started to talk to the group leader (with the child standing nearby) in a loud voice, "He has had a very difficult week. On Monday, he was rude to his teacher and on Tuesday we got a note from the school. Today he had a problem on the bus coming home from school." An effective response to this was to cut the parent off and tell him or her that this is not the place to talk about it, even though the parent may be very frustrated and feel the need to "ventilate," and ask if the parent would like a referral for counseling.

Inappropriate Toy

One mother gave her son clay as an outside toy, saying, "you can toss it like a ball." The group leader had the boy leave it with his parent. Other examples have been Nerf guns, Nazi memorabilia, a pocket knife, and a deflated ball. These were all handled in the same way.

Too Great a Hurry

One parent had to come from work and didn't have time to stop at home for her son to bring a toy. She said she felt it was better to be on time than be late with a toy. While the group leader concurred with arriving on time as being the priority, the group leader suggested putting a ball in the trunk of her car on the night prior to group.

Buying Friends 1

One 11-year-old boy brought in gum bought with his own money for everyone. It was an act of generosity that was unusual for this boy, so the group leader said he could share it with others if everyone kept the gum in their mouths. This turned out to be a serious error in judgment. Gum chewing and the discussion of gum competed with the group leader's instruction. Eventually the boy started blowing bubbles and distracting the group. He became very angry when he was instructed by the group leader to spit out his gum. On the way back from the play deck, one of the other boys kept trying to get him to sell him another piece of gum (the group leader stopped this). Bringing anything other than appropriate toys into the child session has since been prohibited.

Buying Friends 2

An 8-year-old boy brought a bag full of candy in his jacket. He surreptitiously began eating pieces of candy during the didactic instruction and was noticed doing so by his peers. During the deck play activity, peers began asking for pieces of candy. The boy began selectively handing out pieces of candy to peers. The candy was immediately taken away and was given to the boy's mother at the end of the session. The boy's parent advised the group leader that her son had a history of bringing candy to school as a "bribe" to win over friends. The mother also mentioned that the technique had not been successful and that her son was always disappointed when he was exploited by peers promising friendship that only lasted as long as the candy.

Show and Tell

One second-grade boy with Asperger's disorder brought a stuffed animal for "show and tell." The stuffed animal was not age-appropriate for the boy. His parent had obviously encouraged this. The group leader told the mother that the purpose of this intervention is to develop relationships based on skills, not possessions.

Homework Review

Homework review always takes place during the first part of the parent session. The in-group call has such a high compliance rate that starting at one end of the room and going systematically around works effectively. Parents need to be reminded not to expect dazzling conversationalists on this first call.

This may be the first encounter with parents who confess to not doing homework and then soliciting sympathy from others (taking group time on this rather than on how to get it done next time; see "Nobody Was Home" later in this section).

Go around the table and review toys children brought in and phone calls to other group members.[2]

Go around asking the parents what outside game their child is going to bring next week.

Tell them the value of an outside toy assignment: to identify something helpful the child can bring to playgrounds in their area. Playgrounds typically don't supply toys, and a good outside toy will act as a magnet to attract other children. Some toys are better for this than others. A ball is easily shared by two more children (and it's boring to play with it by yourself). Other toys may initially offer a strong attraction for other children—for instance, a Nerf gun. However, after about 5 minutes the children will start arguing over who gets it next.

Clinical Examples of Successful Calls

Mission Accomplished

The mother of a second-grade boy reported that the in-group call went according to schedule. She was concerned that the boys only spoke for 2 to 3 minutes. The group leader assured her that the assignment was fulfilled and that it would be more complex next week.

"Hit It Off" and Attempt to Make Play Date

The mother of a fifth-grade girl reported that her daughter spoke on the phone for 20 minutes with another girl from group and seemed delighted about how the call went. She impulsively asked for a play date with the other girl. The mother appropriately advised her daughter that this wasn't allowed while she was taking the class.

---

[2]Keep in mind telephone call guidelines: No distractions, no TV or siblings in room. For missed appointments on calls: Point out how disappointing it was to other child and ask what the parent will do to ensure the phone call goes better next time.

Potential Problems

Nobody Was Home

One parent of a third-grade girl forgot to have her daughter make the call at the appointed time. The group leader asked the other mother how her daughter felt about this. She said her daughter was quite disappointed. The other parents were asked for suggestions on how to remember to make their calls. One mom said she always did it on a Friday night. Another mom said she has her own mother remind her. The group leader had the mother who had missed the call tell him how she would remember next time. The focus was on what to do differently next time, rather than allowing the offending mother to give her excuse or try to get others to say that missing the assignment was understandable or acceptable.

Anxious Child

A second-grade girl was too nervous to talk to her assigned person. When she made the call, the other girl's dad picked up the phone and she hung up. Seeing this, her mom dialed the call for her and made sure she connected with the other girl. Some parents will rehearse a call right before an anxious child is about to call. Having parents role-playing being the other child has been particularly effective in getting children to overcome the anxiety associated with making their initial phone calls.

Not Scheduled at a Good Time

A second-grade boy refused to make the telephone call: He wanted to watch TV instead. The mom realized she had made a bad plan. She decided not to schedule the call during his favorite program. An alternative in this situation might have been to record the TV show and then he could watch the program at the completion of his phone call.

"Overprogramming"/Overcoaching

The mother of a first-grade boy with Asperger's disorder told him each sentence to say while he was on the call and he simply repeated what his mother had just said. The group leader told the mom that her son was to try this independently. It was acceptable to rehearse the call with her son just before he was to make it, but unacceptable to have a "script" for the telephone call or "feed him the dialogue."

Assignment Too Hard for Parent

The mother of four children said she couldn't do the homework because she was minding all of the children when she scheduled the phone call. So she peeked in briefly to see how the homework was going, but really couldn't monitor the phone call. (She received very little support/involvement from her husband.) The group leader asked her if she could schedule the next phone call when she would be better able to observe. She said she couldn't. The group leader replied that the parents are the main instruments of generalization by exporting each week's learning outside the group. If she is unable to monitor the homework assignments at home, then her child may not actually implement what he is practicing in session. Her reply was that she would "do the best she could." She subsequently complied with most homework assignments.

Parent Handout

There are three main purposes of the handout. The first purpose is to ensure that parents don't talk about their child's faults in front of others. They should be presenting their child as a good playmate instead. The second purpose is to educate parents to adequately monitor the telephone-call assignments for two-way conversations. The third purpose is to enhance parent-child communication by giving parents a "tuneup" on their *active listening* skills. Active listening is a technique by which the parent does only the minimal amount of talking to get the child to share information with them. Promoting active listening is a way to increase appropriate parent involvement in their children's friendships. Parents should have regular active listening sessions with their child about what is happening at school and in the neighborhood. To encourage compliance, the handout suggests parents immediately try active listening on the way home from the group.

1. Tell parents that the children are working on conversation skills in the child session. For the next homework assignment, parents are to focus on the conversational content rather than how children start and end the phone call.
2. Tell parents the first job in a new relationship is to search for shared interests so you know what you can do together. This is a two-way conversation, not an interview (an interview is not between equals).
3. Review the session handout.

Group Leader Guide to Parent Handout— Session 2—Having a Conversation

Goals
(a) To help children develop two-way conversational skills. (b) To help parents and children communicate with each other.

1. A conversation is when two children talk and learn how to enjoy each other. [*Say that this is what the children are being taught concurrently in the child session.*]

Do's

Trade information about each other
  Trade means give an important fact and get an important fact.
  When you answer a question, you may have to ask a question to keep the trade going.
Important facts to find out:
  What do you like to do?—to see what you will do when you get together.
  What you don't like to do?—so you can avoid this when you're around that person.

Don'ts

Don't be a *conversation* hog—let the other person talk too. Give only the facts the person asks for, give the other person a chance to speak.
Don't get *too personal*—don't give information that will make you or others uncomfortable.
Don't be an interviewer—don't only ask questions and not tell about yourself. Give enough so that others get the information they need.

[Pause here for parent questions—make sure they understand two-way conversations. Tell parents they will be monitoring this on the next few phone calls. Parents should listen closely enough to the phone to determine if there is asking and listening going on.]

2. Ways to encourage conversations with your child:

Encouraging

Praising your child (in private) when he or she attempts new skills he or she has learned in group or elsewhere.

Involving your child in decisions about his or her play dates. Select them together.

Talking about and acting respectfully toward other adults, teachers, and children in front of your child.

Listening when *your child wants to talk* about his or her friendships. *

Discouraging

Talking about your child's faults in front of others.

Allowing your child to play with children that he or she doesn't like but who are convenient.

Talking about another adult's or child's faults in front of your child.

Prodding your child to talk when *you* want to talk.

[Pause here for parent questions.]

Parent Assignments

1. *Turn off the car radio and practice listening skills with your child on the way home tonight. First try silence alone and wait to see if your child begins talking. If not, ask your child what happened in session. Parents should have regular listening sessions, going over what happened at school, and so on. [*Tell parents you will be asking them how this went next week.*]

2. Child practices two-way conversations with group member on the telephone. Parent is to listen from afar to the call to see if their child is asking *and* answering questions. If not, then remind them of the assignment. They may not know how to start and end a phone call—this

will come next week. [*Tell parents to make a "big deal" about the phone call to increase its importance. Because the second call deals more with conversation content, parents can help children think of things to say. The best time to do this is just before the call. But they should avoid writing things down, as this will decrease spontaneity. For example, during a call, one child taking notes was heard by his parent to say, "Slow down, I can't write that fast."*]

3. Bring outside toy (except if raining—bring inside toy).

Potential Problems

Mother Not Sure We Can Help Her Son

One mother of a second-grade boy with ADHD asked if we're going to teach the children how to "pick up on social cues." The group leader replied that we don't teach children to pick up on social cues, we teach them the rules of interpersonal etiquette. The children learn that when they follow these rules, people feel good and are more likely to respond to them in a positive way.

Not a Sports Person

The mother of a first-grade boy was concerned about the emphasis on sports. She said her son felt clumsy playing organized sports. She reported that he told her he didn't want to participate in the next session if they were to play sports. The group leader replied that informal playground sports, such as handball, are the major means by which children, especially boys, meet and interact. This is regardless of how good they are at the particular sport. For instance, in handball, most of the time is spent waiting on line to play. If they don't wait on line, then they won't be near the other boys (they can talk to the child next to them while waiting). This class will expose children to this so that they have an informed choice.

At the end of the session reunification, it was clear to the mother that her worries were unfounded: Her son came back from the deck activity, happily bouncing the basketball he had brought.

Child Session Plan 2

On the Way to the Child Session Room

1. The rules of the group start to be enforced by group leaders when the children are lined up to go to the child session room. The parent group leader handles inappropriate toys as a parent problem.[3]
2. Praise children for following rules on the way to the child session room: Walk together, quietly, no running, no bouncing balls indoors, and no touching others. As they seat themselves, write the children's names in one column on the board with room for stars next to each name.

Homework Review

This is the first time homework is reviewed. There are two purposes: first to serve as a reward for children who comply with the homework (they get a star on the board), and second to serve as peer pressure for children who didn't comply—they get to hear how other children did the homework.

The *honeymoon effect* (children being on their best behavior because it is a new situation) usually doesn't last to Session 2. Children start to become disruptive in two ways. Older boys often deal with the nervousness of an unfamiliar situation with sarcasm. This may result in a contagion if it is not firmly handled at the onset with prompts and time outs. Another disruptive behavior that some children may try is telling stories (see Table 10.1).

1. Review the toy brought in by each child.
2. Concentrate on the in-group call—go around and have each child say who they called and what they found out about the other child.

Clinical Examples of Acceptable Homework Reports

Children will report on one or two nice things that they learned about the child they called. Some examples might include that the other child: (a) just bought a new videogame, (b) received a good grade on a test, or (c) got a new pet. The group leader acknowledges homework completion by repeating (using only a few words) what the child found out.

Potential Problems

Tattling

A second-grade girl reported that another girl in the group wasn't home when the call was to be made. As a result, she had to call numerous times.

---

[3]After they are excluded from the child session, the children will not repeat the error, unless the parent supports it.

TABLE 10.1 Children Telling Stories and How Group Leaders Should Handle Them

Example of a child's story: "There was this kid at school. He wanted to do everything. He took the ball away from the other kids. Everybody got mad at him . . . "

Some children want to tell stories (sometimes related and sometimes unrelated to session content). Listening to these stories in their entirety will eat up time, reward the child for monopolizing group time and practicing what is essentially a one-way conversation. If the group leader allows one child to tell a story, then others will also want to do this. Look for ways to cut this off.

Here are some suggestions:
1. Interrupt the story and have the child skip forward to the part that is immediately relevant. Tell the child to go to the end of the story, to sum up and get to how the story ends or to get to the important part, such as, about doing the homework assignment.
2. If totally unrelated, interrupt the child saying, "That doesn't sound like what we're talking about right now. We need to get back to what we're talking about so that we can go to the play deck sooner."
3. If inappropriate (e.g., stories about hitting other children), interrupt the child and tell him or her you don't want to hear the story because it is not appropriate to the group focus. If the child persists (this will generally be due to a maladaptive attempt at negative attention-seeking), give a time out.

The girl continued to emphasize that the other girl had not been home, with the expectation that she might be able to get the girl into trouble. The group leader ignored the "tattling" component and said to her that it was good she persisted (homework noncompliance is addressed in the parent session).

Parent Support of Storytelling

At the end of session, an irate parent said to the child group leader, "My daughter says that you are cutting her off in session and not letting her tell you what is happening in school." The group leader told the parent that this was a class where children had to learn skills to deal with social situations. Our job is to provide group members with skills to avoid problems. Talking about what happened at school was not relevant to material in session and bears some similarities to conversation hogging.

Didactic

Conversational skills that improve peer acceptance are specific to the early stages in relationship development. Practice in having two-way conversations will partially address the tendency of children to "miss social cues." A *Socratic*

method is used (see Table 10.2 for a description of how this method applies to the child session).

1. Say that friends are best made in certain places and times. Use a socratic method to get the following:

   Good places: On playground, in school lunchroom, on the bus to school, on line waiting for lunch, in the schoolyard after school, before and after Scout meetings and team practice.

   Bad places: In the classroom, when you're in the field during a baseball game, in crosswalks or bathrooms.

   Good times: After school, before school, at lunch, after team practice, on telephone.

   Bad times: When the teacher is talking, when the other child is trying to work.

2. Tell them a conversation is when two people talk and learn how to enjoy each other.
3. Ask, "What do detectives do? How is a kid a mystery?"
4. Ask children what's wrong with this conversation: "Hello. I just ate chicken, then played Nintendo, then watched a movie. Oh, my 10 minutes is up. OK, bye." Ask children if that was a conversation? (Answer: No, only one person was talking—he was a *conversation hog*. It's just like a ball hog.) Ask children, what

TABLE 10.2 Using a Socratic Method in the Child Sessions

The *Socratic method* is where the children come up with rules for a situation. It may appear to the children that they are producing the rules when in actuality, the group leader is ensuring that all the rules in the session plan are reviewed. At the end of discussion, or if pressed for time, the group leader states any rules the children did not come up with.

Under certain circumstances it is a useful pedagogical technique for the following reasons:

1. It is a more active and lively way of learning where the children teach each other.
2. Children are made to feel more competent, as they are coming up with the rules.
3. The rules sound more valid to the children because their peers have revealed them.
4. It works well when the issue is not too emotionally laden and there are a few rules to teach.

Actively involve the children in producing the rules and explaining their importance. Keep the list of rules in the session plan as a template for the rules to be taught.

1. If a child says something that can bend a little to fit into one of the rules, accept it and praise the child. Restate the rule as in the session plan. Ask the group, "Why is it a good idea to follow that rule?"
2. If a child says something incorrect, simply say "No, that is not a rule of . . . ," and then ask another child. If you don't correct rules that are wrong it may lead some children to believe what the child said was correct.
3. Do not engage in a "debate" with a child regarding the child's rationale for inappropriate behavior.

the other person is going to think. (Answer: The speaker is selfish and only interested in himself.)

5. The next homework assignment is to *trade information*.

  Do's: *Trade* information about each other. *Trade* means give an important fact and get an important fact. Important facts: (a) What do they like to do?—you need to know this first to see what you will do when you get together. (b) What they don't like to do—so you can avoid this when you're around that person. When you answer a question, you may have to ask a question to keep the trade going.

  Don'ts:

  • Don't be a *conversation hog*—let the other person talk too. Give only the facts the person asks for. Give enough so that they get the information they need.

  • Don't be an *interviewer*—don't only ask questions and not tell about yourself.

  • Don't get *too personal*—Other children only need to know likes and dislikes when you first get to know them. If you tell them too much about yourself at first, it may make them feel less like talking to you.

6. Model trading information, then have children practice: Break children into dyads. Have them "trade information" with the child sitting next to them to see if they can figure out one thing that the other child likes to do and tell the other child one thing they like to do.

  Point out how serious and grown up the children are acting at this time. Being serious when you are getting to know someone makes them feel more like talking to you. Remind children not to get too personal.

Potential Problems

Inappropriate Meeting Place

A fifth-grade boy with Asperger's disorder suggested the bathroom as a place to make friends. He said he would go into the next stall and try to talk to a person he wanted to meet. The group leader asked the rest of the group if this was a good idea. They all said "no." The group leader

stated that the bathroom is a place where children need their privacy.

Bragging About Past Bad Behavior

A sixth-grade boy with ADHD and conduct disorder recounted, "One time I went into the alley behind the school with these guys. We would have got in big trouble if we got caught but we had a great time and they thought that I was cool." The group leader asked the group, "What's wrong with doing something like this?" and solicited appropriate responses from other children. If the child who is boasting about his bad behavior continues to insist that this was acceptable, he would get a prompt, followed by a time out.

Group Disruption

One fourth-grade girl made the girl next to her laugh with unrelated "side talk." She was given one warning and then a time out for persisting. She looked shocked as this was the first time out given in session. The other children in the group appeared startled and then immediately increased their attending.

Homework Assignment

1. "Trade information": Telephone call to find out other group member's interests. Assign each child another (same-sex) child in the group to call.
2. "Bring your thing": Bring a basketball, soccerball, Nerfball, Frisbee, handball, Nerf Vortex, and so on.

Real Play

Rejected children have been deprived of game play. No one picks them or they refuse to let them join in. When they finally get into a game, they might want to show others that they're good, or maybe they might want to get all that pent-up play out in one sitting because they don't know when the next time is coming. They might want to do everything in the game (to the exclusion of other's participation). They might play too aggressively because they see poor sportsmanship on TV and lack a better model of sportsmanship. They may trip another child accidentally at first and then on purpose. They may slap the ball out of each other's hands before they are on the court. They may fake ball throws to each other's faces and then laugh at the startled response of their peer. If the group leader allows this to continue, the children will get more aggressive as time goes on.

not true for kids

Most of children referred for friendship treatment do not have adequate skills to independently play together appropriately in groups, especially in competitive games. At this point in the program, competitive games tend to increase aggression. Having children attempt to decide what they will do will result in indecision and arguments and will usually allow the bossy children to take charge. Therefore the approach advocated during the real play portion of these sessions is to provide structure and instruction on all aspects that the children cannot themselves handle competently and to teach competence on the particular skill being taught. If the structure is decreased below this level, you'll notice that the situation will quickly get out of control.

"Wolf Pack" is heavily cooperative with little opportunity for competition. It's fast-paced and the children get the experience of joining in a team with just a few rules and simple strategies. It is easy to supervise and gets going quickly without lots of instruction about rules. It's a nice prelude to teaching them how to slip into games others are playing (see Chap. 11).

Clinical Examples: Strategies Devised by "Wolves" During the Huddle

1. The wolves split up into two groups, allowing them to work together to catch the deer.

2. The wolves pretend to go after one child. The actual targeted "deer" subsequently becomes relaxed, and then one wolf gives the other wolves a predetermined signal to go after the targeted deer.

3. The group leader will coach the "wolves" to select an "easy deer" to catch in order to increase the size of their "wolf pack" without expending too much energy.

4. One "deer" was a significantly faster runner than all of the "wolves." The group leader suggested that the "wolves" take turns chasing the deer to tire her out.

End-of-Session Reunification

1. Begin by praising the children (as a group) for what they did in this session. Announce to parents, "Today we worked on playing detective and trading information. We also worked on being serious when you're first meeting someone else. I saw a lot of polite and serious behavior in this group. Let's all give the children a big round of applause."

2. Read the in-group call assignments one by one, as in last session, but stop parents from immediately starting to arrange these calls with each other. Continue with, "The major job that everyone has this week is to trade information on the telephone and bring an outside toy for next week."

3. At this point coaches and parent and child group leaders go around the room and have each parent and child agree on the toy to bring for next week.

Children's Friendship Training

Parent Handout—Session 2

Having a Conversation

Goals: (a) To help children develop two-way conversational skills.
          (b) To help parents and children communicate with each other.

1. A conversation is when two children talk and learn how to enjoy each other.

Do's

    Trade information about each other

        Trade means give an important fact and get an important fact (play detective).

        When you answer a question, you may have to ask a question to keep the trade going.

    Important facts to find out:

        What do you like to do—to see what you will do when you get together.

        What you don't like to do, so you can avoid this when you're around that person.

Don'ts

    Don't be a **conversation hog**—let the other person talk too.

        Give only the facts the person asks for, don't get too personal.

    Don't get **too personal**—don't give information that will make you or others uncomfortable.

    Don't be an **interviewer**—don't only ask questions and not tell about yourself.

        Give enough so that others get the information they need.

2. Ways to encourage conversations with your child:

Encouraging	Discouraging
Praising your child (in private) when he or she attempts new skills he or she has learned in group or elsewhere.	Talking about your child's faults in front of others.
Involving your child in decisions about his or her play dates. Select them together.	Allowing your child to play with children that he or she doesn't like but who are convenient.
Talking about and acting respectfully toward other adults, teachers, and children in front of your child.	Talking about another adult's or child's faults in front of your child.
Listening when *your child wants to talk* about his or her friendships.*	Prodding your child to talk when *you* want to talk.

Parent Assignments

1. *Turn off car radio and practice listening skills with your child on the way home tonight. First try silence alone and wait to see if your child begins talking. If not, ask your child what happened in group. Parents should have regular listening sessions, going over what happened at school, and so on.
2. Child practices two-way conversations with a group member on the telephone. Parent is to listen from afar to the call to see if their child is asking *and* answering questions. If not, then remind them of the assignment. They may not know how to start and end a phone call—this will come next week.
3. Bring outside toy (except if raining—bring inside toy)

Children's Friendship Training
Rules for Wolf Pack

Child Session 2

Gather Children

1. Have all children gather in a "huddle."

Assign Sides

2. Pick one child as the "wolf," everyone else is "deer." (The first wolf has to be fast enough to catch at least one deer.)

Tell Game Rules

3. When the wolf tags a deer, he or she becomes another wolf and a member of the "wolf pack." All the wolves in the "wolf pack" work together to transform additional deer into wolves.
4. No "lone wolves." Each subsequent deer that will be pursued is selected by the wolf pack (with group leader coaching/assistance) and wolves can only catch the designated deer.
5. The wolves loudly count down from 5 to allow the deer to prepare for the ensuing chase.

Start the Game

6. Have the deer go out in the "forest" (run away within the boundaries of playing field).
7. Huddle with wolves and get them to pick the next deer they are to catch and come up with a strategy on catching the designated deer.

Core Instruction

8. Constantly monitor and make sure all "wolves" focus on the particular "deer" they are supposed to catch next and that they are following the plan they developed in the huddle. If a child gets distracted, ask, "Who are you supposed to catch next?"
9. Don't allow one child to dominate the huddle and come up with all the "deer choices" or strategies.
10. If all the wolves are not working together, stop the game, have the wolves return to the huddle, and review the rules and game plan.

Core Instruction and Debriefing at the End of Game

11. Ask children how they succeeded in this game. (Answer: The only way to progress in this game is to join forces and work together as a team.)

PART III

CHAPTER

11

"Slipping In"/Reputation/Using Community Resources

Treatment Rationale

The rejected child commits social errors, beginning with how he goes about joining other children at play, and with whom he selects as potential friends. The treatment hypothesis is that teaching children the social etiquette to join other children at play and teaching parents to build social networks to help their child select suitable friends are components that eventually will help improve the child's reputation among the peer group.

11.1 Impediments to Formation of Children's Social Networks

Development of social networks through neighborhood contacts is becoming increasingly difficult. Neighborhood streets, formerly alive with the sound of children playing, are quiet. Parent worries about crime, especially in poorer neighborhoods, lead them to discourage play in front of their house, where children could be more easily accessed by peers (cf. Cochran & Davila, 1992). Increased time occupied in viewing television programming has also reduced the amount of time children are accessible for play. School-aged children average 27 hours of television viewing per week (Bryant & DeMorris, 1992).

Regardless of how much a child watches television, the pervasiveness of television in American culture also means that there is a reduced number of children outdoors for play, even if a family eliminates or restricts the use of television in their own home. (Bryant & DeMorris, 1992, p. 182)

Having children attend a neighborhood school can be helpful in this regard. Attending the neighborhood school may foster friendships among children by providing them with common experiences, plugging parents and children into common social networks, and serving as a springboard for more intimate peer interaction (Bukowski et al., 1996; Rubin & Sloman, 1984). However, many parents feel forced to abandon the neighborhood school and instead take their children to a school that is a considerable distance from the home. A survey of our patients revealed that less than half of the children attended a neighborhood school. This translates into decreased parent involvement in the school, decreased time that children stay after school, and substantially reduced availability of peers from school. Thus, parent choice of schooling for their child may increase their difficulty in helping their child build a peer network.

Factors within schools have also made peer contact more difficult. Classroom size has grown

74

increasingly larger over the years. Children in large classes may have fewer friends than children in smaller classes (cf. Epstein, 1983). The number of hours per weekday that children devote to homework has steadily increased over the past 20 years, decreasing time available for peers.

Decreases in children's accessibility for play and fragmentation of children's social networks have made the parent's role more critical in building a child's social network.

11.2 Making Children's Social Networks Accessible

Lack of accessibility of peers has made it more important for parent social networks to include other parents within easy transport who have children close in age to their child (Ladd, 1992; Rubin & Sloman, 1984). Valuable social support functions also seem to be served by parents' dependable friendships with adults outside the family. The number of such parent friendships has been shown to correlate with the size of their children's friendship networks (Homel, Burns, & Goodnow, 1987).

As indicated earlier, school frequently can't be used by many families as a resource from which to draw friendships, because many parents send their child to schools outside their neighborhood and few parents are willing to drive more than 15 minutes each way to provide a playmate for their child. Thus the neighborhood must be tapped to yield accessible friends. Bryant (1985) found that most friendship resources reported by her 7- and 10-year-old samples were within walking or bicycling distance.

11.3 Problems Found in Rejected Children

The behavior of the rejected child may pose an additional burden upon the development of his social network. Breaches of etiquette (Dodge, Coie, & Brakke, 1983) are undoubtedly the cause of peer rejection and ensuing negative reputation among peers. Once a child attains a negative reputation, subsequent learning of peer etiquette may be more difficult, because the child is cut off from the social network, a major source of instruction. Severed links to the social network

may further decrease the rejected child's awareness of peer etiquette (Erwin, 1993; Ladd & Asher, 1985). Having a negative reputation among peers may produce two secondary effects: (a) It precludes use of the existing social network as a source of peers for more intimate play experiences, and (b) it exposes the child as a target for victimization by verbal (teasing) and physical abuse (bullying) by other children.

Research on Social Networks of Rejected Children

11.4 Effects of a Negative Reputation

Growth in cognitive abilities between first and third grade allows children to begin to differentiate more subtle aspects of reputation (Frankel, 1996; Peevers & Secord, 1973). Rogosch and Newcomb (1989) used an open-ended interview to gather information on components of reputation among first, third, and fifth graders of differing social status. There were many ways children consistently described the reputations of rejected children. These descriptors included "disliked," "excludes others," "nasty or mean," and "immature." Based on discriminant-function analysis, the authors found that the reputation of rejected children was stronger (70.6% correct classification based on descriptors) than either popular (27.8% correct) or neglected children (30% correct). Furthermore, these descriptors became more salient with grade, with a correct classification having 40% accuracy in first grade, increasing to 92% accuracy by fifth grade.

Negative reputations among peers are stable over time (Coie, Dodge, & Kuperschmidt, 1990) and negatively impact a child's ability to resolve conflicts, not only because of the limited skills utilized by the child but also due to the expectations and attributions of peers. Putallaz and Gottman (1981) found that when rejected children attempted appropriate interactions, they were less likely to receive positive feedback from their peers than if a more liked child made the same attempt. Hymel (1986) reported that after committing a transgression, liked 2nd-, 5th-, and 10th-grade children often got the "benefit of the doubt" by peers, whereas rejected children did not.

11.5 Influence of Deviant Friends

Parents of rejected children must be more attentive about whom their child associates. Mutual friends at school tend to form within sociometric categories. Average liked children tend to be mutual friends with average liked children, popular children tend to cross categories (mostly to average liked children), and rejected children have few or no mutual friends (Kupersmidt, DeRosier, & Patterson, 1995; Ladd, 1983). However, the few friends that rejected children make may be problematic. Children with high levels of antisocial behavior tend to find each other and by so doing ultimately increase the likelihood of committing delinquent acts such as drug use (Dishion, Capaldi, Spracklen, & Li, 1995) and committing aggressive acts on others (Grotpeter & Crick, 1996). Disruptive boys who befriend each other increase their disruption and behavior problems (Berndt & Keefe, 1995; Dishion, French, & Patterson, 1995), and antisocial behavior (Patterson, 1986; Patterson, Dishion & Banks, 1984). Vitaro, Tremblay, Kerr, Pagani, and Bukowski (1997) found that moderately disruptive boys with aggressive friends were at greater risk for subsequent delinquency than were moderately disruptive boys without aggressive friends. Girls are more influenced in this regard by their very best friend than boys (Berndt & Keefe, 1995). Dishion, Capaldi, Spracklen, and Li (1995) collected data on 206 children from schools in high-crime areas, assessed at 4th, 5th, and at 12th grade. Active peer support for rule breaking and substance abuse was associated with immediate rises in substance abuse during transition to high school. Ineffective parental monitoring was also highly correlated with children's involvement in a deviant peer network. Dishion, Capaldi, Spracklen, and Li (1995) found that 72% of best-friend dyads in their study were similar in arrest status. They pointed out:

> At the onset of adolescence, antisocial boys tend to coalesce into antisocial peer groups . . . improving the friendships of some of these youngsters may result in deviant peer networks that are more satisfactory, more stable, and perhaps more maladaptive in the long run. (p. 149).

Sabongui, Bukowski, and Newcomb (1998) measured sociometric changes in 229 sixth graders across 6 months of school. They found that changes in a child's popularity were determined by the child's characteristics as well as by the sociometric status of the child's friends. The implication was that associating with sociometrically average or well-accepted children would improve the sociometric status of a rejected or neglected child. Effective treatment for peer problems must therefore involve a shift in the subgroup with which a child interacts, toward more accepted children (Putallaz & Gottman, 1981) and away from peers with antisocial behaviors.

11.6 Implications From Research and Clinical Practice

Rejected children often have the additional burden of having a negative reputation among peers. Parents must be trained to look for this in order to focus efforts at building friendships. They must also help their child screen out undesirable friendships with other children who are rejected and/or have antisocial behaviors. It is important to develop friendships with children who are well behaved and geographically close, usually within 15 minutes travel time. The neighborhood must be tapped for potential friendships, especially if the child has a negative reputation at school.

How to Conduct the Session

Until Now

Almost all parents should be conforming with the program at this point: doing their parts in the homework assignments, and remaining on track in their questions and comments within sessions. Parents and children have started to focus on the functions and process of conversation.

In This Session

Parent conversations with their children, especially active listening (e.g., on the way home from sessions), will be reviewed in the parent group. Children will learn how to start and end a telephone call, and they will be assigned to make their first call to a child who is not in the treatment program. Parental monitoring of telephone conversations to insure that they are "two-way" will continue for several more sessions to ensure that the children consolidate this skill. The major focus for the parent session will be the call to a child that is *not* in the group, as parents will be most nervous about this. This first out-of-group call should ideally be a guaranteed success—someone who likes the child and can talk on the phone.

Training peer entry skills (slipping in) begins in this session. Parents are asked to consider the social resources they have available for their child to use and to start scouting their neighborhoods for suitable places for their child to try joining others at play. Attention is also given to having parents help their child pick suitable friends.

Parent Session Plan 3

Initial Gathering

Check child toys as they come in. Have parents hold toys that are in excluded categories.[1]

Have each parent and child fill out a name tag in large print and put in a visible place on their chest.

Take attendance.

Homework Review

There are only three homework assignments for this session, so that the group leader can keep a leisurely pace in reviewing the assignments with each parent.

1. Review what happened on the way home last week (parent active listening assignment).
2. Review toys they brought in and phone calls to other group members. Ask if there was two-way conversation—was the child asking questions and answering questions? [*Keep in mind there should be no distractions, no TV or siblings in room. For missed appointments on calls—point out how disappointing it was to other child and ask the parent what will they do to ensure the phone call goes better next time.*]
3. Children will sometimes end the inside-group call abruptly. Tell parents that we can only teach one skill at a time and the focus was on the two-way conversation rather than the beginning or end.[2]

Clinical Examples of Homework Compliance

Conversation on the Way Home From the Last Group

One parent reported that she turned off the car radio during the drive home after group. Her daughter was surprised and asked, "Why'd you turn it off?" The parent told her that the group leader told them to. There was a pause and then the child started talking about the group.

Parents Enforcing a Two-Way Conversation

One mother of a third-grade boy noticed that her son was asking questions but not answering during his in-group telephone call, so she reminded him to let the other child ask questions also. The parent of the other child noted that at that point the call went from "one-sided" to "two-way."

Potential Problems

Mother Expecting the Perfect Telephone Call

The mother of a third-grade boy insisted on giving the group details of her son's awkwardness and overall lack of phone etiquette. The group leader interrupted this report and pointed out that improved telephone skills were good things to teach, but the lesson this week focused simply on developing "give and take" in conversation. If her child did that, then the mission for this week was accomplished.

Child Complaints About Sessions

Having parents become more receptive to conversations on the way home from the sessions will sometimes open the door to the "complaint department." One parent said, "My child asked me if he had to come anymore." This was a resis-

---

[1]*Dangerous/aggressive toys*—martial arts toys, Super Soakers, water balloons; *solitary/parallel play*—books, skateboards, toy guns; *too good a toy*—expensive toy that will upset the child if lost or damaged.

[2]Review of the phone calls typically reveal that every child took the call seriously. The group leader should point this out after the third parent reports this.

tant child who was offered a reward that was to be given after coming to the first two sessions. His mother then asked the group if anyone else had this experience. Only 1 of the other 10 sets of parents verbalized a similar experience. The group leader pointed out that approximately 20% of children would not choose to come to sessions. The main factor that keeps these reticent children coming is that their parents verbalize support for the program. Our experience indicates that reticent children actually do as well as the children who like to come. The key factor appears to be completion of homework in predicting successful outcome of program participation.

Parent Handout and Homework Assignments

The handout reviews play resources necessary to carry out play date assignments that will begin in Session 7. Many parents will have these resources, so a cursory review may be all that is necessary. Reviewing this handout sometimes brings up specific questions about the assignments in upcoming sessions, especially play dates. The group leader needs to keep the parents focused on the resources they need to have and defer discussion of these questions to future sessions.

Parents need to rebuild their children's social networks while concurrently ensuring that their child uses important social skills outside the treatment situation. Using good skills will not immediately change peer liking for a child with a negative reputation. Beginning with the call to a child not in the group and over the next few sessions, parents should be taught to identify signs of a negative reputation in the responses from peers at school (children don't invite their child to birthday parties, don't return calls, are not happy to speak with their child on the telephone, and never seem to be available for play dates).

If they have found that their child has a negative reputation, they are instructed to have their children maintain a "low profile" in order to let this reputation abate (while not provoking further negative responses from peers). Instead, the treatment focus will be on establishing friends in a new social situation, among peers with which the child is unacquainted. This is done under parent supervision to ensure that it is done correctly.

1. Tell each parent that their child is learning how to join other children already at play. Next week, they will begin to help this happen at home and in school. If their child has a negative reputation at school, they should find other situations for their child to practice this skill.
2. Review parent handout.

Group Leader Guide to Parent Handout— Session 3—How Parents Support Their Child's Friendships

GOALS
1. To review ways in which parents may help their child's friendships.
2. To develop resources needed for future playmates.

Long term studies show that your child's later adjustment will be better if he or she has two to three close friendships. These are best to have in your neighborhood. Your child's skills at making and keeping close friends improve most from informal one-on-one play dates, not through organized activities such as teams or Scouts. [*Tell parents that right now their children are learning how to join other children already at play. Next week, parents will help this happen at home and in school. Our goals are (a) to give their child the skills to join and maintain group play and (b) to use the groups they join to generate leads for play dates. We are interested in having parents help their children meet well-behaved children. Studies show that having no friends at all may be better than having poorly behaved children as friends.*]

Ways Parents Can Help (You Must Have All of These)
[*Help parents problem-solve if lacking on any resource after each point here.*]

1. A suitable place in house where your child can play with a friend, minimizing intrusions from siblings, if this is a problem.[3]
2. Your child will need interactive activities or games that he or she enjoys and that other children are also likely to enjoy. These include

---

[3]Parents of limited economic resources may lack a suitable place in the house for a play date (lots of people may be living together in one apartment or house).

✓ board games but do not include video games or TV. [*Say that we will not allow video games, computer, or TV. Ask if they have usable board games, action figures, blocks. Sometimes board games fall into disrepair as they are abandoned by boys in favor of computer and video games. These need to be replaced now with newly purchased board games.*] ✗

3. Sources of potential playmates (Scouts, teams, school) from which children can be invited— *have* you will need to draw on one of these in future sessions. [*If parents say they don't have a park or other after-school resource, have them drive around their neighborhood this weekend to look for a park with children playing who are no more than 1 year younger than their child, with whom they would feel comfortable that their child played. Many parks change character with the time of day and day of the week. They may go back to the same park on a different day with better luck. If their child has a negative reputation at school, they must find neighborhood places to practice this skill.*]

4. Time availability for one-on-one play dates— ✓ your child will need to be available for potential play dates for at least 2 to 3 hours on a weekly basis. [*Long-term studies don't show any benefit of activities like Scouts, teams, classes, and such on social adjustment (they are good for meeting new acquaintances). It's more important to carve out at least 2 hours between Friday and Sunday afternoon when children can have a play date than to be involved in numerous scheduled activities.*] [4]

tennis playdate

Parent Assignments

1. Calls to other group members, as in previous sessions. Check for ending call properly: Children are told to listen for a pause in conversation, and then to say that they have to go. [*Have parent check. The ending of the call has two parts (1) notice a pause in conversation (everyone has run out of things to say), then say, "Well, I have to go now, see you in school (etc.)"*]

2. Your child is to have a two-way conversation on the phone *with a child not in the group:* an easy child to reach and for whom you can arrange with parents (e.g., a cousin or child of a family friend). Determine who this will be before you leave today. Resist making a play

date with this child. [*Tell parents the best approach is to have the child make the in-group call first, practicing beginning and ending the call, and then call the child who is not in the group. Criteria ("gold standard") for selecting this child are:*

(a) *The other child should be the same age and sex.*

(b) *Their child's reputation enters into the decision of whom to call. Parents shouldn't have their child call children from settings in which they have a negative reputation. This first out-of-group call should be a guaranteed success— someone who likes the child and can talk on the phone.*

(c) *Go after the "best deal" you can get with each parent. Parents think of someone and suggest to their child at the end of the session. If child has a better idea, they can use the child's idea. The gold standard is for the out-of-group call to be with a same-sex child, within 1 year of age, they haven't talked to in a while that they would like to get to know better. If they haven't done this before, they can try a relative the same age that they haven't seen in a while.* ✗ *relative*

(d) *The child needs to have two-way conversations. Discourage lists of questions, because this promotes interviewing and children lose spontaneity. Parents can prepare their child by going over possible questions to ask right before the call or actually rehearse a phone call with their child.* !

(e) *Cover story for the call: Start the call with questions like what was the homework we had assigned (if they are in the same class at school), what school are you going to in the fall, are you on soccer team, and so on, and launch into trading information. Some children say to the child they are calling that they're making the phone call for a class. However, some children may not like being a "guinea pig," and this also adds an artificial connotation to the call. However, the most important thing is to get the call done.*

(f) *Tell parents to listen for: Was the other child happy to receive the call (if not to a relative)? Could the children figure out things they like to do together? If both answers were yes, then the child called goes on list as a potential play date.*]

---

[4]Time availability may be an issue for middle-class parents who have scheduled their children in back-to-back activities or who want to protect "family time" on the weekends.

3. Bring outside game from home, as in previous session.
4. Look around neighborhood for a place for your child to join other children at play who are the same age as your child (or no more than 1 year younger).
5. Add other needed resources—place to play, interactive toys, free up time in child's schedule.

Potential Problems

Calling for a Play Date

The parent of a third-grade boy asked if her son could call a child with whom the child wanted to have a play date (as an out-of-group call). The group leader asked if the parent's child has had problems with play dates. The mother agreed. The group leader told her either to defer the call to this particular child until the play date at Session 7, or just have her child call to get information now and put off scheduling a play date.

We have generally discouraged parents from allowing their child to prematurely schedule play dates (even though their child might be filled with enthusiasm regarding their successful phone call) due to the high risk of the child jeopardizing a potential new friendship through a poorly set up and supervised play date.

Ill-at-Ease with Phone Calls

The mother of a fourth-grader said her son was very nervous about making phone calls. It was decided that the first out-of-group call would be to their neighbor with whom the child plays frequently and whom the child saw during the past week.

No One to Call

One child insisted that he had no one to call, so a cousin was suggested, just as practice. They were about to visit this cousin for a holiday. The group leader suggested they could utilize the phone call to plan what they would do together during the visit.

Large Age Difference

One mother asked about a selecting a peer who was 4 years older than her child and another parent suggested an older child based on the idea that the older child "has very good skills." The parents' idea was that this older peer would "teach their child." The group leader turned down these suggestions, stating that the teaching has been done in session, and the homework was to have parents continue this teaching with a child who may be a potential friend for their child.

Concern About Meeting Strangers

The mother of a second-grade boy was concerned that her son would meet children in a park with whom she was unfamiliar. The group leader addressed this with two responses. First, the idea was to practice joining other children at play under the mother's supervision. These encounters need not result in friendships. Second, in cases where children had a negative reputation at school, the strategy was to have them seek friends from new sources.

Child Session Plan 3

Homework Review

Although the homework assignments were similar to those reviewed during the last session, children have improved their conversational techniques through being supervised by their parents during the phone call. They have more skills to get information and sustain longer calls. Many children will get excited in telling about the homework.

1. Review phone calls to other group members—go around and have each child say who they called and what they found out about the other child.
2. Check for *trading information*. Liken it to a game of ping-pong or tennis—get information and give information, back and forth.

Clinical Examples of Successful Two-Way Conversations

Mission Accomplished

A fifth-grade girl enthusiastically reported, "We found we have seven or eight things in common. We like pets, playing outdoors, reading, and we like the same TV shows."

A sixth-grade boy with Asperger's disorder reported, "I found out that he's cool. We like the same things: basketball and computers."

Potential Problems

Rigid Time Limit on the Call

One third-grade boy with Asperger's disorder thought the call had to be exactly 10 minutes long. He played detective but punctuated the call with the statements: "got 5 minutes left," "got 2 minutes left," and "time's up, goodbye." The group leader modeled this and asked the group what was wrong. Interestingly, the boy realized his own error when he saw the group leader neutrally portraying the behavior. At the end of session reunification, the child group leader told this boy's parent to remind him before the call that he needed to get and give information and that the duration of the call wasn't important.

"Boy Crazy"

A sixth-grade girl told the other girls in the group she was interested in having a boyfriend. Unlike the other girls in the class, she wanted to call the boys in the class and have boys over for play dates. This may be a way of opting out of dealing with other girls or having the upper hand in relationships with boys. The group leader assigned only girls to call and alerted this girl's mom to monitor phone calls to insure that boys were not a topic of conversation. Discussing boys was also discouraged in class as a case of being a "conversation hog" (because other girls may not want to talk about boys).

Homework Assignment

The children have had two phone calls to group members to get the "bugs" out of their conversa-

tional skills. Now begins the application of techniques to an unsuspecting child outside the group. This call will be more difficult because the other child doesn't have to talk to or be nice to them, or even be home at the time of the call. This first call should be to someone they would be comfortable talking to, so that they are likely to be encouraged for future calls to children outside the group.

1. *Have a two-way conversation on the phone with a child that is not in the group:* The out-of-group call should be with someone they haven't talked to in a while, whom they would like to get to know better. But the first call should be to someone they would be comfortable talking with (someone they have not spoken to who is easy to approach—e.g., an old school friend they haven't seen for a couple of years). Have each child specify who this will be. Tell them they will report an interest they shared with this child next week.
2. They need a cover story for the call. It's best to start the call with things like getting the homework, finding out what school the other child is going to in fall, are they on the soccer team—then launch into trading information. But make the call!
3. Rules for beginning and ending phone calls:
   Begin: Say who you are and ask to speak to the other child. If an answering machine takes the call, leave a message (who you are, who you'd like to speak to [name of child], and your telephone number).
   End: Transition statement (such as "I have got to get to my homework," "Time for me to eat," "I've got to clean up my room," or "I'll talk to you later," and add "See you soon, bye").

Go around the room and ask each child to say how they would begin and end a call.

4. Make partner assignments for the in-group call.
5. Tell children to bring an outside toy again for next session.

Potential Problem

"Boy Crazy"

A fifth-grade girl who had oppositional defiant disorder said she wanted to call boys. The group leader responded that the homework was to call another girl the same age as her or younger. A call to a boy wouldn't count as completed homework.

Didactic

The formal instruction on joining a group of children already at play ("slipping in") begins. Present these steps succinctly and avoid attempting to have the children glean the steps through the Socratic method (as most of the children will not know the steps to join).

Slipping In

When: Try to slip in when others are playing, during lunchtime, before school, or after school is over.

When not: Don't try to play with children when they are working or listening to the teacher (or other adult).

Do: Watch the group *nearby* (show that you're interested in what they're doing without "butting in"), watch what they are doing and what the rules are to participate (are they taking turns, lining up?). Join by *helping them play their game.* Try another group if the group you are watching is playing too rough.

Don't: Ask questions (if you can't tell what's going on, don't bother the others). Don't mention yourself or your feelings (no one's interested). Don't disagree or criticize (you're the outsider and have no right to do so). Don't clown around or be silly (this shows you're not serious about wanting to play and will be distracting).[5]

Clinical Example: Presentation of "Slipping In"

GL: The first thing you're going to do is use your eyes. Decide if you want to play—Are the children you're watching playing by the rules? Are they playing too rough? You might want to find children who don't play rough.

GL: If you decide you want to join them, begin to help them play their game. If the ball

bounces out of play, first make sure it's "ok" to touch the ball. You might ask, "Hey guys, do you want me to get it for you?" Don't make noises that distract others like kicking poles or bouncing balls up and down when you're on the sidelines. Be patient—it may take a while for you to "slip in."

GL: What if a child who is waiting says, " I'm waiting too long? [the group leader exaggerates gestures of anguish and dismay].

[Children are silent]

GL: The answer is, "It's not the other children's problem that you are impatient or irritated." Even though some schools have rules that say "everybody plays or nobody plays," some children "hold others hostage" by walking into the middle of the game and saying "I'm playing" or telling the teacher so that nobody gets to play. This alienates others.

Potential Problems

Belittling the Techniques (Slipping In)

"In my school we don't have to wait to join a game. We can just walk right in." The boy continued to repeat that he didn't need to "waste" his play time by implementing the techniques being taught. The group leader pointed out to this boy that he needed to try the techniques we are teaching. Prompts and time outs were utilized for this disruptive behavior until it ceased.

Real Play

The children will generally take too long to organize games (and they won't know how to do this without being bossy or setting up unfair teams), so prearranged games with simple rules have great utility. You teach the rules to the children quickly and set up the structure to avoid rewarding children who are quick to take charge and attempt to dominate peers. The group leader then has a better grasp of what's going on in the preplanned activity so that the leader can better instruct children as to how to slip in.

Slipping in is practiced in the context of the game "Prisoner."

---

[5]These rules are from Garvey (1984, pp. 164–165). See Chapter 12 for more discussion on slipping in.

Clinical Example: Coaching "Slipping In" Rules

GL [to child held back on the sidelines]: OK. You just came in late and these kids are already playing. What's the first thing you should do?

Child: [quiet].

GL: Figure out the game and rules. What's the game?

Child: Prisoner.

GL: How many kids on each team?

(Child): Four on that side and three on that side.

GL: Who's playing better?

Child: That side.

GL: The ball just came over, what should you do?

Child: Get the ball for them and throw it to them.

GL: Go ahead [child throws ball back]. Which side needs the most help?

Child: That side [pointing to the correct side—the losing side that has fewer players].

GL: Whom should you ask to join and when should you ask?

Child: [points to child holding the ball] During a pause in the game.

GL: Go ahead, ask at the next pause.

Potential Problems

Excluding Others

Some children at play will need coaching not to say "no" when being asked "can I play?" from a waiting child. The correct answers are either "yes," "wait a minute," or "you can join after the next point/at the end of this game." The children are advised that their willingness to allow others to join will enhance their reputation among peers at school or in the neighborhood.

Resistant to Role Playing

Most children will go along with the "pretend" aspect of waiting on the sidelines, if it is introduced with some dramatic panache. But some children will say, "I don't want to play this. This is boring." In response, the group leader says,

"This is the activity, this is what you have to do." Prompts and time out ensue for continued non-compliance.

The Principles Don't Apply in His School

A sixth grader with Asperger's disorder stated after being taught the principles of "slipping in," "In my school kids are aggressive and get into lots of roughhousing—they love to roughhouse when they are just getting to know you." The group leader's reply was, "Your homework assignment this week is to look to join the nicer children at your school and not to 'roughhouse' with them."

Refusing to Participate

On the way to the deck, a sixth-grade boy pouted, saying, "I don't feel like playing." The coaches and group leader didn't look at him and ignored this statement. When the group reached the play deck, he crossed his arms and tried to tell a group leader that he wasn't going to play. Coaches and group leaders continued to ignore this. He sat down on the volleyball court as the group leader was telling the rules of the game to the group. The group leader told him to stand up and come closer. He stood up and came closer, but as soon as the game started, he sat down on the court. The group leader told him to stand up. He complied but didn't start playing. After the game went on for a short while, he began to participate and was disappointed the game didn't continue when time was up.

The Toy as a Tool of Coercion 1

Some children will try to use their own toy to control everyone's play. If things don't go their way, they will attempt to take their toy and leave ("If I don't get to go first then I quit and I'm taking my ball"). A child will try to do this when he is given a time out. In this case, the group leader tells the child that the toy stays in the game while he is in time out. In all cases, the group leader states that once the toy is in play it is everyone's toy.

The Toy as a Tool of Coercion 2

One child insisted that his toy should be selected for use in the upcoming week. The group leader replied that it would be impossible for the leader to use all the toys brought by the group members in the scheduled deck activities. Each week the leader will be picking the equipment that will be used in the game.

End-of-Session Reunification

1. Begin by praising the children (as a group): "Today we worked on beginning and ending a call and slipping into a game other children are playing. I saw a lot of patient children trying to learn these skills. Let's all give the children a big round of applause."
2. Read the in-group call assignments one by one, as in previous sessions, but stop parents from immediately starting to arrange these calls with each other.
3. Continue with, "The major job everyone has this week is to make a call to a child who is not in the group. Agree on this person with your parent."
4. Together with coaches and parent group leader, check with each parent and child about who the child will call outside the group. (Negotiate for the "best deal" and for a "back-up" call in case the first choice isn't home.) Negotiating the out-of-group call may take longer than usual for homework negotiations. Some parents may not realize that their child dis-

likes the child they want him or her to call. Children may suggest someone who doesn't like them (e.g., never returns their calls) or whom the parent thinks is poorly behaved. The parent should suggest an alternative without stating why.

Potential Problems

Calling the Most Popular Child in the Class

The group leader asked a second-grade boy with ADHD who he would call outside the group. When the child said the other boy's name, his mother mentioned that the boy was the most popular boy in her son's class. The group leader said that he needed to come up with another boy who would be more accessible. After some reluctance, the boy accepted his mother's suggestion.

"Parting Shots" by Parents

As parents were leaving the session, one parent approached the group leader, demanding, "I hope you're going to talk to us about how our kids are going to get the phone numbers" (or alternatively, "What happens if he doesn't want to do the outside call?" or, "I can see my son's point that this is too hard to do. There isn't anyone in the neighborhood") In these cases, the group leader suggests that the parent make their best effort at accomplishing the homework as assigned and then bring up the issue during the next parent group to get everyone to help them.

Children's Friendship Training

Parent Handout—Session 3

How Parents Support Their Child's Friendships

GOALS: 1. To review ways in which parents may help their child's friendships
2. To develop resources needed for future playmates

Long-term studies show that your child's later adjustment will be better if he or she has 2–3 close friendships. These are best to have in your neighborhood. Your child's skills at making and keeping close friends improve most from informal one-on-one play dates, not through organized activities such as teams or Scouts.

Ways Parents Can Help (You must have all of these):

1. A suitable place in house where your child can play with a friend, minimizing intrusions from siblings, if this is a problem.

2. Your child will need interactive activities or games that he or she enjoys and that other children are also likely to enjoy. These include board games but do not include video games or TV.

3. Sources of potential playmates (Scouts, teams, school) from which children can be invited—you will need to draw on one of these in future sessions.

4. Time availability for one-on-one play dates—your child will need to be available for potential play dates for at least 2 to 3 hours on a weekly basis.

Parent Assignments

1. Calls to other group members, as in previous sessions. Check for ending call properly: After a pause in conversation, say that they have to go.

2. Your child is to "play detective" on the phone **with a child not in the group**—an easy child to reach for whom you can arrange with parents (e.g., a cousin or child of a family friend). Determine who this will be before you leave today. Resist making a play date with this child.

3. Bring outside game from home, as in previous session.

4. Look around neighborhood for a place for your child to join other children at play who are the same age as your child (or no more than 1 year younger).

5. Add other needed resources—place to play, interactive toys, free up time in child's schedule.

Children's Friendship Training

The Rules for "Prisoner"

Child Session 3

Gather Children

1. Tell the children in advance that coaches and the group leader will be pulling children out to wait on the side lines to practice "slipping in."

2. Tell children when they wait to "slip in" they should avoid complaining about not getting in or engaging in silly or distracting behavior.

3. Children waiting to enter can get the ball when it goes out of bounds to "help the other children to play their game."

Assign Sides

4. Assign equal numbers of children on each side of a volleyball net.

Tell Game Rules

5. The child who has the volleyball calls the name of a child on the other side, then hits or throws the ball up high ("like the golden arches") and over the net in order to give a child on the opposing team a chance to catch the ball.

6. If the child whose name is called or one of his or her teammates catches the ball, he or she remains in. If not, then he or she is out on the sidelines (a "prisoner").

7. If there is only one person left on one of the teams, he or she can call "jailbreak." He or she then throws the ball to the other side. If none of the opposing team members catch the ball, then all prisoners are released on his or her team.

8. If the final player misses a catch, then his or her side loses.

Start the Game

9. Start with all kids playing the game.

10. Pull one child out and have him or her pretend to be a latecomer who is watching a game in progress. (Don't mix up latecomers and prisoners.)

Core Instruction

11. Emphasize whose game it is (the kids at play) and that only the kids at play can let new kids join in (kids shouldn't step into a game and say "I'm playing" or attempt to change the rules or game on entry).

12. Ask the child waiting questions such as "who is winning," or "which team has the most kids," "which side should they try to join" (Answer: losing side, or side with less kids), and "when should you ask to join" (Answer: when a game is completed, or during a pause in the game or after a score).

13. Have the child ask to join after correct answers to questions.

Debriefing at the End of Game

14. Tell children two strategies for eventually getting in: (a) If children are waiting to join and don't get in because the game ends, tell them they can ask to join the *next time* the children play. (b) As the game players are dispersing the child can ask, "Are you going to play this at lunch [or at recess or tomorrow]?"

PART III

CHAPTER

12

Taking "No" for an Answer/ Gender and Age Issues

Treatment Rationale

Some rejected children persist in trying to join peers at play even when it has been clearly communicated that they are unwelcome. This will only serve to make them more unwelcome in the future, as they are showing that they will not consider the wishes of others. Parents may exacerbate this problem by pressuring their child to try to make friends in situations in which they have a negative reputation (e.g., at school). Teachers also may compound this problem, coercing the children at play to accept the rejected child, through lack of understanding of determinants of peer rejection. The treatment hypothesis is that teaching children to accept being turned down will allow a more adaptive approach to this event that may make future entry bids more likely to be accepted. Educating parents as to how children successfully join others at play will focus parent energies on building child skills that are more likely to lead to friendships.

12.1 Joining Others at Play

According to Ladd and Price (1993), the most important aspect of the school playground at recess is that children are free to choose playmates. They can move freely in and out of groups of children who are playing. Serbin, Marchessault,

McAffer, Peters, and Schwartzman (1993) videotaped fifth- and sixth-grade children during 15 minutes of school recess twice per day. They observed that children spent an average of 60% of the time engaged in play (girls 54%, boys 66%) and were alone only an average of 11% of the time. About 70% of play time was spent in groups. Thus, children must be effective in entering a group at play.

Successful entry into a group at play involves not only getting to play with the group but also being liked by the group in order to have a better chance of being invited in on the next attempt. Children who make inappropriate attempts to join will have their entry attempts resisted. Children who enter by coercion (e.g., getting an adult to force the children to let them play) or who impulsively enter and attempt to take over the game will suffer socially in the long run.

12.2 Problems of Rejected Children

A child's entry into groups of children already at play is one of the most challenging situations identified by teachers and clinicians (Dodge, McClaskey, & Feldman, 1985). Ladd (1983) observed third- and fourth-grade children at recess. He found that popular and average boys showed more group play than rejected boys and all girls, whereas popular and average girls showed higher levels of social conversation than rejected girls and all boys. When compared to same sex accepted children, rejected boys spent more time wandering aimlessly, and rejected girls spent more time in solitary play near other children. Rejected children were likely to seek out many different playmates, whereas popular and average accepted children were likely to stay with consistent play partners. This is graphic evidence that joining other children at play is especially difficult for rejected children (Dodge, 1985; Putallaz & Gottman, 1981).

Research on Joining Other Children at Play

12.3 Differences Between Successful and Unsuccessful Entries

Successful entries into a group of children at play begin with low-risk tactics such as waiting and watching the other children play until positive feedback from the playing peers permits entry (Dodge, Schlundt, Schocken, & Delugach, 1983; Garvey, 1984). The following are some rules of etiquette for social entry:

> *The Don'ts:* don't ask questions for information (if you can't tell what's going on, you shouldn't be bothering those who do); don't mention yourself or state your feelings about the group or its activity (they're not interested at the moment); don't disagree or criticize the proceedings (you have no right to do so since you're an outsider). *The Do's:* be sure you understand the group's frame of reference, or focus (are they playing house?); understand the participation structure of the activity; slip into the ongoing activity by making some relevant comment or begin to act in concert with the others as if you actually were a knowledgeable member of the group; hold off on making suggestions or attempting to redirect until you are well into the group. (Garvey, 1984, pp. 164–165)

Accepted children are likely to quietly attend to what the children are playing (Putallaz, 1983), to say things that fit in, to be supportive of others already at play ("He's right—it's his turn"; Coie & Kupersmidt, 1983; Dodge, 1983; Tryon &

Keane, 1991), and to direct statements to each child who is playing (Black & Hazen, 1990). Rejected children are likely to disrupt an ongoing game by asking for information, disagreeing, demanding to include themselves ("I'll take your turn"), or otherwise distracting and criticizing those already at play (Coie & Kupersmidt, 1983; Dodge, 1983; Putallaz, 1983; Putallaz & Gottman, 1981; Tryon & Keane, 1991). Putallaz and Gottman (1981) provided the following example of a rejected girl (Terry) trying to call attention to her own feelings and being ignored by the other girls at play:

> Janet: Okay, I want this one again.
> Terry: This is fun ain't it?
> Janet (to Vera): Do you want this one again?
> Vera: I want this one.
> Terry: This is a nice room ain't it?
> Janet (to Vera): You can have this one here.
> Terry: This is a nice table isn't it?
> Janet (to Terry): Pick your one. (p. 993)

Differences between rejected and accepted children are evident immediately after the unsuccessful entry attempt. Children have been observed to be turned down in approximately half of entry attempts (Corsaro, 1981). Our observations are that rejected children may try to coerce their way into the group that had turned them down, whereas accepted children seek another group of children at play to attempt to enter.

Rejected and accepted children also differ in where they attempt to join with others. Dodge, Schlundt, Schocken, and Degulach (1983) reported that rejected boys were more likely to try friendly approaches to peers in the classroom than on the playground, which was the reverse of the strategy found for popular boys. These classroom approaches were not only likely to be turned down, but if accepted might get both children in trouble with the teacher and lead to future rejection by peers.

12.4 Sex Differences in Peer Entry

In an experiment studying peer entry, Borja-Alvarez, Zarbatany, and Pepper (1991) observed the behavior of the children at play (in this case a board game) as well as the child attempting to enter. Their results suggest that boys would have greater difficulty in the peer entry situation than girls would. They observed that girls at play were substantially more likely than boys to invite an onlooker into their game whereas boys at play tended to ignore onlookers (who had to get the players' attention with relevant comments in order to succeed in entry). They found that girls waiting to enter were more responsive to invitations to join than were boys. Peer entry may be easier when the children at play are well liked. Tryon and Keane (1991) observed that well-liked boys at play tended to ask boys attempting to enter if they would like to join, whereas rejected boys tended to tell boys attempting to enter what to do ("stand here," "wait until we finish").

Some of these results contradict our clinical experience. Parents of girls typically report that their daughters are nearly totally excluded from girls' groups and sometimes find inclusion in boys' groups easier. The discrepancy of our parents' reports from the study findings may be because girls typically aren't playing board games and thus the study girls weren't as concerned about continuing play after the study was over. Also, as presented earlier, girls in a naturalistic setting tend to be engaged more in conversations during free time, whereas boys tend to play games. More naturalistic studies have yielded results consistent with the observations of parents of children in our groups. Eder and Hallinan (1978) noted that 11- and 12-year-old girls were less likely to include an unfamiliar girl in their interaction than the same aged boys.

12.5 Joining Younger Peers

One interim solution for children who are unsuccessful in peer entry is to attempt to join groups of slightly younger children at play. Available evidence, although on preschoolers, suggests this as a promising approach. Furman, Rahe, and Hartup (1979) selected the least interactive 4-year-olds in a day care setting (probably mixing different sociometric categories) to pair with same age or younger aged peers for 10 play sessions over 4 to 6 weeks. Pairing with younger peers normalized the interaction rate (almost every

child improved), whereas same-aged peer pairing had little effect.

It is possible that many rejected children discover this phenomenon for themselves. In comparison to average and popular children, rejected children reported having a larger proportion of younger friends (George & Hartmann, 1996). However, without proper guidance many rejected children become bossy with these younger playmates and may not reap the full benefits of the situation to develop more appropriate skills.

12.6 Cooperative Versus Competitive Games

Many situations that boys try to join at recess are competitive games. Research evidence suggests that rejected boys find this situation especially difficult. Rejected children seem to define the purpose of some games as "to win at all costs," without consideration that the interaction with the game partner must go smoothly if the relationship is to continue (see also the discussion of social goals in Chap. 13; Ladd & Mize, 1983; Renshaw & Asher, 1983). Games with a large component of competition (i.e., with teams) are more likely than cooperative games to evoke this "win at all costs" approach (Gelb & Jacobson, 1988).

Rejected children are likely to behave better when playing cooperative than competitive games. This result has been observed for aggressive (Gelb & Jacobson, 1988; Tryon & Keane, 1991) and rejected children (Markell & Asher, 1984). Rejected boys were less likely to break rules during cooperative as opposed to competitive games (Gelb & Jacobson, 1988). Perhaps as a result of seeing rejected children function better, average children liked rejected children more after daily participation with them in cooperative tasks (Conoley & Conoley, 1983). A productive approach in the early sessions of children's friendship training is to avoid competitive games and focus on cooperative games, until children can be taught to reevaluate their social goals in competitive situations. Meanwhile they can be taught group entry skills, and, once they get in the cooperative games, can maintain positive interactions more easily.

12.7 Cross-Sex Versus Same-Sex Friends

Should rejected children be encouraged to join play groups of the opposite sex? Cross-sex friends seem to be uncommon in elementary school children (Gottman, 1986; Maccoby, 1986; Maccoby & Jacklin, 1987). Howes (1988) found that cross-sex friendships decreased in prevalence across ages 1 to 6. Kovacs, Parker, and Hoffman (1996) found that only a small minority of third- and fourth-grade children (13.5%) reported having cross-sex friendships, with no difference between boys and girls. Fourth through sixth graders report no cross-sex friendships in children who form "cliques" (defined through peer nomination when each member chose and was chosen as a best friend by more than 66% of a small subgroup of children; Hallinan, 1980).

Taking an extreme view, Carter and McCloskey (1984) have proposed that cross-sex friendships violate social norms and may contribute to social ostracism. Ladd (1983) postulated that less socially competent children are more likely to violate gender boundaries. In partial support of this contention, boys have reported being teased more than girls for associating with cross-sex friends (Langlois & Downs, 1979). Gottman (1986) asserts that cross-sex friendships may continue at home but be hidden during school hours. Similarly, Frankel (1996) has observed that boys may maintain best friendships with girls through play dates at home but not group play during school recesses (this was also proposed by Kovacs et al., 1996).

Subsequent research (Kovacs et al., 1996) has not completely supported this contention. Kovacs et al. found two patterns in children who reported cross-sex friendships. One pattern was a rejected child who had a cross-sex friend as their only friend or very best friend. This was consistent with Ladd's (1983) position. But children who had only cross-sex best friends were more socially competent than children who had no best friends at all. The other pattern was that of a well-liked child who reported cross-sex friendships as best (but not very best) friends. These children were also rated as more socially competent than other well-liked children without cross-sex friends. Other evidence also indicates that cross-sex friends may have important contributions to make to social competence of accepted and popular children. Canadian 10- to 12-year-old boys were more intimate with other boys when they participated in more communal activities, less team sports, and had female friends (Zarbatany, McDougall, & Hymel, 2000).

Other determinants of cross-sex friendships have been delineated. Kovacs et al. reported that cross-sex friendships were not significantly related to the number of cross-sex siblings or child self-esteem. Cross-sex friendships were more common among African Americans than among whites, but mainly due to African Americans reporting more friendships in general. Bukowski, Gauze, Hoza, and Newcomb (1993) demonstrated that common interests influence these cross-sex friendships. Fourth- and sixth-grade girls who preferred gross motor play were more likely to have male friends whereas boys who disdained gross motor play were more likely to have female friends. They also showed that cross-sex friendships are driven more by a liking of particular opposite-sex peers than a dislike of same-sex peers.

In summary, it is clear that although cross-sex friendships have beneficial effects upon social competence, friendless children should be encouraged to join same-sex groups playing in public places.

12.8 Parent Roles in Their Child's Peer Group Entry

Parents can make an important contribution to how their children approach the peer entry situation. Parents of rejected, neglected, and average children may differ in how they instruct their children to make new friends and how they supervise their children's attempts at joining play groups. Russell and Finnie (1990) found that mothers of neglected children were less likely than mothers of popular children to give adequate instructions to their child to facilitate group entry. Finnie and Russell (1988) found that mothers of accepted children supervised peer entry by having their child adopt the peers' frame of reference and join the play without disrupting it. In contrast, mothers of rejected children tended to disrupt the peer activities and employed more intrusive, hostile tactics to help their child join the play. Thus it is important to provide parents with the details for how peer-group entry can be successful.

12.9 Implications From Research and Clinical Practice

Previous research justifies the importance of instructing friendless children on how to enter groups of other children at play. Following the rules of etiquette helps ensure acceptance in play groups: (a) waiting and watching while understanding the group's frame of reference and how the group has structured the activity, (b) making relevant comments based on this knowledge, and (c) being supportive of others (when a rejected child is already at play he should be considerate of others attempting to join in; he should acknowledge children who are trying to join, and allow them to enter). Research also suggests that being turned down is commonplace even among accepted children. It should not be viewed as a failure, but rather an occasion to act appropriately so that future bids will be less likely to be turned down. There is a strong indication that slightly younger peers (probably no more than a year younger) may be helpful in the initial acquisition of peer group entry skills. Parents may play a role in maintaining inappropriate types of peer approaches and must be educated as to how children can successfully join others at play.

Research suggests that cross-sex friendships should be maintained but that friendless children should focus mostly on developing same-sex friendships. One reason is that most group play is among same-sex peers.

How to Conduct the Session

Until Now

Children have begun to learn some of the rules for successful peer entry. Parents have focused on where this will take place and have begun to look at their homes and neighborhoods as places in which their children will play with peers. Parents have continued to help their child hone telephone and conversational skills for future use in making play dates.

In This Session

This is the first time parents and children will report on an out-of-group call. The review of homework will emphasize this assignment. The play focus will continue the instruction on joining others who are already at play and accepting being turned down in entry bids. Parents should begin to focus on who should be invited for a potential play date.

Parent Session Plan 4

Initial Gathering

Check child toys as they come in. Have parents hold toys that are in excluded categories.[1]

Homework Review

The goal is to survey other children for a potential play date, so that each week the children should call a different child who is not in the group.

1. There are four homework assignments (not including outside toy) and not enough time to review all in depth. Ask the group as a whole, "Did anyone have a good conversation with their child on the way home from the last session they would like to tell us about?" Review these but don't ask everyone, because this will take too much time.
2. Ask each parent to very briefly tell about two-way conversations during the in-group call. Go into more detail for the assignment for the out-of-group call: Was it a two-way conversation—asking questions and answering questions?[2] Was the other child interested or excited by the call? Did the children have things to talk about? The *affect* of the other

---

[1]*Dangerous/aggressive toys*—martial arts toys, Super Soakers, water balloons; *solitary/parallel play*—books, skateboards, toy guns; *Too good a toy*—expensive toy that will upset the child if lost or damaged.

[2]It's more important to have a good out-of-group call than an in-group call, because the child may *want* to know the child he or she is calling outside the group, whereas calls to group members are not by the child's choice and are only for the purpose of practice.

child is important. If the other child was known from school and rude to their child on the phone, it could be a sign of a bad reputation. On hearing a negative experience like this from a parent, state the following to the group: "If a child has a bad reputation and he or she starts doing everything right, it will likely still take a couple of months for others to realize this and stop avoiding him or her. If he or she tries harder to be friendly and forces the issue, it will guarantee a failure experience. In this case, the best thing is to 'lay low' and find some other place for your child to practice skills where the other children don't know him or her. It's better for him or her to have a chance to join rather than a guaranteed failure with children he or she knows."

3. Ask about neighborhood parks they found for "slipping in" homework (if a parent found none then the parent should try again this week. Ask other parents in the group for help, if necessary, with locations of good parks).[3] Tell parents their child will be ready to attempt to "slip into" other children at play in their neighborhood after the next session.

4. Next out-of-group call—have parents identify a child who has potential to be invited as a playmate for the next out-of-group call (the "gold standard")—perhaps someone their child used to play with and hasn't seen in a while.[4]

Clinical Examples of Homework Compliance

Examples of Successful Out-of-Group Calls

Parents generally do a nice job of supervising "give and take" in conversations. One mom prompted her third-grade boy with a whisper to let the other child speak. Another passed her fifth-grade daughter a note saying, "you need to ask questions."

A fourth-grade boy had a class project to do with another boy. He called this boy and asked his questions before they started talking about the project at school.

A third-grade girl was to get together with girls she hadn't seen in a while for an Indian Guide reunion. She called one of the girls she was about to see prior to the reunion.

A fifth-grade girl had a negative reputation in school and in her Girl Scout group. The mom picked a girl from the girl's kindergarten list she hadn't played with in a long time. This family had moved 60 miles away. The call went successfully.

Perfunctory In-Group Call, Then Good Out-of-Group Call

Two fourth-grade boys in the group talked to each other for about 2 minutes (shorter than the 10-minute phone call that has been encouraged). Then each went on to have a successful call with a boy outside the group. The group leader emphasized that this was a complete success because it was more important to have a good out-of-group call.

Avoiding Telephone Tag

A mother of a second-grade boy reported that her son tried to call a neighbor across the street twice without success. She then called the other mom herself and arranged to have her son call when she knew the other child would be home. The children were then able to talk to each other on the phone.

Increasing Incentive

A mother of a third-grade boy reported offering her son $3 if he brought home three phone numbers of other boys he liked at school.

Potential Problems

Unsupervised Out-of-Group Call

The mother of a fifth-grade boy with ADHD said

---

[3]Bad places for joining: (a) the beach, on vacation—because children come from all over and may not provide sustainable friends; (b) children being supervised by an adult (e.g., birthday parties)—because the adult may interfere; (c) the library, bookstore—because people expect silence.

[4]If children were not able to call a child outside the group, select a closer friend or cousin, just to break the ice and have a success. If they were able to make a call to a child they know slightly and it went well, have them select another child for this week, so that they can add to their list of potential play-date candidates. You should continue to make the "best deal" to get them to approach the "gold standard" more closely on each successive call.

her son made a play date from his out-of-group call, but that she was not home to supervise this call. The group leader pointed out that parents need to be there to attend to how the call was received by the other boy and ensure the child had a two-way conversation. Did this play date come about because her son coerced it and the other boy didn't think it was a good idea? Did the other child insist on the play date even though her son wasn't thrilled about it? The quality of the exchange was unknown, yet this was very important information. The mom agreed to supervise all future calls.

Child Evading Supervision

A fifth-grade girl insisted on privacy for her out-of-group call. The mom acknowledged that she wasn't even sure if her daughter had actually made the call. The group leader said that privacy might be a reasonable request if her daughter had many previous appropriate calls that had been monitored by the mom. The group leader emphasized that the mom needed to hear how the phone call went and that she could tell her daughter that unsupervised phone calls would not count as completed homework at this time.

Supervised but Not Controlled by Parent

A sixth-grade boy called several other boys. During each call, he insisted on asking each one for a play date. His mom reported that she knew that this was inappropriate, but didn't know how to stop him. Another mom in the group suggested giving him a date for which he could make the play date (in 3 weeks).

Calling at a Bad Time 1

One fifth-grade girl waited until the last minute to do the out-of-group call. She made the call while she had a guest over. The group leader pointed out the breach in etiquette and suggested that the mom make her do it earlier next week, perhaps saying she couldn't watch her favorite TV show until her homework assignment had been completed.

Calling at a Bad Time 2

A second-grade girl reached a girl from her class while the other girl was entertaining three friends. She continued to have a two-way conversation in spite of this. The mom said she would encourage her daughter to make an appointment to call back at a better time if this happened again.

Awkward Conversation

One fifth-grade girl (functioning socially at about third grade) called another girl she hadn't spoken to in a year. She abruptly started asking questions as if conducting an interview, such as "What do you like to play?" and "What movies do you like?" Mom said this didn't go over very well with the other girl because the other girl expected that her daughter already knew this information based on their previous experiences together. After thinking briefly about this, the mom devised a strategy to make the phone call less formal and uncomfortable by refreshing her daughter's memory about the last time that her daughter and the call recipient were together and by rehearsing, asking things like "What have you been doing since last year?" and "Do you still like Britney Spears?"

"Boy Crazy"

A mother of a fifth-grade girl complained (in private to one of the group leaders) that the topic of conversation her daughter was having with another girl during their in-group call was how the other girl was kissing boys after school. Her daughter didn't wish to talk about this and the mom didn't wish to bring it up in session and possibly make the other girl's mom feel uncomfortable. The group leader suggested that the mother tell her daughter that she could say, "Talking about boys is not our homework assignment." During homework review the other girl's mom was urged to monitor her daughter's calls more closely.

Parent Handout

The handout for this session educates parents on the specific "rules of etiquette" that average and popular children use when they join groups of children at play. This is done so that parents will have an adequate foundation when supervising the "slipping in" assignment that will be made during Session 5. It may give parents a clearer idea of what to look for when they search their neighborhood this week for places for their child to carry out the assignment next week.

Group Leader Guide to Parent Handout— Session 4—How Children Make New Acquaintances

GOAL
To inform parents about group entry strategies taught to their children.

Studies have identified the ways popular and accepted children successfully join groups of other children at play. The strategies they have are much different from those of children who are frequently rejected. [*Tell parents that we will teach their child to do what the accepted/popular children do. Demonstrate how competent adults meet new people, using a parent sitting near the group leader: "Suppose you're at a party, where you don't know anyone and people are talking in groups of two and three. First you walk up close enough to show that you are interested and listen for how interesting and at what level the conversation is (demonstrate a comfortable distance with the parent sitting near you and only look at this parent while you say the next lines). You are seeing if you would like to join and figuring out how you can contribute. How do you know you have been accepted? The others start looking at you when they talk, ask questions, or direct statements to you (as you are talking, look away from the parent and toward the rest of the group). If they don't, then perhaps they don't want outsiders in their conversation. If you don't like the conversation or can't contribute or they don't look at you, then walk on to another group. No one's feelings will be hurt. If you hang around, you wait for a pause in the conversation and say something that contributes. Popular/ accepted children do this: younger children through play and older children through conversation. Neglected children don't get close enough to show they are interested. Rejected children barge in, play keep-away with the ball, and get others upset."*]

Do's and Don'ts of Group Entry
1. When and where:
   Do try to join in when others are playing, during lunchtime, or before or after school.
   Don't try to play with kids when they are working or listening to the teacher (or other adult).
   [*Rejected children try to make friends at the wrong times and places. If your child is rejected at school, he or she probably has a bad reputation. For now, don't encourage him or her to make friends at school, but rather to practice skills with new children.*]
2. How:
   Do watch the group *nearby* (show that you're interested in what they're doing without "butting in") and understand what they are doing (playing house, basketball) and what the rules are to participate (are they taking turns, lining up?).
   Do praise the other kids (great shot, nice try . . .)
   Do join by *helping them play their game.* Wait for a break in the activity and say something that shows you know the game (Do you need another guy on your team?).
   [*Which side do you pick to try to join—the winning side or the losing side? Rejected children pick the winning side—the side that needs the least help. They go into play with the strategy "win at all costs," whereas the accepted/popular children go in with the idea that maintaining continuing relationships is more important than winning.*]
   Don't ask questions for information (if you can't tell what's going on don't bother others); don't mention yourself or your feelings (they're not interested at the moment); be serious when meeting new children (clowning around tells them you're not really interested in playing).
   [*Through watching on the sidelines, children should figure out the game structure without intruding on the game.*]
   Don't disagree or criticize or tell them what to do (you're the outsider and have no right to do so).
3. *Take "no" for an answer*—On average, children are told this 50% of the time. [*This is not "rejection," it is being turned down. If they accept*

this gracefully, they will be more likely to be allowed in the next time.]⁵

4. Successful group entry can only be done by the child. Direct attempts by parents to help will generally be unsuccessful or counterproductive. [Tell parents they are to just watch from a distance.]

5. Your child will be asked to slip into a group of children after *next* session.

Parent Assignments

1. Calls to other group members as in previous sessions.
2. Play detective with a new person outside the group.
3. Bring outside game from home as in previous session.
4. Drive around your neighborhood looking for a playground with children the same age as your child or 1 year younger. Do not discuss this with your child until after next session.

Potential Problem

Talking About Feelings About Being Turned Down

The father of a third-grader with Asperger's disorder asked, "Are you going to talk about the child's feelings about being turned down?" The group leader replied, "We focus on what to do rather than on feelings. Focusing on what to do teaches children behaviors that are likely to pay off. Focusing on their feelings is likely to be a distraction from the true task at hand and may magnify those feelings. You're lucky to get children to focus on one thing at a time."

Child Session Plan 4

Homework Review

1. Review in-group and out-of-group calls—each child says who they called and what they found out about the other child. Check for *trading information* and how they *began and ended the phone call.*

2. *Call a new child that is not in the group* (tell them it might be someone they might invite over for a play date—but they are *not* to make play dates yet). Have each child specify who this will be. They will be asked to present a shared interest next week.

3. Discuss the "cover story" for the call—getting the homework, "What school are you going to in the fall?," "What time is the soccer practice/game?" and then how to launch into trading information. The most important goal is to get the call done.

4. *Level of disclosure:* Tell children, "When you are just getting to know someone, you need to find things you both like and dislike. You also need to keep some secrets—getting too personal too fast will not be liked by children you barely know." Have children discuss examples.

Clinical Examples of Homework Compliance

Examples of Reports of Trading Information

"He likes soccer and I like it, but neither of us are on soccer teams." "His favorite sport is basketball and we were on the same basketball team." The group leader praised the children for not getting too personal.

Examples of Call Endings

"He [the other boy] had to go eat dinner."

A third-grade boy with Asperger's disorder: "I thought eating dinner while talking was a little dangerous, so I said I have to go eat dinner now, bye."

A third-grade girl: "Well, I have to go visit my cousin now."

The group leader praised the children for explaining to their peers why they had to dis-

---

⁵The most difficult point for some parents is the idea that their child may be turned down in their entry bid. The group leader should distinguish this from "rejection" and "normalize" the experience, pointing out that peers will also turn down children who are popular.

continue the phone call. The very last things said could be, "Call you later" or "See you at school."

Potential Problem

Overexclusion

One fifth-grade girl said she only wanted to call a specific other girl because "She's my new best friend." The group leader discouraged this by saying that the homework is to call another girl and that it is important to get the homework done. The group leader asked whom else the girl would call next week if she couldn't reach her first choice.

Didactic

Last session focused on steps to group entry. This session will continue to practice group entry and teach children how to view and handle being turned down.

1. Say that you're going to practice "slipping in" this week and review the following with the children:
   Do slip into an activity by making a relevant comment or begin to act in concert with others (get the ball for them when it goes out of bounds and throw it back). Wait for a break in the activity or before it begins. When asking to play, say something that shows you know the game ("Can I play Capture the Flag too?" "Do you need another guy on your team?"). *Don't* tell them what to do or make suggestions until you're playing for a while.
2. Peers may not want to play just then but they may want to play later. Ask the group, "How many times will other kids usually say 'no' if you ask to join 10 different groups of kids playing?" (Answer: 5—about ½ the total number of requests.)
3. Have children think of reasons for being turned down. Use a Socratic method. Make sure you cover all the reasons in the chart below. [6]

Reasons for being turned down	What to do next time
(a) Something you did to them before (rejected them, got them in trouble with the teacher, etc.)	Treat others as you would have them treat you
(b) Disobeyed one of the rules for 'slipping in'	Use the rules next time
(c) Other child too popular, too athletic, not interested in the same things you are	Pick other children
(d) Other child doesn't want to meet new friends	Pick other children
(e) They misunderstood what you wanted to do	Say it differently, e.g., they say "no" and you point out that they are short two people on their side
(f) You played too rough and hurt other kids	Watch out for others and show concern when they are hurt
(g) They didn't feel like playing with you just then	Try again later

[6]Some children will say, "because they're mean." Although this may be true, it is more instructive to show them that their behavior can have an effect on current as well as future attempts to enter groups of children at play. The leader continues to ask, "What might a child have done to make other children say 'no'?"

Homework Assignments

1. Trade information during the in-group and out-of-group calls.
2. Bring outside game.

Real Play

This portion has them attempt to join and get turned down in order to practice the new idea presented during the didactic portion. Setting up two concurrent games adds more realism to practicing seeking other children playing after being turned down. Try to avoid having the children at play saying no, because you want to teach them to invite others in, consistent with what well-liked children do in this situation.

1. Soccer/Basketball (see rules sheet)
2. Taking "No!" for an answer.

End-of-Session Reunification

1. Announce to parents, "Today we worked on 'slipping into' a game other children were playing. I saw a lot of children waiting patiently to slip in. Let's all give the children a big round of applause."
2. Assign the in-group calls one by one, as in previous sessions, but stop parents from immediately starting to arrange these calls. Continue with, "The major job everyone has this week is to make a call to a child who is not in the group. Agree on this person with your parent."
3. Check to make sure each child and parent agree on whom to call.

Children's Friendship Training

Parent Handout—Session 4

How Children Make New Acquaintances

GOAL: To inform parents about group entry strategies taught to their children.

Studies have identified the ways popular and accepted children successfully join groups of other children at play. The strategies they have are much different from those of children who are frequently rejected.

DO'S AND DON'TS OF GROUP ENTRY

1. When and where:

   Do try to join in when others are playing, during lunchtime, or before or after school.

   Don't try to play with kids when they are working or listening to the teacher (or other adult).

2. How:

   Do watch the group *nearby* (show that you're interested in what they're doing without "butting in") and understand what they are doing (playing house, basketball) and what the rules are to participate (are they taking turns, lining up?).

   Do praise the other kids (great shot, nice try . . .)

   Do join by **helping them play their game.** Wait for a break in the activity and say something that shows you know the game (Do you need another guy on your team?)

   Don't ask questions for information (if you can't tell what's going on don't bother others); don't mention yourself or your feelings (they're not interested at the moment); be serious when meeting new children (clowning around tells them you're not really interested in playing).

   Don't disagree or criticize or tell them what to do (you're the outsider and have no right to do so).

3. **Take "no" for an answer**—50% of the time children are told this.

4. Successful group entry can only be done by the child; direct attempts by parents to help will generally be unsuccessful or counterproductive.

5. Your child will be asked to slip into a group of children after the **next** session.

Parent Assignments

1. Calls to other group members as in previous sessions.
2. Play detective with a new person outside the group.
3. Bring outside game from home as in previous session.
4. Drive around your neighborhood looking for a playground with children the same age as your child or 1 year younger. Do not discuss this with your child until after next session.

Children's Friendship Training

Rules for Soccer

Child Session 4

Gather Children

1. Tell the children the plan is for them to get "turned down" the first time they try to slip in and then be allowed to play after the second time (with another playing group).
2. Gather children in two groups for two concurrent games (such as one small game of soccer and one game of basketball or handball).

Assign Sides

3. The group leader chooses children for each team.
4. Assign the two teams as evenly as possible, based on children's athletic talents and pick the first goalies (children seldom want to be goalie because the goalie stays in one place).

Tell Game Rules (Soccer)

5. Children have to pass constantly between at least two children.
6. Children are not allowed to bump, play with physical aggression, kick a ball directly into another child, or dive at the ball recklessly (give prompts and time outs for this).
7. Do not keep score and direct children not to.
8. Excessive and inappropriate celebration after scoring receives time outs—even though some children will complain that they are mimicking World Cup/professional soccer behavior.

Start the Game

9. Start the second game (handball or basketball) using two or three children (better done out of view of the soccer players). Tell the children playing that this is an informal game with no teams.
10. Start the soccer game. Encourage each team to rotate goalies regularly and by themselves. If this doesn't happen spontaneously, help them do it.
11. Monitor the soccer game closely. If one player is left out of scoring goals, stop the game and ask the team how they are going to work the child into the next goal.
12. Consequences: Ball hogging or trying to keep score = 2-minute time out; Aggression, excess bumping, and dangerous play = 5-minute time out.

Core Instruction

13. Coach the children on the sidelines to attend to the game and retrieve the ball if it goes out of bounds and return the ball to the players ("help them to play their game").
14. Ask the child on the sidelines questions such as "who is winning," or "which team has the most kids," "which side should you try to join" (Answers: losing side, or less kids), and "when should you ask to join" (Answers: when a game is completed, during a pause in the game or after a score).
15. Have the child ask to join but intervene and pretend someone has turned the children down, then have the child go to the other (basketball or handball) game and join successfully, after having the child watch the game and figure out when to ask to join. Pull two children out of the basketball/handball game saying they just tried to join and were turned down. Take them over to the soccer game and have them watch and join successfully.
16. After the initial two children join, pull two more children out, saying that they just got turned down when they asked to join and repeat the "slipping in" procedure until all of the children have practiced "slipping in" and cycled through the soccer and basketball/handball games.

PART III

CHAPTER

13

Rules of a Good Sport/Social Goals

Treatment Rationale

Utilizing the proper steps to joining other children at play will only take children to the beginning stage of being a good playmate. Good sportsmanship will help children to be enjoyed more by their playmates. Some children seem more consistent in their good sportsmanship than others. Others seem to "forget." Good sportsmanship can be seen as a set of goals and priorities. It is clear that by second or third grade, children can formulate goals and devise strategies as to how to obtain their chosen goals. The treatment hypothesis is that children become better playmates by better prioritizing their goals for interactions to obtain satisfying continuing relationships with peers.

13.1 Definitions and Nature of Social Goals

It is useful to think of a child's approach to peers as determined by goals that the child hopes to gain from the interaction. *Social goals* can be operationally defined as objectives that children strive to attain or avoid in different social situations. Research has shown that social goals are situation-specific (e.g., McFall, 1982; Renshaw & Asher, 1983). For instance, hostile goals may be absent from first meetings but present in conflict situations. Social goals, together with skills,

knowledge and attributions of other's intent, are thought to guide children's behavior and values (cf. Erdley & Asher, 1996; Zarbatany et al., 1990).

Good sportsmanship can be defined as a set of social goals that elevate the importance of relationships with game mates over the outcome of the game. Good sportsmanship is especially important in competitive games. Competing in order to achieve task mastery (i.e., "I'm improving at this game") is distinct from competition motivated by social comparison (i.e., "I'm better than you"). Peer nominations of third graders (Tassi & Schneider, 1997) indicated that task mastery was associated with acceptance and prosocial behavior, whereas social comparison was associated with being rejected and being seen as aggressive. Thus, good sportsmanship is a set of goals and priorities that include close adherence to the rules of the contest in order to master the skills and hone one's own abilities, while being considerate of others.

Research on the Influence of Social Goals

13.2 Using Social Goals to Predict Peer Ratings

The presence of social goals can be inferred from consistencies in behavior. However, it is more convincing to show that responses geared to assessing social goals in a question-and-answer format correlates with overt behavior. Melnick and Hinshaw (1996) interviewed 6- to 12-year-old boys with ADHD and comparison boys about their social goals before they were about to play a game of "foosball." Correlation with peer liking was positive for the stated goal of "wanting to cooperate" and negative for "not afraid of trouble," despite the observation that many of these boys reported wanting to be liked by others. The social goal of avoiding conflict with best friends discriminated children with more versus fewer best friends (Fonzi, Schneider, Tani, & Tomada, 1997; Rose & Asher, 1999).

13.3 Social Goals of Different Types of Children and Situations

Researchers are beginning to catalogue the more salient social goals of different types of children in different situations. During competitive game play, rejected children seem to attach a high priority to "winning at all costs," without consideration that the interaction with the game partner go smoothly so as to continue the relationship (Ladd & Mize, 1983; Renshaw & Asher, 1983). Aggressive boys prioritize the goals of retaliating, making others look bad, having themselves look strong, and protecting themselves (Erdley & Asher, 1996; Lochman, Wayland, & White, 1993). Erdley & Asher (1996) found that withdrawn children attach a high priority to the goal of staying away from a child to which they attribute hostile intent. In a situation in which the intent of another child is ambiguous (knocking over of a child's project), both aggressive and withdrawn children tended to attribute hostile intent, whereas children lacking either of these characteristics tended to attribute accidental intent (Erdley & Asher, 1996). Subsequent responses were different since aggressive children gave precedence to retaliation whereas withdrawn children gave precedence to avoidance.

Melnick & Hinshaw (1996) noted that prior to competitive game play, highly aggressive boys with ADHD rated "not afraid of trouble" and "having fun even if it means breaking rules or teasing kids" much higher than the low-aggres-

sive boys with ADHD and comparison boys. Conversely, a lower proportion of highly aggressive boys chose "playing fair" than ADHD boys without aggression and comparison group boys (1996, p. 177). This suggests that aggression rather than ADHD is more directly related to peer problems in this context.

Children who differ in social status may attach differing priorities to prosocial and antisocial goals (Erdly & Asher, 1996), based partly on how successful they feel they will be obtaining them. Crick & Ladd (1990) found that rejected third- and fifth-grade children tended to focus more on goals that obtained tangible rewards and less on relationship-enhancing goals in comparison to average status peers (cf. Renshaw & Asher, 1983). Crick & Ladd (1990) hypothesize that this was because rejected children doubt their ability to enhance relationships (i.e., "I might as well just concentrate on winning the game because none of these kids will want to be my friend anyway"). Related to this hypothesis, Perry, Perry, and Rasmussen (1986) found aggressive children to be more confident than nonaggressive children that aggression will reduce subsequent negative behavior from peers.

13.4 Interventions Focusing on Changing Social Goals

Games with a large component of competition (i.e., with teams) are more likely than cooperative games to evoke a social goal of "winning at all costs" in socially rejected children (see also Chap. 12.6; Gelb & Jacobson, 1988). Supporting this observation, Conoley and Conoley (1983) found that sociometrically average children liked rejected children more after daily participation with them in cooperative as opposed to competitive tasks. There was no evidence of generalization to competitive situations, probably because no attempt was made to change social goals in these more problematic situations.

Two studies demonstrated that changing social goal orientation was a powerful intervention for rejected children. Oden and Asher (1977) focused on coaching children to have fun and make sure the game partner had fun as well. The positive impact of this instruction remained at the 1-year follow-up, despite it being a brief intervention (six 25-minute sessions). Hupp and Reitman (1999) used a token system to increase sportsmanlike behaviors and suppress poor sportsmanship for three boys diagnosed with ADHD, aged 8 to 10 years. The program was effective in increasing good sportsmanship and improved game performance. The program also increased the boys' interest in basketball.

13.5 Implications From Research and Clinical Practice

Giving precedence to relationship-enhancing rather than competitive social goals correlates with peer acceptance. Rejected children give a higher priority to goals that obtain tangible rewards, often using aggressive strategies, such as commands and threats. It is possible to modify children's social goals. Studies that have done this have demonstrated positive, lasting, and generalizable results after only a few sessions. Giving rejected children more confidence that they can attain goals involving relationship enhancement may increase the priorities they attach to these goals.

In Session 4, the focus was on joining others at play by "helping them play their game." Implicit in this social goal is that the game belongs to the children at play and that they may have good reasons not to include a child. But social goals are situation specific, and the children need to prioritize goals such as "help everyone to have fun" in order to have more satisfactory continuing relationships as a result of how they behave during game play.

How to Conduct the Session

Until Now

Parents have monitored three out-of-group calls, helping their child practice two-way conversations and starting a list of potential play dates with other children who were happy to receive the call. Children have practiced "slipping in" and what to do when their entry bids are turned down. Parents have scouted their neighborhood for places for their child to "slip in." Parents have also learned how successful children slip into a group and how they handle being turned down.

In This Session

Children are taught the rules of a good sport, in order to modify their social goal priorities to be consistent with continuing relationships with peers. Parents are given specific instructions on how to help their child do the "slipping in" assignment, given for the first time in this session. Token rewards are introduced to distract children from their previous primary social goals.

Parent Session Plan 5

Initial Gathering

Check child toys as they come in. Have parents hold toys that are in excluded categories.[1]

Homework Review

1. There are four homework assignments (not including outside toy) and not enough time to review all in depth. Tell parents that you want them to focus on (a) the out-of-group call, (b) two-way conversations during in-group and out-of-group calls, (c) neighborhood parks they found for the "slipping in" homework, and (d) only a perfunctory "Was the in-group call done, did it go OK?" (no more details than this).

2. *Probes for out-of-group call:* Were there pauses after your child spoke when he was listening to the other child's answer? Was the other child interested or excited by the call? Did the children have things to talk about? Whom might your child call for this week's assignment?[2]

3. *Neighborhood resources for the "slipping in" assignment:* Ask each parent: Did you go by a park last week and see children the same age or slightly younger than your child playing as a group in this location?

---

[1]*Dangerous/aggressive toys*—martial arts toys, Super Soakers, water balloons; *solitary/parallel play*—books, skateboards, toy guns; *Too good a toy*—expensive toy that will upset the child if lost or damaged.

[2]The "gold standard" is a child they haven't called before who has potential to be invited as a playmate or someone they used to play with and haven't seen in a while. Accept the "best deal" toward this.

Clinical Examples of Finding Neighborhood Parks for "Slipping In"

One parent had a park across the street from their home.

Driving around and actually looking to see what age the children were at local parks helped another family. They had to come back several times and found that children the right age tended to play in the afternoon on Saturday.

Another parent targeted before and after team practice.

Homework Assignment

Parents have been well prepared for the "slipping in" assignment—scouting for a place over the past 2 weeks, decreasing the importance of their child being turned down, and today, learning the steps to supervise their child's group entry. Parents typically don't have many questions at this point.

Group Leader Guide to Parent Assignment—Due on Sessions 6–9

GOALS
1. To increase your child's ability to join play groups.
2. To help your child make new friends.

Studies show that over 50% of attempts by children to enter playgroups are turned down. This is not rejection. Accepted/popular children experience this and look for other children to play. Rejected children try to coerce children to let them into their play. Neglected children don't get close enough to try. [*Tell parents you have been teaching this to their children.*]

Your child should attempt to join a group of children the same sex as him or her, the same age or younger. Attempting to join a group of younger children (no more than 1 year younger) may be helpful:

1. Studies have shown that many children with peer problems may benefit in the long run from play with slightly younger children.
2. Children are more likely to be accepted by younger children.

At the End of This Session
1. Decide with your child where and when he or she will attempt to join a group of children at play. Older children (fourth graders and above) may prefer to so this at school/camp. During recess, before or after school, during after-school activities, or at a playground are good choices for the place. The time should be as soon as possible (tomorrow or this weekend are best). [*Review again bad places: (a) the beach, on vacation – because children come from all over and won't live close enough to make sustainable friends (b) children being supervised by an adult (e.g., birthday parties) – because the adult may interfere (c) the library, bookstore – because people expect silence.* Good places: *(a) neighborhood park, (b) unstructured after-school program, (c) before or after team practice, (d) before or after scout meeting, (e) at church/temple. Children don't have to play for long and don't have to be invited in, just go up to the edge of the group, watch, and make the attempt to slip in at an appropriate opportunity. Have parents say where and when they will try this.*]
2. Bringing a toy may help break the ice. Use only an outside toy that your child has been bringing here.

At the Time of the "Slipping In" Assignment
1. Remind your child of the rules: (a) Watch first before joining; (b) Praise other children or wait until a break in the game and try to join; (c) if they say no, say nothing but go to another group of children; (d) Act serious when joining. [*For children who are shy/anxious, step 1 is all that is necessary on this week's homework assignment.*]
2. Your child must try this by himself or herself. *Do not try to help in any way.* For younger children (first through third grade), you may watch from a distance, so that the other children do not see you (in which case, bring a magazine with you to pretend to read). Older children might prefer to do this assignment when you are not present (but they have to join children with whom they don't ordinarily play). [*Parents of older children should remind the child in the morning before school and later get all the details.*]
3. Your child is *not* to try to enter a group of older

children or to bring a peer or sibling with him or her.

After the Child Attempts the Assignment
1. If your child begins to talk with you about it, *praise* any attempts to do the assignment or any discussion of what your child was supposed to do.
2. If the group did not accept him or her; encourage your child with comments like "That's too bad, maybe it will work next time," or, "It sounds like it was a hard thing for you to do."

Don't criticize in any way or tell your child to try something different.

Potential Problem

Concern About Old Patterns of Behavior

One mother of a fifth-grade boy with Asperger's disorder expressed concern about her son's tendency to barge into other children playing. She was reassured to know that he had been taught appropriate steps in previous sessions before the "slipping in" homework assignment she was about to do with him.

Child Session Plan 5

Homework Review

1. Review in-group and out-of-group phone calls—each child says who they called and what they found out about the other child.
2. Check to see that the level of disclosure was not too deep, not too personal. Check for trading information and how they began and ended the phone call. Have each child present a shared interest he or she found during the call.

Didactic

The last three sessions demonstrated how easy it is to get children to obey rules for peer entry. These were discrete steps that many children

didn't previously take. Once invited into a game, the children's social goal priorities may interfere with playmates' enjoyment of the game. In contrast to discrete steps, it is necessary for them to learn rules that govern their behavior throughout play.

The didactic portion gets them to reevaluate their social goals through use of the "rules of a good sport." The Socratic presentation together with practice in the real play segment (with token reward) makes for quick learning.

1. Ask, "What happens if we are not well behaved *after* we join other children at play?"
2. As an introduction to the rules of a good sport, have the children come up with things that they can say to praise others during play ("nice try," "good shot," . . .). Practice in session.
3. Ask children how it makes them feel to get praise like this from others.

Introduce rules of a good sport using a Socratic method (see Table 10.2).

Rules of a Good Sport [Keep in mind the template for these rules]:
- *Praise another kid's behavior,* for example, nice try, great shot, high-five. Kids who are really good at something often praise others, too.
- *Say what you want others to do—no refereeing* (refereeing = telling others what not to do or calling excessive penalties such as "double dribble" "foul" "cheating," etc., like a referee).
- *If bored, suggest a change in activity or having a turn.*
- *Let others have fun too* (e.g., stay in your own area of the field, don't try to jump in front of other kids and catch all balls everywhere).
- *At the end of a game* tell the kids on the other team it was a good game.

4. Tell children about tokens they will get during the real play portion of the session: They will earn tokens for following the rules of a good sport: that is, for praising another child's behavior ("nice try," "good shot"), no refereeing, suggesting a change in activity when bored, and letting others have fun. The tokens count the same as stars toward the final party.

Clinical Example: Presenting the Rules of a Good Sport

GL: Last week we worked on taking "no" for an answer, this week we'll work on being a good sport. What compliment can you say before or when you get into a game?

Different children: "Good job." "Nice try." "Really cool football you have there." "At the end of the game, you can say, 'Good game.'"

GL: Those are good things to say. What about children who brag at the end of the game? What if they say, "I scored the most points so I'm the best basketball player?"

Child: We don't like bragging.

GL: No one likes bragging. What's a "referee?"

Child: Someone who is always making calls like "double dribble" "foul" or "out of bounds." You know, spending all their time telling the other kids what they are doing wrong.

GL: What happens if kids try to be a "referee?" What might other kids do?

Child: They get mad because they don't want to be bossed around.

GL: That's right, they would make other kids mad and "refereeing" isn't their job. Supposing you're bored, how do you change the game? Do you tell the others, "We're doing it this way now?"

Different Children: "No, you're not the boss of them." "They won't like it."

GL: We're going to practice all of these things when we go out to play. This time for homework you're going to "slip into" a group of children playing in your neighborhood. They can be the same age or a little younger than you. It can be after or before school, or at a park.

Homework Assignment

1. *Try* to slip into a group of children with whom you are not familiar.[3] Children are to *try* to "slip in" to a group of same-age or younger acquaintances. They don't have to actually be invited into the game in order to complete the assignment. "Slip in" with kids they only know "so-so."

2. Out-of-group and in-group calls (make assignments).
3. Bring an outside toy.

Potential Problems

Trying to Modify/Nullify the Assignment

Children may ask, "How about if I do the homework with kids that I already know?" or "How about kids that are older than me?" The group leader responds to these responses with a repetition of the original assignment.

Examples of Children Telling Why They Can't (Won't) Do the Assignment

"I know all the kids in my class (parents say he plays alone)." "There are no kids that I don't already know." "In my school you're not supposed to play after school."

The group leader avoids generating solutions for the dilemma presented by the child because frequently the child is simply trying to be excused from doing the homework assignment. Instead, discussion of how the assignment will be done is explained in front of the child's parent at the end-of-session reunification.

Overly Selective Regarding Playmates

A fifth-grade girl said she couldn't do the assignment because "I don't like the kids that stay after school to play." The group leader replied, "Where else can you go where there are kids so that you can practice 'slipping in'? Tell me where the nice kids are."

Real Play

Tokens make their debut this session. Table 11 presents guidelines for delivering tokens. Just before the real play portion is the time to introduce tokens. Don't worry about explaining this too much, as the children won't grasp the change

---

[3]Trying is more important than actually getting in, as it allows the child to be turned down and go elsewhere.

TABLE 13.1 Delivering Tokens—Child Sessions 5, 6, 10, 11

The main purposes of token rewards are to get children to:

1. Start using didactically taught skills.
2. Divide the attention of children between the game and the reward. In so doing, we have observed that the children are unable to maintain their initially counterproductive social goals. For example, the social goal of "winning at all costs" is difficult to focus on if a child is also concerned about earning tokens for good sportsmanship.

Description of Tokens
Tokens should be unique (don't use pennies or standard poker chips) so that children won't be tempted to inflate their count with chips they have at home. However, if they're too unique (we have used plastic tokens with a hole in the center that resemble Japanese coins) they will start to disappear.

When to Give Tokens
1. Tokens are given for any behavior related to the rules of a good sport.
2. Do not give tokens for anything else, e.g., eye contact, saying other person's name, etc., as this will dilute the focus on good sportsmanship.

How to Give Tokens
1. Move in and out of play among the children, much as a basketball referee does.
2. Receiving a token should cause only a momentary disruption of the child's attention to the game.
3. Speak telegraphically to state why a child earned a specific token, while handing the child the token. Examples: "for being gentle just now," "for giving a 'high-five.'"
4. Withhold tokens if children look or ask for one after doing a desired behavior (but praise them for the behavior). Some children will begin "performing" in front of the coaches with the sole desire of obtaining the token and losing focus on the other aspects of the game being played.
5. If a child argues with you over not being given a token, give them a prompt followed by a time out if the arguing continues.

Debriefing
1. At the end of play, count only the total number of group tokens, adding each child's tokens to the total. Have all the children count along.
2. Avoid comparisons between children or pointing out who received the most tokens, as this will foster a counterproductive form of competition.

in procedure until group leader and coaches actually start dispensing them.

At first, children might be surprised or puzzled when they receive an individual token. This is partly because they are overly focused on their initial social goal. After a few tokens are given, the coaches and group leaders begin to become "invisible" to the children. This is a sign they have oriented toward playing the game and are attending to the other children in the game.

The children are to briefly practice joining, but mostly concentrate on being a good sport in the context of "Magic Johnson Basketball."

End-of-Session Reunification

1. Praise the children (as a group) for what they did in this session. "Today we worked on "slipping in" and being a good sport. I saw a lot of friendly and considerate behavior in this group. Let's all give the children a big round of applause for their courtesy."
2. Read off the in-group call assignments one by one, as in previous sessions. Stop parents from immediately starting to arrange these calls with each other.
3. "The major job everyone has this week is to

go to a place and try to 'slip in' with children you haven't played with before. Agree on where you will do this with your parent."

4. Negotiate the place for the "slipping in" assignment and an out-of-group call with each parent and child. Accept a place out of parent's view for fourth graders and above. First ask the child. If the child doesn't produce a response that meets with parent agreement, then the parent is asked for ideas and the group leader has the child pick one he or she likes the best.

Clinical Example: Negotiations With a Girl With a Negative Reputation at School

GL [to child in front of mom]: Who are you going to call for your out-of-group call?

Child: Doreen.

GL [to mom]: Is Doreen OK?

Mom: Yes. She has known Doreen from kindergarten but hasn't seen her since.

GL [to child]: Where are you going to try to "slip in"?

Child: I'll do it at recess at school. [In the parent session, mom has said her child has a negative reputation at school.]

GL [to mom]: Is that OK?

Mom: How about the park across the street from our house?

Child: I do it all the time at school.

GL: I think it's time for you to branch out and meet new kids. You can do it at school for practice if you would like, but in order for it to count as homework, you should try it at the park. Remember you only have to try. If they say "no" then you still get credit for doing your homework.

Child: O.K.

Potential Problem

Parent Not Adhering to "Slipping In" Criteria

One mother of a fifth-grade girl picked a local bookstore for the "slipping in" assignment, despite the group leader recommending against this venue. She insisted that the bookstore in her neighborhood would fit the criteria as a good place for her daughter to slip in. Because this was hard to dispute, the group leader waited until the end-of-session reunification and asked the daughter if she wanted to do the "slipping in" at the bookstore. She hesitantly said "yes." However, after the group leader asked her if other girls would gather around and do group activities in the bookstore, she said "no." The group leader subsequently negotiated a park as the location for her assignment.

Children's Friendship Training

Parent Assignment—Given on Session #5

Due on Sessions 6–9

GOALS: 1. To increase your child's ability to join play groups.
               2. To help your child make new friends.

Studies show that over 50% of attempts by children to enter playgroups are turned down. This is not rejection. Accepted/popular children experience this and look for other children to play with. Rejected children try to coerce children to let them into their play. Neglected children don't get close enough to try.

Your child should attempt to join a group of children the same sex as he or she, the same age or younger. Attempting to join a group of younger children (no more than 1 year younger) may be helpful:

1. Studies have shown that many children with peer problems may benefit in the long run from play with slightly younger children.
2. Children are more likely to be accepted by younger children.

At the End of This Session:

1. Decide with your child where and when he or she will attempt to join a group of children at play. Older children (fourth graders and above) may prefer to do this at school/camp. During recess, before or after school, during after-school activities, or at a playground are good choices for the place. The time should be as soon as possible (tomorrow or this weekend are best).
2. Bringing a toy may help break the ice. Use only an outside toy that your child has been bringing here.

At the time of the "slipping in" assignment:

1. Remind your child of the rules: (a) Watch first before joining. (b) Praise other kids or wait until a break in the game and try to join. (c) If they say no, say nothing but go to another group of kids. (d) Act serious when joining.
2. Your child must try this by himself or herself. **Do not try to help in any way.** For younger children (first through third grade), you may watch from a distance, so that the other children do not see you (in which case, bring a magazine with you to pretend to read). Older children might prefer to do this assignment when you are not present (but they have to join children with whom they don't ordinarily play).
3. Your child is *not* to try to enter a group of older children or to bring a peer or sibling with him or her.

After the child attempts the assignment:

1. If your child begins to talk with you about it, **praise** any attempts to do the assignment or any discussion of what your child was supposed to do.
2. If the group did not accept him or her, encourage your child with comments like "That's too bad, maybe it will work next time," or, "It sounds like it was a hard thing for you to do."

Don't criticize in any way or tell your child to try something different.

Children's Friendship Training

Rules for Magic Johnson Basketball

Child Session 5

Gather Children

1. Tell children that tokens will be given to those who praise others, give "high-fives," follow any "rule of being a good sport" or are considerate of others.

Assign Sides

2. The group leader chooses sides of two and three players of approximately equal ability, to start.

3. Keep the rest of the children on the sidelines as children who are about to "slip in."

Tell Game Rules

4. Rules of a regular basketball game are used, except the primary emphasis is on cooperative team play. The following behaviors earn prompts and time outs:
   - Stealing the ball or attempts at it.
   - Aggressive physical contact (e.g., fouling others by slapping instead of just blocking or excessive, stifling defense that intimidates the other child).
   - Excess celebration after a score.
   - The ball must be passed at least once prior to a goal being scored.

Start the Game, Monitor and Control Nehavior

5. Children who "ball hog" excessively lose their opportunity to shoot any baskets (they are only allowed to rebound, dribble, and pass the ball to others).

Core Instruction

6. Have the children figure out which team needs the most help, as well as when to ask and who to ask in order to "slip in." Then allow them to slip in.

7. Tokens are given for any behavior related to the rules of a good sport. Do not give tokens for anything else, such as eye contact, or saying other person's name, as this will dilute the focus on good sportsmanship. How to give tokens:

   (a) Move in and out of play among the children, much as a basketball referee does.

   (b) Receiving a token should cause only a momentary disruption of the child's attention to the game.

   (c) Speak telegraphically to state why a child earned a specific token, while handing the child the token. Examples: "for being gentle just now," "for giving a 'high-five.'"

   (d) Withhold tokens if children look or ask for one after doing a desired behavior (but praise them for the behavior). Some children will begin "performing" in front of the coaches with the sole desire of obtaining the token and will lose focus on the other aspects of the game being played.

   (e) If a child argues with you over not being given a token, give the child a prompt followed by a time out if the arguing continues.

Debriefing at the End of Game

8. Count only the total number of group tokens, adding each child's tokens to the total. Have all the children count along. Avoid comparisons between children or pointing out who received the most tokens, as this will foster a counterproductive form of competition.

9. Ask children if they had a good time. Ask why they had a good time (Answers: Because they made sure other children had a good time, everyone had an equal opportunity to shoot the ball, and no one was getting injured or intimidated by rough play).

PART III

CHAPTER

14

Rules of a Good Sport/Positive Statements

Treatment Rationale

Training the appropriate steps to take in joining other children at play and training parents how to supervise initial group entries will promote situations outside of treatment. However, children's interactive skills must continue to be bolstered to ensure that other children continue to enjoy their company, after they let them join their play.

14.1 The Importance of Positive Statements to Peers

Positive interactions begin with entry into a group (Dodge, Pettit, McClaskey, & Brown, 1986; Tryon & Keane, 1991) and persist in helping children avoid conflict. Hartup, Glazer, and Charlesworth (1967) found that 4-year-old nursery school children emit three to five times as many positive reinforcers (approval, affection, and submission) as negative reinforcers (noncompliance, criticism, attack, interference) in unstructured play. They suggest that the positive tone also helps diminish conflict when it begins. According to Hartup and Laursen (1993), children will continue to interact after conflict is over if affective intensity is low and conciliation is employed. In contrast, standing firm, strong affect, and an inequitable outcome result in discontinu-

ation of further interactions between two children.

Research on Positive Statements and Peer Status

14.2 Negativity in Rejected Children

Frequent use of praise and agreement are both essential to being liked by other children. Hartup and Laursen (1993) found that a child's observed positive reinforcement rate correlated with the proportion of "liked most" peer sociometric nominations but was uncorrelated with the proportion of disliked nominations. Likewise, negative reinforcement rate correlated with the proportion of "disliked most" nominations but was uncorrelated with the proportion of "liked most" nominations. During dyadic interaction in a game, Putallaz and Gottman (1981) found that popular second and third graders disagreed less with each other than rejected second and third graders. In response to disagreement, the popular children were more likely to state the rule of concern of the game and provide an acceptable alternative for the other child, ("you're not supposed to do that, you're supposed to do this first"—a "stop" and then a "go" statement), whereas the rejected children were likely only to state the reason for the disagreement without including the relevant rule (e.g., "you can't do that"—only a "stop" statement).

14.3 Implications From Research and Clinical Practice

Rejected children are least equipped with skills to deal with times when they must structure their own activities with other children. These situations demand more positive approaches to peer interactions than rejected children typically have in their repertoire. In contrast, they more readily produce negative behaviors such as criticizing peers. *Refereeing* is when friendless children impulsively state rule violations while neglecting to praise their peers. Thus, it is imperative to have children identify negative behaviors (refereeing) and replace them with good sportsmanship ("high-fives" and other praise).

How to Conduct the Session

Until Now

Children have focused on being considerate of others when and after attempting to join others at play. They have begun to practice doing and saying positive things to others during play, and adjusting priorities on their social goals before entering into play.

In This Session

This is the first session in which parents and children report the results of the child's attempt to "slip in" with others at play. Now the emphasis is on skills that will sustain interaction after successful entry into the play of others. Parents will need help if the choice for a place to do the "slipping in" homework did not work out. Children will concentrate on maintaining positive interactions (praising) with the help of the token rewards during the real play portion of the session.

Parent Session Plan 6

Initial Gathering

Check child toys as they come in. Have parents hold toys that are in excluded categories.[1]

Homework Review

Parents typically require most of the session to review their child's first attempts at "slipping in" and suggestions for the next attempt (The session handout takes little time.) Expect that between 30% and 80% of parents will report that the "slipping in" assignment was successful (and be ready to celebrate their excitement with them).

1. There are three homework assignments (not including outside toy) and not enough time to review all in depth. Announce to parents that you want them to focus on (a) the "slipping in" homework and to a lesser extent (b) the out-of-group call (only dwell here if there was a problem), with (c) only a perfunctory "Was the in-group call done, did it go OK?" (no more details than this—this will be last time the in-group call has been assigned).
2. Ask first for success stories on the "slipping in" assignment. Then get other parents to report. Where did the children attempt to slip in? Were parents either able to observe it or hear the details from their child? Don't accept parents' unelaborated descriptions—have them go over the details so they know you are serious about getting parents to observe their child.[2]
3. Go around to each parent and ask (a) "How did the out-of-group call go?" (b) "Did the inside the group calls go OK?" ("yes"–"no" answers here), and (c) Have parents identify a child who has potential to invite as a playmate for the next outside group call. Someone they met in the joining assignment might be appropriate. They can set up a play date and schedule the play date for no earlier than 2 weeks from now.

---

[1]*Dangerous/aggressive toys*—martial arts toys, Super Soakers, water balloons; *solitary/parallel play*—books, skateboards, toy guns; *too good a toy*—expensive toy that will upset the child if lost or damaged.
[2]Bad places: (a) the beach, on vacation—because children come from all over and offer a low likelihood of evolving into sustainable friends; (b) children being supervised by an adult (e.g., birthday parties)—because the adult may interfere; (c) the library, bookstore—because people expect silence. Good places: (a) neighborhood park, (b) after-school unstructured program, (c) before or after team practice, (d) before or after Scout meeting, (e) at church/temple.

Clinical Examples of Successful Homework Compliance

A mother reported that her sixth-grade boy looked outside their house, saw someone skateboarding, and went out and skateboarded next to him.

A mother of a third-grade boy reported he was waiting on the sidelines at a neighborhood park when others were playing Frisbee. When the Frisbee was overthrown he asked to get it for them. They said "yes" and then invited him to play.

A mother of a fifth-grade boy said her son told her he tried to slip in while children were playing at recess in his new school. He said he was turned down at first. She reported that our point about being turned down 50% of the time helped him walk away gracefully (and not feel too bad). He said that he tried again later and the group let him in.

A mother of a third-grade girl diagnosed with oppositional defiant disorder watched her slip into a group of boys. After letting her daughter play for a while, she took her aside and reminded her daughter that the assignment was to slip in with girls. To her surprise, her daughter then slipped in with girls. The mom was pleased at the absence of disagreement and the ease with which her daughter was subsequently able to slip in with same-sex peers.

A mother of a third-grade girl reported seeing girls milling around before her daughter's ballet class. One girl did a slide. She heard her daughter give a compliment by saying "Cool!" and then her daughter and several other girls practiced sliding together.

A mother of a second-grade boy saw her son in the schoolyard before school started watching other children playing handball. Her son cheered the others and was let in quickly.

Potential Problems

Wrong Place

A third-grade boy's parents took him to the beach so that he could practice "slipping in." He found two brothers playing in the sand and "slipped in." However, the brothers' father went over and told him to leave. The group leader used this to point out how difficult the beach is to "slip in" and had the other parents suggest a local park for this parent to try for next week.

Child Needed Extra Help

The parents of a fourth-grade boy with ADHD said he had no trouble joining but staying in was the problem. This actually occurred because he didn't join correctly. The group leader asked the mother if he waited on sidelines first. She said no, her son just went in and asked if he could play. The group leader added that the next time the mother should have her son wait with her and not let him join until he could tell her information such as what the rules of the game are and who's winning and losing.

Child Afraid to Do the Assignment

A shy third-grade boy was afraid to do the assignment. The group leader said this was the mother's opportunity to give him a "tuneup" and make sure he does this appropriately. The group leader suggested all the child would have to do for this homework is to get up close to others at play (wait on the sidelines). That would be the extent of the assignment for this week.

Parent Giving Up

The mother of a fifth-grade girl said her daughter told her she joined at school but couldn't give the details. The mom accepted this as fulfillment of the assignment, despite reporting in previous sessions that her daughter had a negative reputation at her school. The group leader had the mother agree to get her daughter to try to "slip in" before softball practice. The mother said she would bring her daughter to practice early. However, the mom verbalized her concern that her daughter would again refuse to do the assignment. The group leader offered to spend extra time at the end of the session helping her and her daughter to agree on a place other than school for "slipping in." The group leader would let her daughter know that attempting to "slip in" at school would not count as the assignment.

Parent Noncompliance 1

One mom of a fifth-grade boy said her son refused to tell her what he did for the assignment—only that he did the homework. The mother had said in the previous session that her son would attempt to "slip in" before baseball practice and that she would take him early in order to insure this. The mom reported she had made these arrangements but had only dropped her son off at practice and then left. She gave excuses as to why she couldn't "hang around." The group leader had her promise to supervise for the next assignment.

Parent Noncompliance 2

One mom saw her son wait on the sidelines but not initiate a request to join. She walked over to "help him join by asking other children for him." The group leader asked the group what they thought. Several other parents voiced their opinions that her son needed to do this himself.

Homework Assignment

Next week begins the instruction on good host behavior on play dates. This session begins instructing parents on good and poor toys and games for play dates. Reviewing this handout (inside toys to bring for next session) should take no more than 10 minutes and generally poses no problems.

In contrast to the outside toys, which tend to be staples across generations, inside toys are constantly evolving. New toys are being developed all the time. If the toy doesn't appear to fit in any category in the parent homework assignment handout, then a good strategy for group leaders is initially to allow a child to bring it in and to have the child group leader watch how it affects the quality of play. If the toy encourages interactive play with lots of cooperative verbal interchange and is easily shared, then allow it. If the toy is used in an exclusive or bossy fashion, tell the child to play with something else, inform the parent (at the end of the session) to avoid this toy for subsequent sessions and to curtail its use on play dates.

Pass out parent assignment for session 7–9 (no parent handout for this session).

Group Leader Guide to Parent Assignment—Due on Sessions 7–9

GOALS
1. To help your child search for potential best friends.
2. To assist your child in the appropriate social use of games he or she has during informal one-on-one play dates.

Right Now and at the End of Every Session
1. Continue arranging assigned telephone calls to children who are not in the group as before. [*Announce: Next time the children will be working on being good hosts on play dates so we need an* inside *toy.*]

Before Each Friendship Group Meeting
2. Have your child select a game to bring in next time that he or she can play well and that he or she *would be likely to play with at home with another child.* This must be a game that two children can play and that encourages interaction between the children; for example, a board game, action figures, Jengo, Mancala, Connect Four, Battleship, Sorry, Parcheesi, or Uno. We will be using this to help your child learn how to play more appropriately with other children in one-on-one situations.

Indoor Games to Exclude

Games that are not advisable for a play date:
Obsessions—Any game on which your child is so hooked that he or she no longer cares if he or she is playing with someone else. Video and computer games are always in this category. Video games and computer games are typically a small part of many boys' play dates, but children in our group tend to have a lot of trouble changing activities once they start playing these.
Trades—Pokemon cards. Children may trade them and later regret the trade as unfair. These activities make for hurt feelings all around.
Provocative games—water pistols, anything that shoots projectiles, martial arts toys or objects.
Solitary or parallel activities—books, drawing or arts and crafts, watching TV or videotapes.
Require more than two to play—Twister, Clue.
[*Tell parents we will be focusing on play dates when only one child will be invited at a time.*]

Games that are not suited to our sessions:
[*Tell parents these may be good for longer play dates, but there's not enough time in our sessions.*]
Too specialized for most kids—Dungeons & Dragons, Magic Cards; these are not games that are known by everyone—they limit whom you can play with.
Too complicated for many kids—If your child wants to bring chess or Mastermind, he or she needs to first find out if anyone else in our group knows how to play them. If not, don't bring them. Teaching other kids how to play a game is not a good way to make closer friendships with others—the teacher tends to dominate.
Too much time to set up—Your child may spend the whole time setting them up and not get to play it during the session, such as for Monopoly.

Potential Problem

Too Avid an Interest

On intake, the mother of a third-grade girl reported that her daughter was so fascinated by playing with Barbies that she would not change the play activity when her guest asked. The group leader told the mom that Barbies should not be allowed on play dates and in sessions until it was clear that this girl could easily transition to what a guest would want to play.

Child Session Plan 6

Homework Review

1. Briefly review in-group and out-of-group calls—ask all children who they called.
2. Briefly check for *trading information* and how they *began and ended the phone call.*
3. *Review attempts to "slip into" a group of children with whom they were not familiar.* Ask: Where did you go to try to "slip in"? What game were the other kids playing? How did you ask to join? Which side did you join (winning or losing)? What did the kids do [let you in]? [When entry was turned down, add] What did you do next?[3]

Clinical Examples of Children's Reports of "Slipping In"

A second-grade boy reported that he was good at handball. He subsequently waited in line with children about to play handball and successfully "slipped in." The group leader asked, "Was it fun?" He replied "yes."

A fourth-grade boy reported joining after school when he saw two boys were playing Karems. He said he stood nearby, waited for the end of the game and asked to play the winner. He was allowed to play.

A second-grade boy with Asperger's disorder joined others who were playing "shark tag." Although he was initially worried about playing this game, he waited on the sidelines long enough to determine that what they referred to as "biting" each other was actually just tag. He figured this out before he asked to join.

Examples of Children Handling Being Turned Down

A third-grade girl reported, "They said 'no.' I said OK. I played on the swings for a while and asked nicely later. They let me play." The group leader said, "You handled being told 'no' well. You waited and it paid off when you asked the next time."

A second-grade girl reported that she approached girls playing jump rope. They turned her down. Another girl came along and they asked together. This time the girls playing said "yes."

A fifth-grade boy said, "I tried to slip in with kids playing volleyball. They said 'no.' So I went to another group and they said 'yes.' The group leader replied, "If at first you don't succeed, try again."

A third-grade boy said he tried to join two other boys who were playing. One said "yes" and the other said "no," so he didn't join. The group leader praised him for not entering the game when one child disagreed, saying it would be easier next time he wanted to join them because he respected both their wishes.

---

[3]It is important to continue to normalize being turned down and the response of trying to join another group of children or the same group of children at a later time.

A fifth-grade boy reported, "They said 'No, we're in the middle of a game.' So I went away." The group leader pointed out, "That was nice of them to tell you why—that they were in the middle of the game. When could you come back?" The boy replied, "At the end of the game."

Potential Problems

The only problems encountered in this segment are children who say they didn't do the homework or report that they did when they actually did not. Comparisons with parent reports sometimes are inconsistent. Usually, but not always, the child will say he or she did the assignment and the parents will say the child didn't. Compliance with the homework is addressed in the child session only by using peer pressure (hearing other children in the group reporting success). Excuses such as "we were too busy" or "I had too much school work" should be ignored and addressed at the end of session reunification with the parent present.

Didactic

1. List things children can say to praise others during play. Have children practice saying what they came up with.
2. The group leader has children recall the rules of a good sport from the last session using a Socratic method (See Table 10). Keep in mind the template for the five rules here:

   (a) *Praise another kid's behavior,* for example, "nice try," "great shot," "high-fives"—kids who are really good at something often praise others too.
   (b) *Say what you want others to do—no refereeing* (refereeing = telling what not to do or calling violations/penalties, etc.). Coaches prompt this and suppress group members pointing out rule violations.
   (c) *If bored, suggest a change in activity or having a turn.*
   (d) *Let others have fun too* (e.g., stay in your own area, don't try to catch all balls everywhere). Who should have fun? (Answer: Everybody.)

   (e) *At the end of a game* tell the kids on your team and the other team it was a good game.

Homework Assignment

1. Slip into a group of children with whom you are not familiar. Have each child say where he or she will do this. (Note: The in-group call is no longer assigned.)
2. Bring an *inside* toy next time: a board game, Jengo, Mancala, Connect Four, Battleship, Sorry, Parcheesi, or Uno. No video games, trading or Magic cards, or anything that shoots something. Have each child say what he or she will bring.
3. Out-of-group call.

Real Play

Only one game is chosen for this segment in order to focus on good sportsmanship. "Slipping in" practice no longer takes place, as children have done this for homework.

1. Have children play soccer or basketball (see rules sheet).
2. Tell the children it will be a "friendly" game—no keeping score and everyone gets to play.
3. Group leaders should be ready to prompt rule violations—instances of playing referee and not allowing others to participate (e.g., ball hogging).
4. Use tokens for following the rules.

Clinical Examples of Good Sportsmanship

Giving a "high-five" to a team member making a score.
Saying "nice try," "good shot."
Children who pass the ball to others.

Potential Problem
Argument Over Not Getting a Token

A fifth-grade boy told another boy in a flat tone "nice catch" and looked over to the group leader.

The group leader praised him but did not give him a token. He then asked, "I said 'nice catch.' Don't I get a token?" The group leader reiterated, "That was an good compliment, keep it up."

End-of-Session Reunification

1. Announce to parents: "Today, we worked praising other children. I saw a lot of good sports in this group. Let's all give the children a big round of applause."
2. "The major job everyone has this week is to go to a place and try to 'slip in' with children you haven't played with before. Agree on where you will do this with your parent right now. Remember, you are also to call a new person for your out-of-group call and have a two-way conversation in order to come up with games to play, and bring an *inside* toy next week."
3. Go around and negotiate inside toy, out-of-group call, and place to join in with each child. Accept a place out of parent's view for fourth graders and above (but the child should not join his or her usual play group).

Potential Problems

Refusing to Do the Homework

A fifth-grade boy had previously refused to try to "slip in" while his mother was watching or to tell her details of his attempts at school. The group leader had him choose which way he would do the homework assignment—either do it in front of the mom (who will be a far distance away) or tell her about it, so it will count as the homework. He chose to tell her the details and complied with this.

Parent Intrusion on Token System

A fifth-grade boy with Asperger's disorder tearfully told his dad that he only got one token although he felt that he deserved a lot more. His dad became concerned about his son's distress and asked the child group leader for an explanation. The group leader told him the purpose of the tokens is not for group participants to compare and compete. The dad and his son were able to accept this clarification.

Child Attempt to "Split" Group Leader and Parent

A sixth-grade boy was telling his mom after the session that he couldn't "slip in" because he didn't get to practice it in the session. His mom asked the child group leader in front of the child if this was true. The child was looking down at the floor as the group leader told his mom that this was not true and that her son had participated in extensive practice during the session.

Children's Friendship Training

Parent Assignment—Given on Session 6

Due on Sessions 7–9

GOALS: 1. To help your child search for potential best friends.
2. To assist your child in the appropriate social use of games he/she has during informal one-on-one play dates.

Right now and at the end of every session:

1. Continue arranging assigned telephone calls to children who are not in the group, as before.

Before each friendship group meeting:

2. Have your child select a game to bring in next time that he or she can play well and that he or she **would be likely to play with at home with another child.** This must be a game that two children can play and that encourages interaction between the children: for example, a board game, action figures, Jengo, Mancala, Connect Four, Battleship, Sorry, Parcheesi, or Uno. We will be using this to help your child learn how to play more appropriately with other children in one-on-one situations.

Indoor games to exclude

Games that are not advisable for a play date:

Obsessions—Any game on which your child is so hooked that he or she no longer cares if he or she is playing with someone else. Video and computer games are always in this category. Video games and computer games are typically a small part of many boys' play dates, but children in our group tend to have a lot of trouble changing activities once they start playing these.

Trades—Pokemon cards. Children may trade them and later regret the trade as unfair. These activities make for hurt feelings all around.

Provocative games—Water pistols, anything that shoots projectiles, martial arts toys or objects.

Solitary or parallel activities—Books, drawing or arts and crafts, watching TV or videotapes.

Require more than two to play—Twister, Clue.

Games that are not suited to our sessions:

Too specialized for most kids—Dungeons & Dragons, Magic Cards; these are not games that are known by everyone—they limit whom you can play with.

Too complicated for many kids—If your child wants to bring chess or Mastermind, he or she needs to first find out if anyone else in our group knows how to play them. If not, don't bring them. Teaching other kids how to play a game is not a good way to make closer friendships with others—the teacher tends to dominate.

Too much time to set up—Your child may spend the whole time setting them up and not get to play it during the session, such as for Monopoly.

Children's Friendship Training

Rules for Magic Johnson Basketball

Child Session 6

Gather Children

1. Tell children that tokens will be given to those who praise others, give "high-fives," follow any "rule of being a good sport," or are considerate of others.

Assign Sides

2. The group leader chooses sides of equal number of players of approximately equal ability, to start.

Tell Game Rules

3. Rules of a regular basketball game are used, except the primary emphasis is on cooperative team play. The following behaviors earn prompts and time outs:
   - Stealing the ball or attempts to do so.
   - Aggressive physical contact (e.g., fouling others by slapping instead of just blocking or excessive, stifling defense that intimidates the other child).
   - Excess celebration after a score.
   - The ball must be passed at least once prior to a goal being scored.

Start the Game, Monitor and Control Behavior

4. Children who "ball hog" excessively lose their opportunity to shoot any baskets (they are only allowed to rebound, dribble, and pass the ball to others).

Core Instruction

5. Tokens are given for any behavior related to the rules of a good sport. Do not give tokens for anything else, such as, eye contact or saying other person's name, as this will dilute the focus on good sportsmanship. How to give tokens:
   (a) Move in and out of play among the children, much as a basketball referee does.
   (b) Receiving a token should cause only a momentary disruption of the child's attention to the game.
   (c) Speak telegraphically to state why a child earned a specific token, while handing the child the token. Examples: "for being gentle just now," "for giving a 'high-five.'"
   (d) Withhold tokens if children look or ask for one after doing a desired behavior (but praise them for the behavior). Some children will begin "performing" in front of the coaches with the sole desire of obtaining the token and losing focus on the other aspects of the game being played.
   (e) If a child argues with you over not being given a token, give the child a prompt, followed by a time out if the arguing continues.

Debriefing at the End of Game

6. Count only the total number of group tokens, adding each child's tokens to the total. Have all the children count along. Avoid comparisons between children or pointing out who received the most tokens, as this will foster a counterproductive form of competition.

7. Ask children if they had a good time. Ask why they had a good time. (Answers: because they made sure other children had a good time, everyone had an equal opportunity to shoot the ball, and no one was getting injured or intimidated by rough play.)

Making a Best Friend/Play Dates

Treatment Rationale

The best way to form a close friendship is through organizing and frequently carrying out successful play dates for two children who like each other. As noted in the foreword, we define *play date* as an appointment made between two children to play in the home of one of them. The most effective means of having successful play dates is for parents and children to collaborate in having them (Frankel, 1996). Friendless children may be unable to utilize play dates effectively to build friendships. Thus, they and their parents must be trained how to accomplish this.

We define the *host* role as a collection of rules of etiquette that gives deference to a child invited on a play date as a guest. The social role of host is helpful in promoting successful play dates. Both parents and children have some conception of good host behavior. Ladd and Hart (1992) reported anecdotally that when parents invite children to their homes, they put their child in the role of the host. They expect their child to be concerned about the needs and wishes of their playmates and to ensure that the guests have a good time. The treatment hypothesis is that knowledge and use of certain rules of host etiquette can be an effective means of avoiding conflict and quickly resolving the search for common ground

activities. Putting the child in the host role will allow the child to have more harmonious play dates and will clarify to parents how to more effectively supervise these play experiences.

15.1 Definitions of Friendship Levels

We define three levels of friendship for the purposes of this chapter: *friend*, *favored few*, and *best friend*. A *friend* is someone with potential to be invited for a play date in the home. Friends usually engage in social contact in public places, such as schoolyards and lunchrooms. A *best friend* is a close, reciprocal, and ultimately confiding relationship.

Girls are reported to be more likely to have best friends than boys are (Doyle, Markiewicz, & Hardy, 1994; but cf., Benenson, 1990, and Cairns, Perrin, & Cairns, 1985, who reported no differences); however, this may oversimplify the social relationships of boys. Unlike girls, who typically have a few best friends who are also best friends with each other (*cliques* or *friendship circles*), boys have another level of friendship, the *favored few*, from which they draw one or two best friends (Berndt & Hoyle, 1985; Frankel, 1996). The stability of boys' best friends is less than that of girls', but the durability of boys' favored few may be the same as girls' friendship circles.

15.2 The Importance of Best Friendships

Best friend relationships are perhaps the most enduring social outcomes of middle childhood. Having one or two best friends is of great importance to later adjustment. Valuable best friends are intimate, affectionate, loyal, and available (Furman, 1985). Best friendships become stable by about the fourth grade (cf. McGuire & Weisz, 1982), although children report having a best friend much earlier than this. Between 78% and 89% of elementary school-aged children have best friends (Kovacs et al., 1996; Malik & Furman, 1993; Putallaz & Gottman, 1981). According to the results of Bryant (1985), 72% of 7- and 10-year-olds rated a peer as among the "top 10 most important people in their lives" and 45% rated at least 3 peers in the top 10.

Best friends can buffer the impact of stressful events (Brown, Bhrolchain, & Harris, 1975; Miller & Ingham, 1976), mitigate the stress associated with parental divorce (Lustig, Wolchik, & Braver, 1992) and protect against loneliness (e.g., Parker & Asher, 1993; Renshaw & Brown, 1993). Having a best friend improves self-esteem and decreases anxious and depressive symptomatology (Bagwell et al., 1998; Bishop & Inderbitzen, 1995; Buhrmeister, 1990). Best friends can also protect children against victimization by peers (Hodges, Boivin, Vitaro, & Bukowski, 1999). Children with best friends are more altruistic and have better skills in explaining emotions. Best friends may foster the development of greater social competence. Asher and Renshaw (cited in Gottman, 1983) reported that children who are accepted by peers and have best friends have greater social competence than children who are accepted by peers but have no best friends.

It is plausible that greater social competence, altruism, and enhanced skill in explaining emotions are prerequisite to having best friends. However, one line of research seems to support the role of best friend in subsequent development of these abilities. Best friends have been observed to teach each other relationship skills: Although conflicts with acquaintances can inhibit future social interaction, conflicts among best friends and their resolutions are associated with subsequent increases on measures of social problem solving (Nelson & Aboud, 1985).

15.3 Problems in Quality of Best Friendships

Parker and Asher (1993) found that many third-through fifth-grade children who are rejected, but who have best friends, have a lower quality of best friendship. These children are more likely to report loneliness than are accepted children who have a best friend. This is probably because these children tend to have best friends who are themselves rejected (Nangle et al., 1996). In a survey of fifth and sixth graders, George and Hartmann (1996) found that 77% of rejected children reported having at least one reciprocal friend. However, these reciprocal friends were more likely to be younger and less likely to go to the same school when compared with reciprocal friends of accepted children.

15.4 Prevalence and Importance of Play Dates

The term *play date* has recently been introduced to our social vernacular (Ladd, 1992; Parke & Bhavnagri, 1989). Newson and Newson (1976) found that 72% of upper-middle-class mothers reported that their child had friends play in their home "most weeks." Lougee and Kenniston (1975, reported in Gottman, 1983) found that about 55% of boys and 90% of girls 6 to 8 years old reported playing with their friends at home. Ladd and Hart (1992) reported that 81% of parents made play dates for their children.

Play dates may be of great value in increasing the number of friends a child has and reducing susceptibility to negative peer influence. Parents who invite peers into their homes have children who have more play dates in both theirs and their peers' homes (Ladd, Hart, Wadsworth, & Golter, 1988), have children with a larger range of playmates and more consistent play partners (Ladd & Golter, 1988), and have children with closer and more stable friendships (Krappman, 1986, cited in Ladd & Hart, 1992). Steinberg (1986) reported that peer pressure had less effect on "latchkey" children who played at a friend's house when compared to children who describe themselves as "hanging out."

Research on Play Date Processes

Most formal studies of play date processes have employed preschoolers and their mothers. We have used this literature together with the first author's direct observations and informal interviews (cf. Frankel, 1996) to develop the intervention described in this chapter. Clearly, more research in this area would be helpful in further refinements of this session.

15.5 Parent Social Networks, Interpersonal Skills, and Play Dates

Lack of accessibility of peers has made it more important for parent social networks to include other parents within easy transport who have children close in age to their child (cf. Chap. 18 for more on peer networks; Ladd, 1992; Rubin & Sloman, 1984). The number of such parent friendships has been shown to correlate with the size of their children's friendship networks (Homel et al., 1987). However, it is just as likely that children's friendships lead to parent friendships as the reverse. Our recent survey data have supported that mothers of children without friendship problems are more likely than mothers of rejected children to make their own friends through child-centered activities (Frankel, 2002a).

Studies of the initiation of play dates find that most (82%) parent initiators of play dates for 4- and 5-year-old children were mothers (Ladd & Golter, 1988; Ladd & Hart, 1992). Play date initiations weren't correlated with parent employment or with children's involvement in child care. Ladd and Hart (1992) noted a total frequency of play dates at about 9.5 for the 16 days studied. However, this frequency may have been inflated due to a Hawthorne effect. Contacts initiated by children not directly studied averaged 1.8 during this period, so that a truer frequency may be about 1 to 2 play dates per week.

Mothers' interpersonal skills have been found to correlate with children's social competence (Prinstein & La Greca, 1999). Mothers of rejected children tended to elicit less positive affect from other mothers (Ladd, 1992), suggesting impairments in their ability to form functional social networks with the parents of potential playmates for their children. The quality of mother's

best friendships correlated with child popularity and quality of child's best friendships (Doyle et al., 1994). This suggests that a secondary goal of treatment is to educate parents, especially mothers, on the skills necessary to further their children's friendships. In the course of this intervention, the mothers may learn through their children's experience how they might enhance their own friendships or at least relate better to the parents of their child's friends.

15.6 Play Date Success

Parents with good interpersonal skills and a supportive social network will find it easier to arrange play dates. However, the key link for the development of sustained best friendship is frequent *successful* play dates, rather than frequent incidental contact between friends during community activities. A *successful* play date results in sustained mutually pleasurable interchange (cf. Gottman & Parkhurst, 1980) and (usually, but not always) subsequent reciprocal play date invitations by the guest.

In two landmark observational studies, Gottman (1983) observed child behavior on play dates. Gottman found that play date interaction frequently fluctuated between information interchange (finding games of mutual interest—common-ground activities) and interactive play on the currently established common-ground activity. Gottman reported that those children who "hit it off" were more efficient in the search for and transition to common ground activities. A major tool used by children for this search involved "two-way conversations." Gottman et al. (1975) demonstrated that accepted children are better at this skill than rejected children. Our clinical experience has been that children can establish common-ground activities in telephone conversations prior to a play date ("What should we play when we get together?") and can maintain them for up to 2 hours in play at the time of the meeting.

15.7 Nature of Parental Supervision on Play Dates

According to Ladd and Hart (1992), over 85% of play dates are supervised by at least one parent.

Research suggests the nature of parental supervision is important. Ladd and Golter (1988) suggested that mothers who join into play may inhibit their child's social development, whereas mothers who supervise peripherally (without joining in play) help their children achieve more optimal socialization effects. They found that preschool children who were peripherally supervised were better liked than children whose mothers joined in play.

Many parents of rejected boys inadequately supervise their child's play, despite continued problematic episodes (Ladd & Golter, 1988; Ladd et al., 1992). Mothers of rejected children may fail to teach their child conflict management skills and rules of behavior (Kennedy, 1992), and/or may allow their child to control play coercively (Ladd, 1992). Our clinical experience has indicated that parents are aware of the conflict but don't think they should intervene or don't know how to make an effective intervention.

15.8 Video Games and Play Dates

Video games have recently pervaded the culture of boys and is an activity that needs to be addressed on play dates. A survey of elementary school children by van Schie and Wiegman (1997) found a negative relationship between time spent playing video games and prosocial behavior. Video-game use was not found to correlate with popularity among elementary school boys (Sakamoto, 1994), which implies that children who do not play them regularly are not at a disadvantage in regard to peer acceptance.

Although most (77.2%) of 11- to 16-year-old boys play videogames, about 10% of video-game players might qualify under criteria of addiction (Phillips, Rolls, Rouse, & Griffiths, 1995). Examples of play-date behavior reported by parents prior to our treatment are often consistent with this picture: Rejected boys may elect to continue video-game play even after the guest tires of it (while either making statements such as "I need to get to the next level" or ignoring the peer completely).

Rejected children may become so passionate about a game that they are more prone to get into arguments while playing it. They may pick a game they know better than the guest and use their advantage to boss the guest around and criticize the guest's poorer performance. Also, video games with violent themes may at least temporarily increase aggressiveness when compared to nonviolent videogames (Schutte, Malouff, Post-Gorden, & Rodasta, 1988).

15.9 Implications From Research and Clinical Practice

Having at least one or two best friends serves as a buffer against stress, and improves social competence. Play dates are common. Children who have them regularly tend to have a larger range of playmates than children who rarely have play dates. The first few play dates are especially important in determining who will go on to be best friends. Avoiding conflict and finding common-ground activities are key. Mothers play a key role in initiation and supervision of play dates. The intervention should focus on helping mothers supervise and intervene appropriately in their child's play dates, as well as networking with parents of potential friends for their child. Having the child assume the role of host helps to eliminate conflict, clarifies parent supervision, and promotes friendships. Although definitive studies have not been done on children with friendship problems, we advocate that parents bar the use of video games from play dates for children in our program.

How to Conduct the Session

Until Now

The children have met new playmates in their neighborhood through the "slipping-in" assignment. The children have developed two-way conversational skills on the telephone, at first with other members of the group, and then with neighborhood children who are potential friends. Through telephone calls, the children have selected other children who were receptive to talking with them. Parents were told to maintain a list of potential play date guests (and their phone numbers) for use in arranging play dates.

In This Session

In this session all these components come together. The children will receive training on "good host behavior" using the inside games they brought from home. The parents are taught how to coordinate a play-date invitation with their child and how to prepare for and monitor the play date.

Parent Session Plan 7

Initial Gathering

This is the first time children have to bring in games that can be played inside their home. The most frequent problem is due to parents forgetting that the homework assignment has switched to bringing an inside toy (and bring an outside toy instead). Boys with ADHD sometimes bring violent toys. Children with Asperger's disorder tend to bring inappropriate toys (stuffed animals, balloons, objects that they have made, magic tricks, etc.). Educating parents as to the inappropriateness of these toys is an important part of the treatment.

1. Check for inside toys as they come in.
2. Chess or Mastermind may be allowed only if the child checked with the group last week to see if anyone else knows how to play.
3. Have parents hold toys that are in excluded categories.[1]

Potential Problems

Bringing a Prohibited Toy 1

One parent, despite our instructions to the contrary, allowed her son to bring a "Nerf gun" with six projectiles. It is likely that she was encouraged by the amount of attention the toy had brought to her child in the past. All the children from the group immediately gathered around to examine the "Nerf gun." After the children left the parent room, the group leader asked what was wrong with toys like the "Nerf gun." The other parents in the group offered the following: "The toy is easily broken by others," "It would

involve policing the turn-taking of others," and "It would introduce aggression between the boys."

Bringing a Prohibited Toy 2

A mother of a 10-year-old boy was not able to say "no" to her child's insistence on bringing a handheld video game, even though she knew better. Neither child nor parent was surprised when the group leader had the boy leave the toy with his mother. After the children left the room, the group leader asked the mother how she would keep the toy out of subsequent sessions (and play dates). The group leader offered to continue being the "bad guy," as far as bringing appropriate toys to session, but the mother needed to have the resolve to enforce this on upcoming play dates.

Bringing a Non-Toy Object

One family of a 9-year-old boy brought an old golf ball just so the child would have an object that marginally qualified as completing his homework assignment. It appeared that the boy did this with his parent's encouragement. During the homework review portion of the parent session, the parent agreed to buy two new toys that the child would bring into the next session and have available at home for play dates.

Homework Review

The out-of-group call and the results of the "slipping in" assignments represent two sources of children to invite for the upcoming play date. These are the focus of homework review.

1. There are two homework assignments (not including inside toy) and not enough time to review all in depth. Tell parents that you want them to focus on the "slipping in" homework and the out-of-group call.

---

[1]Obsessions, trading cards, water pistols, anything that shoots projectiles, computer games, video games, books, arts and crafts, Magic cards, Dungeons & Dragons, Monopoly, Clue, or Twister.

2. Ask first for success stories on the "slipping-in" homework assignment. Ask where the children attempted to slip in and whether parents were either able to observe it or hear the details from their child. Then get the other parents to report.[2] Debriefing questions to ask parents:

(a) [For parents of children with negative reputations at school]: Did the child with a bad reputation try to meet children in a new setting so that the child would be more successful and "take the heat off" making friends where the reputation was negative?

(b) Did the child get a possible play date phone number from a child he or she slipped in with?

(c) Go around to each parent asking how the out-of-group call went.

(d) In the course of their turn, discuss with any parent not complying with the inside toy assignment what the parent will bring in next time.

Potential Problems

The Child Who Was Telephoned Was Rude

A fourth-grade girl telephoned another girl in her class. It was a short phone call. The girl in her class did not ask any questions and quickly said she had to go. When the parent recounted this, the leader suggested that this was an indication that the children would not get along on a play date and an invitation would likely be a mistake. The parents were upset that their child was treated like this. But the group leader cast this in a positive light: "There was no chemistry between the children. Not all children should be friends with each other. It is better to determine this through the phone call than being repeatedly turned down in requests for play dates or in the midst of a play date that is deteriorating. The time will be better spent by you in looking for someone else to invite over."

The Child Who Refused to Bring a Toy

One sixth-grade boy did not want to bring any of his games to the session because he didn't feel

he had any board games good enough to bring (most of the games had pieces missing). The boy said he would like to play the game Sorry, so the group leader encouraged the parent to go with the child to a toy store to buy Sorry and two or three other reasonably priced board games to have available for the next play date.

Parent Handout

There is no parent handout for this session, just the parent assignment. Notice that only one session of practice with the children in good host behavior comes before this homework assignment. That is because the parent's supervision of the play date is the major active treatment component. The parents should get the idea that this is the way to do all play dates, not just ones done for homework for this intervention.

Ideally the process works as follows: The child picks someone he or she really likes. The parents ensure that this is a well-behaved child (and gently vetoes all others). The child calls and tests the water (does the other child like him or her?). If the feelings are mutual, then the parent offers to make all the transportation arrangements with the other child's parent.

Group Leader Guide to Parent Assignment—Due on Sessions 8–12

GOAL
To increase your child's ability to become better friends with acquaintances.

Studies show (a) informal play dates are most beneficial to social development, (b) one or two such play dates per week is sufficient for these benefits, and (c) parents and children who plan play dates together maximize these benefits. [*Tell parents: "In this session, we are teaching your child how to be a good host. Your part of the next homework is to make sure your child uses this in your*

---

[2]Keep in mind: Bad places: (a) the beach, on vacation—because children come from all over and may not be appropriate to make sustainable friends; (b) children being supervised by an adult (e.g., birthday parties)—because the adult may interfere; (c) the library, bookstore—because people expect silence. Good places: (a) neighborhood park, (b) after-school unstructured program, (c) before or after team practice, (d) before or after Scout meeting, (e) at church/temple.

home during a play date you will supervise in a very special way."]

At the End of This Session

1. Decide with your child on a new child to invite over. Your child must want to play with this child and this child should be well behaved for you. [*Tell parents the "gold standard" for the child to be invited over is someone who:*

1. *Their child would like to play with.*
2. *The parent believes would like to play with their child (i.e., was happy to receive the inviting call).*
3. *Is well behaved.*[3]
4. *Is not family or extended family.*
5. *Is within 1½ years of age of their child, or in the same grade.*
6. *Is within a 10-minute drive from their house (to encourage reciprocation).*
7. *Is the same sex as their child.*

Have parents think of "back-up" playmates, in case their child suggests an inappropriate child or no child (research shows it's better to have no friend than a friend who values antisocial behavior). Best is a new playmate never played with individually before (perhaps someone the child has known for a while but never invited over). Next best is someone they haven't invited over in a long while that used to be friends. Third best is someone they invite over rarely. Fourth best is a present good friend.][4]

2. Decide on possible times when you can supervise the activity for about 1–2 hours. (Future play dates with the same child may be longer). [*Ask, "Who has other children in their household?" Parents who do, have to come up with a plan for what to do with siblings. For the first play date, accept the mother's statement, "We won't allow his little brother to go near," or "We'll make a play date for his sister at her friend's house," or "Dad will take his little sister to the park." Stress how important it is for a parent, especially the mom, to be present during the entire play date in order to train the child on the rules for a good host and to be ready to support the play date.*]

Making the Play Date

1. Your child is to have a two-way conversation with the other child first (to determine if they like each other, have mutual interests, and have something to do on the play date). Then your

child is to make the invitation to the other child. [*Stress that this telephone call doesn't have to result in a play date, and shouldn't if the children don't hit it off or can't think of anything they both like doing together. This is the only out-of-group call this week.*

Have parents think of a good rationale to tell the guest for why there will be no video games or TV. Good examples are, "My mom doesn't allow me to play video games or watch TV on play dates" or "I'm on restriction from videogames and TV." The parent should monitor this call within earshot to make sure that the child handles it appropriately and arranges to play games other than video and computer games. Tell the parents that the children already have been made aware of this prohibition. It has been presented to them as a necessary part of the homework.][5]

2. You are then to check with the child's parent to finalize the date and time of the play date. [*This play date should be no longer than 2 hours (but may be extended slightly if going very well). The parent should offer to pick up the guest before the play date and, if necessary, drop him or her off after the play date. Parents should defer accepting invitations to the other child's house until they are confident that their child will act appropriately. This can only be ensured through three or four successful play dates supervised by the parent. Furthermore, a play date at another child's house would not qualify as completing the homework, because it puts the child in a "guest" rather than "host" role on the play date.*]

Immediately Before the Play Date

1. Have your child decide what to play with his or her guest—something that will keep them busy for the play date. Ask what they decided on during the telephone call. Choose interactive

---

[3]Play dates with another child who has behavior problems or who gets in trouble at school should be avoided. On the other hand, shy children are good candidates. Remember, play dates between intervention group members are prohibited, so continue to be firm about this.

[4]Some children will have had ongoing play dates until now with long-time friends. These will not count as the homework, unless this turns out to be the "best deal." In any case, now is a good time for parents to start supervising play dates with long-time friends in the manner described in the homework handout, especially if there are frequent arguments on play dates.

[5]The most anxiety-provoking aspect of the play-date homework assignment is the ban on electronic media (*Note*: A CD player or other music is allowed on play dates.) Some parents will doubt that they can enforce this. It's important for children to experience that *they* and not the game they play are the reason that their friends come over.

games. Prohibit Nintendo, watching TV/videos, and computer games.

2. Have your child hide any games or toys that he or she does not wish to share or play with, or that are noninteractive. [*Say that once hidden, the games can't be retrieved until the guest leaves. The child may choose not to hide them on the next play date.*]

3. Ask your child to repeat the six rules of being a good host:

1. *The guest gets to pick the games you play.* Put away games you don't want to play with before the guest arrives.
2. *Praise the guest's behavior* ("nice try," "great shot").
3. *No refereeing* (don't criticize the guest).
4. *If you're bored, suggest a change in activity or having a turn* (make a deal).
5. *Let the guest have fun too* (take turns, share toys).
6. *Be loyal to your guest.* If another child stops by or calls, thank them for coming by (or calling), and tell them you are busy now and will get back to them later. Do not leave the guest alone.

During the Play Date

1. You are to monitor within hearing range but not so that the children can see you. [*Stress how important it is for a parent, especially the mom, to be present during the entire play date in order to train the child on the rules for a good host and to be ready to support the play date.*]

2. If your child breaks a rule, you should step in and remind her or him about the corresponding good host rule. [*Tell parents: At the time of the play date, parents have to be available to immediately enforce good host rules. When the parent hears an argument, their child criticizing the guest, TV or video games on, or another child at the door, they are to intervene by telling their child to step outside the room where he or she is playing for a moment. After the child steps out, the parent is to ask, "Remember the rules for a good host?" If the child can repeat the rule (don't criticize the guest . . .) then the parent asks if the child can do that now. If the answer is "yes," then they can send the child back. If not, then keep the child out until he or she agrees to follow the rule. Children are usually compliant in this context. If the child isn't able to repeat the rel-*]

evant good host rule, then the parent states it simply (as is done immediately before the play date).

A successful initial play date may involve several parent interventions when the child breaks good host rules. The number of times parents have to intervene should decrease over successive play dates. This is the teaching function of this play date.

If a child wanders off in the middle of a play date, one of the following may have happened:

1. *The child didn't hit it off with the guest and wishes to disengage from an unpleasant experience. The parent should ask if the child likes playing with the guest. If the answer is "no" then it's time for snacks and waiting for the end of the (short) play date. This is why the first play date is short.*
2. *The child couldn't resolve a decision with the guest to switch to a new game. The parent should enforce the good host rule. (The guest gets to pick).*
3. *The play date went beyond the attention span of a child with ADHD. Consider a medication dose before the play date or consider shorter play dates, but for now remind the child of the good host rule.*]

Immediately After the Play Date

1. If the play date was a success, try to get to know the other child's parents. Try to talk with them when they pick up their child. [*Encourage parents to get to know the guest's parents if they want the child as a friend for their child. Saying something nice about the other child is a good icebreaker. Remember, parents should defer accepting invitations to a new child's house to a future time when they are more confident that their child will act appropriately.*]

2. After the other child has left, praise your child for something he or she did well during the play date. Ask your child if he or she would like to invite that playmate over again.

Potential Problems

Parent Uncomfortable With a Short Play Date

One parent asked how she could arrange something for only 1½ hours with another parent ("Wouldn't they be expecting more?"). The group leader replied that most parents would want to be cautious on the first play date, and that she could say to the other parent that this time period was available for her right now.

Embarrassment Over Enforcing the Rules of a Good Host

A mother of an 11-year-old boy was concerned that her son would be embarrassed if she had to take him aside to remind him of a good host rule in front of his playmate. The group leader replied that now is the chance for this "tuneup." It is better to have the guest see a social error is corrected rather than have it continue to ruin the play date.

Parents Evading Assignment

Parents have asked if it's okay to do the play date at: (a) a birthday party, (b) a family get-together, (c) the hotel pool when they are out of town, or (d) with a cousin who is 5 years older than the child. The group leader responds with statements such as "Our goal is to develop friendships outside the family but within your neighborhood among children who consider themselves as equals. So we need to stick to the guidelines."

The Child Who Planned Her Guest's Activity

A mother of a third-grade girl reported that on previous play dates, her child would write a list of all the games she wanted to play with her guest before each play date. During the play date, the guest typically did not want to follow this list of activities that was being imposed on her. Her daughter would then become upset and refuse to play. Our solution was to have the girl call the intended guest *before* writing this list so that they could compose the list of games together. We reemphasized that the priority for play date game selection would be what *the guest* wanted to play (that her daughter also liked).

Adverse Living Conditions

One single mom lived in an apartment with lots of adults (and some children) living in every room. There was no place to go in the apartment where playmates could be alone. She elected to take the children to a quiet area of a nearby park at a time when much younger children (supervised by parents) dominated the park. They would bring some games and the mom would watch nearby (pretending to read a magazine or book) as they played together. This was a reasonable solution to her space problem.

Using Swimming Pools for Play Dates

One parent of a 7-year-old girl asked if using the swimming pool was a possibility. The group leader asked if there already were children in the neighborhood who seemed to come over to their house with the primary purpose of getting to use the pool. The mom acknowledged that this had occurred. Other parents in the group verbalized their concerns about doing this. The group leader recommended that for the first play date, it would be better to establish that the child being invited for the play date genuinely wanted to play with the *child* rather than simply to use the pool.

Child Session Plan 7

On the Way to the Child Session Room

1. In the parent meeting room, some children will start playing with the games they brought during the initial gathering. They don't have the good host skills yet and this may delay the start of the child session (as they put the game back in the box to take to the child session room), so the group leader should discourage this. Do this by telling the children that they will be leaving momentarily.
2. Tell the children to hold the board games firmly so as not to spill the contents on the way to the child room.

Homework Review[6]

1. Briefly review the out-of-group calls—ask each child who they called. Briefly check for *trading information* and how they *began and ended the phone call.*
2. *Review attempts to "slip into" a group of children with whom they were not familiar. Ask, "Where did you go to try to slip in? What game*

---

[6]The review of the out-of-group calls and "slipping in" assignments now have immediate relevance in generating children to invite for the play-date homework assignment.

was played? How did you ask to join? Which side did you join (winning or losing)? What did the kids do (let you in)? (When entry was turned down, add:) What did you do next?"

Homework Assignment

1. Bring an inside toy again next time.
2. Play dates: Pick a child to invite over for an hour or two. Call this child as the out-of-group call. Have a two-way conversation to determine which games to play before asking the other child over.

Didactic

Friendless children may think that a play date is a chance for *them* (as opposed to them *and their guest*) to do fun things or that their guest will be their "play slave" (who is there for the purpose of entertaining and meeting their needs). The concept of "host" puts children in a role with which they are somewhat familiar. Sometimes children have never thought of themselves as a host when another child comes over. For children who have seldom or never had play dates, good coaching and supervision can help them avoid the mistakes that can occur from simply being overly excited and overwhelmed about finally having someone at their house.

1. Ask the children the difference between "host" and "guest." (Answer: The host's job is to make sure the guest has a good time, to listen to the guest. The most important thing is the guest has fun. The guest is not a "play slave.")
2. Tell the children they are going to have a play date (use the term "get-together" for older children) as the homework assignment. They will use the out-of-group call to find out about, and set up, what the guest wants to do (i.e., the games they want to play) and to have guest bring games they don't have that the guest wants to play. *No* video games, computer games, or TV will be allowed.[7]
3. When their guest first gets to the house, they should give a tour of the house showing where bathrooms and kitchen are and ask if the guest is thirsty, and so on.

4. Present the "Rules for a Good Host," using a Socratic method (see Table 10.2). Keep in mind this template for the six rules.

Rules for being a good host (when you invite someone over to play):
(a) *The guest gets to pick the games you play.* Put away games you don't want to play with before your guest arrives. *Computer games/Nintendo/TV etc. are off limits.*[8] They are to concentrate on getting to know each other by talking.
(b) *Praise the guest's behavior,* for example, nice try, great shot.
(c) *No refereeing.* Don't criticize the guest. The guest is "always right" except when the guest wants to do something dangerous.
(d) *If you're bored, suggest a change in activity or having a turn.* (You may have to make a deal—"How about if we play _____, and then we can _____").
(e) *Let the guest have fun too* (take turns, share toys).
(f) *Be loyal to your guest.* If another child you know stops by or calls, thank them for coming by (or calling), and tell them you are busy and will get back to them later. Do not leave your guest alone.

5. Say to the children, "To help you be a better host, it's always a good idea to think of toys that you don't want the guest to play with. For instance, you just put together a Lego airplane and you don't want your guest to take it apart. Who can think of other examples?" (Have the children think of toys they wouldn't want to share.) Then add, "These are games that you want to keep out of sight of the guest. Your parents will help you find some place to

---

[7]While younger children tend to remain silent, older children often react negatively to the ban on electronic media (TV, Nintendo, Game Boy, and computer). They will often frantically come up with reasons why they will be "social outcasts" if they don't have these available on play dates. They will try to prevail on their parents not to enforce this rule. Stand firm by this rule.

[8]The group leader answers "no" to both of the following: "How about following the rules for the two-hour play date and then playing Nintendo after it is over?" "How about if you have two controllers for your Nintendo and both of you can play?

put them right before your guest comes over. After the guest has left, you can get them."

Clinical Example: Presenting the Good Host Rules

GL: What is a host?

Child: You show kids around.

GL: Why do you do that?

Child: If you are nice to a kid, they are going to want to come back. First do what the guest wants to do.

GL: The most important job for a host is to make sure that the guest has a good time.

Child: Then they'll tell other kids that you're a good person.

GL: That's right. In your out-of-group call you're going to ask them what games they want to play.

GL: What if they want to play a game you don't have?

Child: Ask if they can bring it.

GL: What about telling the guest they're a cheater?

Child: They won't want to come over again.

GL: What's the first thing you ask when they come in? Supposing they had a 32-ounce drink before they came over and a long ride in the car?

Child): [Laugh] Show them where the bathroom is.

Child: Offer food.

Potential Problems

Examples of Debate on the Rules of a Good Host

Child: What if they don't treat me like that when I'm at their house?

GL: Only have play dates with kids that don't mistreat you.

Child: How about a play date at their house.

GL: The play date needs to be at your house because you are learning to be a good host.

Child: Why not have an overnight?

[Note: Some children are so desperate for friend, they don't want to let them go].

GL: You're just getting to know each other and you want to go slow.

Examples of Worries Children Have on Play Dates

The guest damages the host's toys:

Put away toys that you don't want the guest to touch before the guest arrives.
If guest is doing it on purpose, ask him to stop.
If this doesn't work, tell your parent.

The guest brings dangerous objects:

First, tell them to put it away.
If the guest doesn't listen, tell your parent.

The guest wants to play with another child in the neighborhood:

On the first play date, tell them "let's do that next time."

If this happens again next time, you don't have to invite this guest over anymore.

The guest cheats:

Ask the guest what the rule should be.
Choose someone else for a future play date if the guest is a chronic cheater.

Real Play

Most features of an actual play date are captured here. When group leaders monitor host and guest, it makes it easier for parent monitoring at home.

1. Break up into same-sex dyads. *One child is picked to be the guest, the other is the host.* They then play games they brought in (the guests decide which game). Praise the host for deferring to the guest's choices, saying the *host* has the hardest job.
2. Have them decide which game is played first and when to switch games (the guest always gets to choose).

3. If there is enough time, host and guest can switch roles.
4. Give a 2-minute announcement before the child session is over and play has to stop. At the two-minute mark, group leaders may say, "The guest's mom just came to pick him up so the play date (get together) is ending. In two minutes it will be time to stop playing and put away the toys." Follow up in 2 minutes with, "It's time to put away all toys now."

Potential Problems

Extra Girl and Extra Boy

If you have one girl and one boy left over after dyads are paired up, you may combine them as a dyad on a play date (while reminding them that they will be inviting same-sex guests to their actual upcoming play date).

Odd Number of Children

Make one same-sex triad with host, guest, and onlooker and rotate children through, with host becoming guest, onlooker becoming host, and guest becoming onlooker. This is not a great solution, but the best that can done under the circumstances.

Only One Toy Available for the Dyad

It is important to have at least two toys, so that children can negotiate which one they play with. In this case, take the toy not used from another dyad and offer it as a choice (ask permission of the owner first).

Refusing to be the Host

One 8-year-old boy refused to be the host. This was treated the same as any noncompliance or disruptive behavior. He was told once that he needed to practice being the host. He refused and was told, "This is your first prompt." He still didn't comply and was told to take a time out. Upon his return, he reluctantly agreed to be the host.

Ownership of a Toy as Instrument of Coercion

A seventh-grade boy with conduct disorder brought his deck of cards. He dominated the game by demanding his choice of card games ("These are my cards and I get to pick the card game"). When the group leader had him put his cards away and use another boy's cards, this behavior stopped.

Tantrums When a Child Lost the Game

One third-grade boy with Asperger's disorder pounded the table, started crying, and yelled, "You cheated" at the other player (who was the "guest") when he lost a game of "Connect Four." The group leader gave him an immediate time out. At the conclusion of the time out, the boy reentered the room and immediately began arguing again with his peer and calling him a "cheater." A second time out was administered. When the boy returned from the second time out, he had stopped crying and arguing and was subsequently able to engage in the exercise.

End-of-Session Reunification

1. Announce, "Today we worked on being a good host. I saw a lot of good host behavior in this group. Let's all give the children a big round of applause."
2. "The major job everyone has this week is to make a play date [use the term "get-together" instead of play date for older children] with someone you've met during the "slipping in" assignment or someone you've been wanting to play with but haven't recently. Agree on this person with your parent. Remember, you are to call this person for your out-of-group call and have a two-way conversation in order to come up with games to play. This will be your only required out-of-group call. *You are not allowed to play video games, or computer games, or watch TV during the play date.*"
3. Negotiate play date guest and toy for next session with each child in front of each parent.

Get child and parent to agree on both. Choosing a playmate may involve some extended negotiations. If the child can't think of anyone and won't accept the parent's suggestion, tell them that you will come back to them after going around the room. Sometimes the pause in negotiations facilitates an eventual agreement.

Children's Friendship Training

Parent Assignment—Given on Session 7

Due on Sessions 8–12

GOAL: To increase your child's ability to become better friends with acquaintances.

Studies show (a) informal play dates are most beneficial to social development, (b) 1 or 2 such play dates per week is sufficient for these benefits, and (c) parents and children who plan play dates together maximize these benefits.

At the End of this Session:
1. Decide with your child on a new child to invite over. Your child must want to play with this child and this child should be well behaved for you.
2. Decide on possible times when you can supervise the activity for about 1–2 hours. (Future play dates with the same child may be longer.)

Making the Play Date:
1. **Your child** is to have a two-way conversation with the other child first (to determine if they like each other, have mutual interests, and have something to do on the play date). Then your child is to make the invitation to the other child.
2. **You** are then to check with the child's parent to finalize the date and time of the play date.

Immediately Before the Play Date:
1. Have your child decide what to play with his or her guest—something that will keep them busy for the play date. Ask what they decided on in the telephone call. Choose interactive games. Prohibit Nintendo, watching TV, and computer games.
2. Have your child hide any games or toys that he or she does not wish to share or play, or that are noninteractive.
3. Ask your child to repeat the six rules of a good host:
   (a) **The guest gets to pick the games you play**. Put away games you don't want to play with before the guest arrives.
   (b) **Praise the guest's behavior** ("nice try," "great shot").
   (c) **No refereeing** (don't criticize the guest).
   (d) **If you're bored, suggest a change in activity or having a turn** (make a deal).
   (e) **Let the guest have fun too** (take turns, share toys).
   (f) **Be loyal to your guest**. If another child stops by or calls, thank them for coming by (or calling), tell them you are busy now and will get back to them later. Do not leave the guest alone.

During the Play Date:
1. You are to monitor within hearing range but not so that the children can see you.
2. If your child breaks a rule, you should step in and remind him or her about the good host rule.

Immediately After the Play Date:
1. If the play date was a success, try to get to know the other child's parents. Try to talk with them when they pick up their child.
2. After the other child has left, praise your child for something he or she did well during the play date. Ask your child if he or she would like to invite that playmate over again.

Resisting Teasing

Treatment Rationale

Resisting victimization becomes important during the later portion of the treatment program, after better friendship skills have been trained, but before the child's negative reputation at school (if present) has died down. Many rejected children are the targets as well as the perpetrators of negative behavior. The treatment hypothesis here is that children can be effectively trained to resist teasing in a manner that will deter the perpetrator (while not encouraging the child to tease first or tease back) and perhaps gain support from peers and adults who are onlookers. Parents should also be taught to support this intervention.

16.1 Importance of Protection from Victimization

We define a *chronic victim* as a child who is nominated by peers as being "picked on." Victimization is highly stable across the elementary school years (cf. Hodges, Malone, & Perry, 1997). Perry, Kusel, and Perry (1988) reported about 10% of third- through sixth-grade boys and girls were classified as extremely victimized through physical and verbal intimidation. They found age and sex differences were nonsignificant. However, other authors have found victims are more common among boys (Boulton & Smith, 1994; Boulton & Underwood, 1992; Olweus, 1993). Children's victimization scores were negatively correlated with peer liking, and were positively correlated with peer dislike. Schwartz, Dodge, Pettit, and Bates (1997) found that victimization ratings by peers were negatively correlated with social preference (number of liked nominations – number of disliked nominations) and positively correlated with aggression. In a longitudinal follow-up study, Hodges and Perry (1999) found that third- through seventh-graders who were withdrawn, physically weak, and rejected by peers were most likely to be victimized by peers, with each of these factors contributing to the level of victimization. Similarly, Boulton, and Smith (1994) found that the self-esteem (cf. Harter, 1982) of boys nominated as chronic victims was significantly lower in athletic competence than either aggressive children or children who were not nominated as either aggressive or victimized.

Surprisingly, Perry et al. (1988) found that neglected children were relatively unlikely to be victimized, and Boulton and Smith (1994) did not find any significant relationships between victimization and any sociometric category. In contrast to the submissive profile usually associated with chronic victims, Salmivalli and Nieminen (2002) presented research suggesting that victims who fought back were common. Complicating the picture even further, rejected children can be chronic victims and/or perpetrators. In studies of victimization among fourth and fifth graders, rejected children had victimization scores about four times greater than popular and average children (Perry et al., 1988; Ray et al., 1997). Rejected boys were found to victimize their mutual friends more than any other combination of sex and sociometric status (Ray et al., 1997).

This chapter and treatment module focus on victims of teasing, because we have found a highly effective intervention that can be taught to the chronic victims to stop it. Most victimization involves teasing, so training effective responses to teasing can have a substantial impact. In contrast, a different intervention has been found effective for bullying. Bullying and aggression are not synonymous. Victimization by and perpetration of aggression are handled in Chapter 19.

16.2 Definition and Victims of Teasing

Teasing is defined as disparaging remarks directed to another child. Younger boys tease primarily by name-calling. Older boys tease by disparaging the victim or the victim's family (Frankel, 1996). Teasing may be humorous, but the humor is a sarcastic comment made at the expense of the victim. It is frequently done in front of onlookers. Although physical victimization declines between third and sixth grade, teasing is higher in frequency than physical victimization during third grade and remains constant through sixth grade (Perry et al., 1988).

Parker and Seal (1996) reported that friendless children were perceived by their peers as having greater difficulty handling teasing than children who had friends. Feldman and Dodge (1987) demonstrated that rejected children had poorer quality responses to teasing than popular children. Therefore, it is of prime importance to train the friendless child in nonaggressive but effective ways of handling teasing.

16.3 Bullying

Bullying is defined as repeated (once per week or more) attempts to inflict unprovoked injury or discomfort at one and the same victim by one or more specific other peers (Olweus, 1993). Results of surveys of bullies and victims reported by

Olweus (1993) indicated that 3% of all children were victims of bullying, 2% were bullies, and 0.3% (extrapolating) were both victims and bullies. Salmivalli and Nieminen (2002) found that 10.6% were bullies, 6.2% were victims, and 1.9% were both.

Discrepancies among researchers as to the prevalence is largely due to differing definitions. For instance, Boulton and Smith (1994) reported prevalence of bullying ranging from 30.1% to 57.8% of boys, depending on the criteria (i.e., the proportion of peers agreeing that a target child was a bully). However, they defined bully as "someone who often picks on other children, or hit them, or teases them, or does other nasty things to them for no good reason" (p. 318). This definition probably includes children who are generally aggressive, because it does not specify that the aggression is directed toward a consistent victim. On the other hand, Salmivalli and Nieminen (2002) trained their respondents to exclude children of equal strength who get into fights with each other, but to include as bullying "when the feelings of one and the same student are intentionally and repeatedly hurt" (p. 34). Frankel (1996) distinguished between *frequent fighters* (i.e., aggressive-rejected boys; cf. Chap. 19) who are nonselective in their targets and generally aggressive (cf. Patterson, 1986), versus bullies, who are very selective in targets and not generally aggressive (Olweus, 1993).

Other authors have drawn a similar distinction between perpetrators of reactive (provoked) versus proactive (unprovoked) aggression (Dodge & Coie, 1987; Salmivalli & Nieminen, 2002), classifying bullying as the latter. The two types of aggressive children differ in other respects. For instance, boys with reactive aggression do not tend to associate with each other, whereas boys with proactive aggression do (Poulin et al., 1997). Salmivalli and Nieminen (2002) reviewed evidence suggesting that bullies have good skills at deducing what others might be thinking and have above-average social intelligence.

Rican (1995) found that among sixth graders, both bullies and victims were rejected more than other children were. For girls, sociometric status of bullies was higher than that of their victims (see relational aggression in Chap. 14), but for boys, the sociometric status of bullies was lower than that of the victims. Boys are more bullied than girls are (Boulton & Underwood, 1992; Crick & Grotpeter, 1996). Sixty percent of boys who were bullies in Grades 6–9 had at least one conviction by the age of 24.

Victims of bullying report that teachers do little to stop it. Victim and bully status is stable across ages 9–16 (cf. Boulton & Smith, 1994, for a review). Bullying mostly takes place on the way to and from school (Olweus, 1993). The incidence at school correlated with ratio of adult supervisors during recess but was not related to physical characteristics of the victim. Victims of bullying among 8- to 9-year-olds were more likely to play alone rather than participating in larger groups (Boulton, 1999).

Bullying is not a condition that victims can resolve successfully by themselves. Encouragement to "just punch him once in the nose as hard as you can" by fathers to their sons almost always leads to disastrous results. Unlike the Hollywood scripts of many films (such as *Karate Kid*), most children do not have the ability to contend with a bully in a physical showdown. It is almost always necessary for adults to actively intervene, with serious consequences being implemented to deal with physical harassment and violence. Therefore it is not a part of the current program. For a more detailed discussion of an effective program, see Olweus (1993). Frankel (1996) presented parts of this program in a form that can be readily employed by parents.

Research on Teasing

16.4 Teasing Within Different Subgroups

Research on teasing suggests it is common in elementary school, with some teasers and teased pupils in every classroom. Well-liked children tease in less critical, more prosocial ways than rejected children (Keltner, Young, Heerey, Oemig, & Monarch, 1998). Children are more aware than teachers of who the teasers and the teased are (Aho, 1998).

Research suggests that teasing is more distressing to girls than to boys (Keltner et al., 1998). Interpretation of this is unclear. This research may reflect an artifact, because the authors did not extract relational aggression (see Chap. 9) from teasing (Crick, 1995). Cash (1995) examined the recollection of childhood appearance-related teasing by adult females. Most teasing was about facial characteristics and weight. Although peers perpetrated most teasing, teasing by brothers was also common. Women who reported having had more severe teasing about physical appearance in childhood held more dissatisfying body images as adults.

16.5 Effective Ways of Handling Teasing

The dominant motivation reported by perpetrators of teasing is their pleasure at the discomfort of the victim (Warm, 1997). Although accepted children tend to employ humor or assertion in response to being teased (Perry, Williard, & Perry, 1990), rejected children tend to get angry, upset, or physically aggressive (cf. Shantz, 1986). This reaction probably motivates the perpetrator to continue, even if the victim uses physical aggression (cf. Shantz, 1986). Kochenderfer and Ladd (1997) observed victimization and asked for response strategies in 199 kindergartners. They found the strategy of "having a friend help" was associated with reduced victimization, whereas "fighting back" was related to stable victimization.

Scambler, Harris, and Milich (1998) had children between 8 and 11 years old view videotaped interactions of one child being teased by two other children. They saw the victim respond either with humor, by ignoring, or with hostility. Subjects rated the humorous response as the most effective, followed by ignoring, and the hostile response as least effective. Furthermore, the victim's response to teasing significantly affected the rater's perceptions of the friendliness and popularity of the teasers and victim.

Children have been taught to develop humorous or assertive coping responses to teasing. Goodwin and Mahoney (1975) presented the earliest documented use of this approach. Boys in a residential treatment setting took part in a "taunting game" in which the other boys tried to make the target boy angry. Coping responses were first modeled on a videotape. Then the boys took turns being the target. Results showed that all boys were able to develop coping responses and subsequently reduce disruptive behavior in their classroom. Lochman and Wells (1996) recently replicated this approach.

16.6 Implications From Research and Clinical Practice

Bullying and teasing are vastly different phenomena, although frequently lumped together by the media as well as researchers. Different approaches are effective with each. Teasing is far more common than bullying. The chronic victim of teasing can be taught effective nonaggressive responses. In teaching responses to teasing, the clinician must be careful to draw distinctions between teasing, relational aggression, and statements of a child's ineptness (e.g., "You aren't good at handball"). The goals of the perpetrator are different within each of these categories. The goal of relational aggression is dominance and control of the other child's actions. The goal for statements of a child's ineptness is to express irritation during a frustrating experience (e.g., vastly disparate abilities in handball). The goal for teasing is to get the victim upset. This latter goal is thwarted by the techniques advocated in this chapter.

Children see a humorous response by the victim as the most effective response to teasing. Rejected children are unlikely to use humor but more likely to get upset when teased. They can be taught to use more effective responses. Group leaders must be careful not to inadvertently teach children to tease back (i.e., improve their teasing ability), because some victims of teasing are on occasion the perpetrators and are more likely to be teased because of this.

The parent role in the child's vulnerability to being teased has not been empirically explored. We find that parents contribute to the child's vulnerability in two ways. Parents may advise ineffective responses to teasing, such as "tell the teacher," "tease back," or "hit the bully as hard as you can," which may exacerbate teasing (being labeled a "tattletale" or becoming aggressive). Parents may also make it difficult for the child to ignore teasing in order to defend the family honor or may focus on the child's feelings about being teased ("Just tell her that it hurts your feelings when she says mean things to you"), which also tends to validate the teaser. Thus it is critical to involve the parent in the understanding and training of effective responses to teasing.

How to Conduct the Session

Until Now

Parents have supervised their children in their first structured and supervised play date during the previous week. It is hoped that children's feelings of social competence have improved as a result of play date successes. Children with a negative reputation are learning that they don't have to put all of their "eggs in one basket," that basket being the peer group at school. Children are also learning that other children will want to come over to play with *them* rather than just sit and play videogames.

In This Session

Parents will give their first report of how the structured play date went. Count on the parents, not the children, to supply the crucial details of this play date. Often, the parents will need feedback on how to "fine tune" these play dates to increase their potential benefits. In addition to helping the children formulate and practice their response to teasing (with parent support), this session will also continue practice of the rules of a good host.

Parent Session Plan 8

Initial Gathering

Check child toys as they come in. Have parents hold toys that are in excluded categories.[1]

Homework Review

You may notice at the beginning of this session that the affect of the parents has changed. Many of them will have positive reports of how they witnessed their child have a good play experi-

---

[1]Obsessions, trading cards, water pistols, anything that shoots projectiles, computer games, video games, books, arts and crafts, Magic cards, Dungeons & Dragons, Monopoly, Clue, or Twister. Chess or Mastermind is allowed only if they checked with the group last week to see if someone else knows how to play.

ence. Much of the work going on from this point is getting parents to "fine tune" their observation and supervision of the play date. They need to be ready to intervene to keep their child on track as a good host. Parents are not used to letting their children play by themselves, monitoring closely enough to identify when they should intervene, and then limiting their intervention to effective prompts for their child.

1. There are two homework assignments (not including inside toy), and not enough time to review all in depth. Tell parents that you want them to focus on (a) the out-of-group call, which led up to (b) the play date.
2. Parents typically need reminding that the out-of-group call is specifically for the purpose of organizing the play date and that they should be monitoring this also. Ask about the out-of-the group call: (a) Was the other child interested or excited by the call, (b) did the children have things to talk about (in a two-way conversation), and (c) did the children come up with things to do together on play date? If yes to all, then parents should have arranged the play date. If no to all, then they should have helped their child select another playmate.
3. Ask who had a successful play date experience and have them report first. Recount the first play date: (a) Was a parent there to supervise? (b) Did the parent have to intervene to enforce the good host rules? Did the child comply with the rule? This is the teaching function of this play date—having to enforce rules helps the children where and when they need it the most. (c) Review the different activities that the children did. How did the exclusion of video game and TV work? (d) Did the child want to invite his or her playmate back? Elicit testimonials for how this was a better quality play date. (e) Did the parent get to know the other child's parent a little bit?
4. Tell parents a play date should be easier on the parent than supervising their child alone. It is a self-esteem booster—especially if their child found another child with similar interests and entertained him or her on his or her own. The child should know that another child came over just to play with him or her, not just to play with neat video games.

Clinical Examples of First Successful Play Dates

The mother of a fifth-grade boy with oppositional defiant disorder was surprised that her son was well behaved with his guest while at the same time he was curt with his mother.

Despite a bad reputation at school, the classmate of a shy fifth-grade girl agreed to have a play date. She spoke with a girl at school to set up play date. The moms called each other to set up details. During the play date, the girls played "catch" with balloons, and played "dress-up" and "fashion show" with mom's clothing. They then sang on her karaoke machine. Both girls had a great time.

Successfully Fending Off Peer Pressure for Videogames

A sixth-grade boy with Asperger's disorder complained on the way home from the previous session, "If we don't play 'Dragon Ball Z,' that will make me look like a dork to my guest." His mom replied, "Tell them your mom is a huge witch and doesn't allow you to play 'Dragon Ball Z.' They have moms too. They'll understand." During the subsequent play date, the boys played Monopoly. The boy made popcorn for his guest. He felt good about the play date.

Reminding About the Good Host Rules

An 11-year-old boy with ADHD telephoned a boy who insisted he only liked TV and homework. With his mother coaching him, he told the other boy, "Well I'd like to have you over but my mom says we can't watch TV. Instead we have to make a plan of three other things we can do." They were able to make a list of possible things to play. One of the games the other boy wanted to play was Monopoly. He first said, "That'd take too long." Then he paused and said sarcastically, "*Sure,* we can play Monopoly." His parent pulled him aside and reminded him of the good host rule (a little prematurely but appropriately). He then said to the other boy, "I really mean it—we can play Monopoly."

At the time of the play date, they played

Monopoly, then baked cookies and sang songs from a "Weird Al Yankovic" album. The boy continued playing songs from the album despite his guest's obvious boredom. His parent (listening from another room) came in, pulled him aside, reminded him of the good host rule, and took away the lyric sheet. He began again to do what his guest wanted. The other boy had a great time. The parents reported a much happier play date than any play date that involved Nintendo. The next day the other boy was waiting for him at school when his dad dropped him off.

First Play Date Without Baby Sister

A second-grade boy with ADHD had a charming younger sister who would take over any play date he had with a friend. On this play date, one parent took the sister to a movie while the boy had his guest over. The boys played in the back yard, digging in mud. At one point the boys were so far away that the mom couldn't hear what was going on. So the mom checked on them by bringing shovels out. Her son took the bigger shovel and the mom whispered into his ear, "be a good host." He quickly gave his guest the bigger shovel. Her son was clearly elated, even after the play date was over.

Overcoming Child Resistance to Making the Call for a Play Date

The mother of a fourth-grade boy said her son wanted a play date with another boy but was afraid to call him. Despite her efforts, he refused to make the call. So during the day, when she was sure no one was home at the other child's house, she called and left a message that her son wanted to speak to the other boy. She told her son she did this. Her son was pleased when the other boy returned the call and had no difficulty in having a conversation, and the play date was set up.

Potential Problems

Saving Face After Failing to Do the Assignment

The mother of a third-grade boy said her son didn't have a play date but had a sleep-over at someone else's house. She began saying how much better it seemed (but how could she know since she wasn't there to supervise?). The group leader cut her off, saying he wanted to hear about completion of homework from others in the group.

Parent Breaking a Play Date Rule

A bright third-grade boy with autism found common interests with a boy in his class during his out-of-group call. The other boy accepted his invitation for the play date. His parents were surprised. Because they weren't sure their son would offer enough on the play date to keep the other boy interested, they took the boys bowling for the first hour, in clear opposition to the instructions on the handout. The remainder of the 2-hour play date went well. The boy let his guest choose the activities. They gave his turtles a bath and took them for a walk. They then played "hide and seek." His guest asked to stay overnight, but was told they couldn't that night. Mom realized that the trip to the bowling alley was unnecessary and could have interfered with their friendship (if they didn't have enough time to play by themselves).

Imposing Mother, Shy Child

The mother of a shy second-grade boy reported that she felt her son was too shy to complete his homework as assigned, so she took the initiative (as she has done for the last 2 years) and tried to arrange a play date directly with another child's mom (without first consulting her son).

The group leader asked her how her son was doing, "slipping in." She said he occasionally joins in but says he usually waits on sidelines and considers the children he is watching as "playing too rough." The group leader pointed out that her son may have good taste in being uncomfortable with more aggressive children's play. Because he is able to "slip in" sometimes, he may have found one group who plays at a comfortable level for him and the mom should respect that. The group leader also pointed out that the mom needs to take a back seat and encourage her son to initiate the play dates so that she doesn't make it too easy for him.

Problems Recognizing Emotional Cues

A mother of a sixth-grade boy with Asperger's disorder reported that her son didn't know if his guest had a good time. The group leader responded that the mom may have to teach him which cues would indicate this: (a) His guest asked to stay longer, and (b) the mom observed the guest laughing, smiling, and complimenting her son on his games.

Play Date in the Neighborhood Instead of at Home

A second-grade girl did not establish what she and her guest would do before the play date. The girls played indoors at first for about 30 minutes. They then went down her street to play basketball. Two other girls in the neighborhood approached them when they were outside. She asked her guest if she wanted to continue playing just with her. Her guest said "no" and asked the others to join (this resulted in a violation of the play date rule for the guest—remain loyal to your host). The group leader advised that she plan her activity on the phone before the play date, keep the play date inside her home, and maintain loyalty to her guest.

Guest's Parent Wants to Drop Off Sibling for Babysitting

A mother of a second-grade girl reported that the mother of the guest asked if the younger sister could be dropped off also. The group leader pointed out that it was inconsiderate for a guest's parent to ask this on first play date. The parent was urged to politely refuse this, saying something like, "I'd love to do a bigger get-together later but right now I would just like to have the two girls."

If this happens during the phone call to schedule the play date, the parent can request another time when it would be convenient for the guest's parent to drop off only the invited child. Other parents in the group wondered if the guest's mother does not value play dates or is blackmailing the mother with child care just to get her child a play date.

Parents Not Handling Play Date Consistently

Parents of an 8-year-old girl with ADHD had to alternate which parent accompanied her to sessions because of the mom's work schedule. Although the mom was well aware of her daughter's social problems, the dad maintained during the first sessions he attended that his daughter didn't need the program. However, this changed when he monitored her play date for this assignment. He saw that his daughter chose to play a magic show and proceeded to boss her playmate around for the whole play date (the dad didn't follow instructions to intervene). During this session, he asked how he could change this behavior. The group leader pointed out how several instructions in the handout would handle this.

Parent Attempts to Structure the Play Date

One father said he left a huge puzzle out and had the children figure out 10 pieces. The group leader said that although it was good to have the puzzle out, greater benefits accrue when the children learn to structure play activities themselves.

Another parent suggested art activities. The group leader asked the other parents if they could think of why these activities were not conducive to play dates. One parent suggested that artwork tends to be parallel rather than interactive play.

Play Date Out of Desperation (Poor Guest 1)

The mother of a third-grade girl reported that she didn't like the girl who had been invited (out of desperation) for the past week's play date. The guest played well for the first hour but then became bossy and verbally hostile. Her daughter wasn't enjoying the play date and asked her mother privately when it would be over. The mom had her persist for the allotted time period. The group leader said that her daughter had good sense and that mom should have ended the play date early by offering snacks and a video until the guest's mom picked her up. The group leader pointed out that this was one reason to keep the first play date short. The mom was urged not to invite this girl over (especially if her daughter didn't want to play with her) and to have different girls over for the next couple of play dates. This might provide her daughter with better alternatives.

Poor Guest 2

One mother of a fourth-grade boy said that the guest argued with her over the video-game prohibition. The group leader pointed out that this was a "red flag" for a bad choice for friendship and play dates: Even children who don't listen to their own parents will usually listen to parents of the host. Noncompliance and arguing with an unfamiliar parent are often evidence of serious behavior problems.

Poor Guest 3

A father of a sixth-grade boy reported that he didn't have a play date. The reason was that his guest was suspended from school and grounded by his parents. The group leader pointed out that this was probably a poor choice for a friend right now. He had the dad think of another child that was better behaved to invite over for next week.

Child Attempts to Use Deception to Circumvent the TV Prohibition

The mother of a second-grade boy said her son told her that the child group leader said it was "OK" to watch TV while the children were having snacks. The mom said she didn't hear about this and that it wasn't "OK" on this play date. The group leader clarified that TV was not to be used at any time during these initial play dates and that there had not been any directions to watch TV "while having snacks."

Homework Assignment

1. Next play date: Parents should help their child select another playmate with which the parent is comfortable, not a child with behavior problems. Parents are to try a few different playmates before the class is over, so their child will have a choice of whom they want to

play with based on actual experience. Reiterate two things for the parent to look for when monitoring the out-of-group call: (a) Did the children come up with things to do together on play date? (b) Was the other child enthusiastic about this? If the answer is "yes" to both, then the parent should get on the phone to arrange a play date with the other child's parent. An out-of-group call does not have to end in a play-date appointment being made. If child called was rude then move on and call someone else. Maybe the next call will be better.[2]

2. Remind parents that the first play date should only be 1 to 2 hours. It's easier to extend a short play date going well then to cut a play-date disaster short. It's better to end the first play date on a good note than to have a long play date end in disaster.

Parent Handout

There are two main points to this handout: (a) Parents can reduce teasing by "backing off" on having their child defend the "family honor." (b) Parents can give booster sessions, practicing "make fun of the tease" with their child.

1. Review parent handout.

Group Leader Guide to Parent Handout— Session 8—Effective Ways to Resist Being Teased

1. Children will pick on others to tease chronically because they find it fun to watch their victim's reactions. Reactions that spur on perpetrators usually involve "losing one's cool" or not knowing what to do.
2. More effective strategies against perpetrators involve making teasing less fun for them but not getting them angry.
   (a) Walking away may sometimes work,
   (b) Telling the teacher or other authority fig-

---

[2]*Best* is a new playmate never played with individually before (can be someone the child has known for a while but never invited over). *Next best* is someone they haven't invited over in a long while who used to be friends. *Third best* is someone they invite over rarely. *Fourth best* is another present good friend.

ure tends not to work for children past first grade, because peers will tease them about this ("tattletale").

3. An effective strategy we have taught your child is to *make fun of the tease.*" What they will be doing is making fun of the perpetrator's inability to tease well. This is different from teasing back: The child does not sink to the level of the perpetrator, and may gain support from onlookers for this. [*Tell parents that the idea is to show that the teasing doesn't bother the child (even if it does) and that the child has a competent comeback for any tease the perpetrator might have. Children can do this with short, snappy comebacks (they shouldn't get tangled up in an overly wordy or complicated comeback) or with voice tone or actions indicating disdain. They need enough different comebacks so that the perpetrator will think:"There's plenty more where that came from. This is no fun for me." Having an effective comeback will make the children feel much better and more in control. Treating teasing in a matter-of-fact way rather than as onerous and intolerable also helps take the "punch" out of it. Review the distinction between teasing back (which provokes more teasing, injures the child's reputation, and potentially escalates into a physical altercation) and "making fun of the tease" (which can't be used as a tease itself, but results in a sense of mastery and often gains support from onlookers).*]

Examples:

Child response: That's so old it's got dust on it.

Child response: And your point is . . .

Child response: Talk to the hand 'cause the face ain't listening.

Child response: Whatever . . .

Child response: I fell off my dinosaur when I first heard that.

Child response: Can't you think of anything else to say?

Child response: So what?

Child response: Big deal!

Child response: Tell me when you get to the funny part.

Child response: Thanks for sharing.

Child response: [Exaggerated yawn, covering mouth, stretching motions.]

Child response: Huh? Huh? Huh?" [Exaggerated pretending to not hear the teasing.]

Child response: Boo Hoo Hoo. [said flatly while hand is rubbing eye in exaggerated pretend crying.]

Child response: I don't get it.

Child response: Yeah, and . . .

The essential elements are:

Showing the tease does not bother the child (demonstrating an unconcerned attitude).

Having a series of short, humorous responses to successive teases.

Not sinking to the perpetrator's level by making personal attacks on him.

[*Encourage parents to take turns teasing the group leader while the group leader models comebacks. At the end of this demonstration, add that the child can also use this in response to teasing from a sibling.*][3]

Parent Assignment

1. Play date and phone call with a new child.
2. (Optional) You and your child may practice "making fun of the tease," if your child agrees. [*Tell parents they should not use an actual tease in practice to avoid teaching their child to tease back. They should use a benign or nonsense tease like "your mamma" (mothers are doing the practice so that this will make no sense). The idea is to get children to practice a variety of comebacks.*]

Clinical Example of Parent Supporting Teasing Resistance

Taking the Pressure Off of the Victim

The mother of a fifth grader reported that her son was teased about her being "fat." She said she could tell her son, "No matter what bad things another boy says about me, I don't want you to

---

[3]Using the technique when brother or sister is the teaser helps by having the child experience success in a more controlled setting before trying it at school.

get into a fight about it. It's not going to hurt my feelings."

Potential Problems

Wanting to Delve Into Hurt Feelings

Parents may want to recount how they delved into the feelings that their child had about being teased in order to provide empathy. The group leader should stress that talking about feelings may validate the teasing (by conveying to the child that he or she should be upset) and may also distract the child from focusing on an effective comeback at the time he or she is teased. Having an effective comeback will make the children feel more in control of the situation when it next arises. Treating teasing in a "matter-of-fact" way rather than as a catastrophic emotional event also helps takes the "punch" out of it.

Defending the Family Honor

A foreign-born mother of a third grader with ADHD had difficulty understanding why her son shouldn't defend the family's honor when a child used family insults as the content of teasing. The group leader pointed out that the more her son felt he had to "defend his family," the more enjoyment the perpetrator would have teasing him. Her choice was whether to keep insisting he "stick up" for his family or use the techniques in the handout and have the teasing quickly die down.

Child Session Plan 8

Homework Review

Many of the children will be reporting positive play experiences without having to resort to playing video games. This will win many "converts" who can be counted on to support this during the session and peer pressure will become a supportive factor.

1. Ask if any child had a chance to "slip in" and call on children who raise their hands to volunteer reports of homework compliance.

2. *Review play date.* Ask who did play date homework and pick only children who did.[4] Allow them to tell about their play date only if it followed the rules. If the child gives an example of a play date in or just outside the home, then allow the child to continue. If it was anywhere else or the child talked about playing video games, then it wasn't a play date according to the assignment.

3. Questions to ask: Who did you play with? Did you call first to figure out what to do? Tell me one or two things you decided to do. Did you actually do what you had previously decided for the play date? Who got to pick the games? Did your guest have a good time? Did you have a good time?

Clinical Example of Review of the Play-Date Homework

GL: Who did the play date homework last week?

Child: I did. I had a child over that I saw last year.

GL: Did you call first to figure out what to do?

Child: Yes. We decided to ride our bikes.

GL: Is that what you actually did on the play date?

Child: Yes.

GL: That's great that you figured out on the phone that you both wanted to ride your bikes. Did your guest bring over his bike?

Child: Yes.

GL: Great, did you play anything else?

Child: We played "hide and seek" in my back yard.

GL: Whose idea was it?

Child: My guest's.

GL: Terrific. It sounds like you were being a good host! Did your guest have a good time?

Child: Yes.

GL [writing a star on the board next to the child's name]: Did you have a good time?

Child: Yes.

---

[4] Ask who did the play-date homework, as opposed to who had a play date, because children may try to substitute any peer contact. In having the children review their homework, they communicate to each other the advantages and attainability of successful play dates.

Potential Problem

Examples of Homework Not Done

A fourth-grade girl said she went to the movies with a friend. The group leader interrupted and said that was nice to do but that wasn't the homework assignment. The group leader then asked if there was a play date in the home as the homework play-date assignment called for. The homework had not been done.

A third-grade boy said his friend didn't want to play anything but video games and his mom caved in and let them play. The group leader cut this off, reiterated the electronic game prohibition, and then asked if anyone did the homework assignment. (The group leader discussed this with the mom at the end-of session reunification.) Another child began to talk about his appropriate play date.

Didactic

The focus of this session is to help the child identify causes of teasing in a way that will facilitate his or her feeling competent producing humorous and assertive responses in the face of teasing from their peers at school.

Between the introduction of teasing and the description of what to do about it is a critical time in the session. During this time, the group leader should *take care not to use a Socratic presentation or to recognize children who are raising their hands with suggestions about what they do in response to teasing.* Children may offer inappropriate responses. Once said, they may argue with the group leader.

The group leader instead should convey that teasing is not a "big deal" unless they allow it to be a "big deal." Instead, most of the time is spent on the "comebacks," which children will generate. Children will enjoy this part of the session and will be more likely to use the comebacks they practice.

1. Draw a box with about six buttons on it (the "button box") on the board and two lines to a Nintendo controller. Ask, "Why do kids tease?" After two or three children give answers (if none are correct), the group leader says, "Kids tease because they want to get you

upset and 'lose your cool.' So that maybe you'll cry, yell, hit, get in trouble or look foolish. They are also doing it to show off in front of other kids. They may even say to the other kids, 'watch what I'm going to do.'" Do we want to provide the entertainment for kids who are teasing us?" (Answer: "No.")
2. Discuss "button box". Each button is something that children can say or do that gets us upset. Children who tease figure out which "button" to press and then press that "button." If we cry and such, they will come back and press that button again and again. Everyone has a different "buttons."
3. Have the children tell at least one "button" that children (not necessarily they) get upset with.
4. Erase the line drawn from the controller to the button box. "What we need to do is break the wire so that other children can't control us. We have to disconnect these buttons. Don't give the teaser an easy job." [*Don't answer any questions until you get through step 6.*]
5. "We want children to be able to have something to say back without doing to them what they are doing to you. If you tease back, you will get in trouble too. If we can say something back to them that's funny and not get upset, they'll look for someone else who will put on a better show for them and is easier to tease."
6. Good comebacks are short, don't make you look silly and show the attitude "I don't care." They don't even have to have words—for instance, a shoulder shrug. (Demonstrate shaking head and shrugging shoulders.) Say the comebacks below and list them on the board.

Examples:

Child response: That's so old it's got dust on it.

Child response: And your point is . . .

Child response: Talk to the hand 'cause the face ain't listening.

Child response: Whatever . . .

Child response: I fell off my dinosaur when I first heard that.

Child response: Can't you think of anything else to say?

Child response: Who cares?

Child response: Huh?

Child response: So what?

Child response: Big deal!

Child response: Tell me when you get to the funny part.

Child response: Thanks for sharing.

Child response: [Exaggerated yawn, covering mouth, stretching.]

Child response: Huh? Huh? Huh? [Exaggerated pretending to not hear the teasing.]

Child response): Boo hoo hoo [said flatly while hand is rubbing eye in exaggerated pretend crying].

Child response: I don't get it.

Child response: Yeah, and . . .

7. Ask each child to pick a comeback to use and go around room and "tease" each child with the expression, "your momma." Some children will try to formulate their own comebacks. If they fit the criteria of making fun of the tease without teasing back, then accept them.

8. Praise them when they sound confident and use a good comeback. Correct them when they attempt to tease back.[5] Discourage talking about specific teases.

Clinical Examples of Practicing "Making Fun of the Tease"

Child: Whatever . . . [Said with an unconcerned tone while shrugging shoulders].

GL [repeating response with voice tone that had been used]: Whatever. What a great tone! It really shows that you don't care and teasing isn't going to get to you.

Child: I would say repeatedly, "Huh?" [putting hand next to ear in a half-hearted pretense of difficulty in hearing].

GL: The other kid might say something like "Are you deaf?" or "You must be hard of hearing!" but then they will likely get frustrated and storm off. That's what you want to happen.

Child: Talk to the hand [she looks away and puts up her hand, turning the palm toward the teaser] because the ears ain't listening.

GL: [laughs and repeats the comeback.]

Potential Problems

Examples of Incorrect Comebacks

Some older children may have trouble focusing on this, in which case the group leader attends to the children who are participating. Others may actually tease others in the group ("I heard a really great one today—"You're sister is so ugly . . . "). Group leaders should be ready to give immediate time outs for this breach.

A fifth-grade boy recounted that he knew one boy who would swing at him when he said something back after being teased. The group leader recommended a comeback that was minimally embarrassing or provocative to the peer with poor impulse control, such as, "Whatever . . . ."

A fifth-grade boy said he had tried the technique and it didn't work: He ignored the teaser but the teaser said another tease. The group leader said that he had to persist and to practice several comebacks. Delivering one comeback may not be enough.

A third-grade boy with Asperger's disorder was extremely silly in his role-played response to teasing (at school, this probably would have provoked even more teasing). The group leader cut him off by saying in a neutral voice, "That's not making fun of the tease." The group leader then called on someone else in the group. By the end of the session, after being cut off twice, he finally came up with two good examples and the group leader praised him.

Homework Assignment

1. Have each child name a likely perpetrator, if the child wants to. Have them practice the technique on the perpetrator next week or with parent. *Do not practice this during any telephone calls.*

---

[5]Be careful to quickly correct comebacks that are really teasing back or inept responses (particularly overly verbose, intellectualized responses—e.g., "I said to him, 'Maybe we really haven't evolved very far from our simian cousins'").

Real Play

The children usually show improvement on their good host behavior as they have had a play date supervised by their parents between the last and current sessions.

1. Assign the children to guest and host dyads as in Session 7 to practice good host rules, making sure that each child gets a turn at being the guest and host across Sessions 7 and 8.
2. The group leader may go around to each dyad and ask whose idea it was to play the game they are playing. Verify that the child assigned as guest picked the game.
3. Praise hosts who followed the guest's suggestion.

End-of-Session Reunification

1. "Today we worked on making fun of the tease. We also worked on being a good host on a play date. I saw a lot of good host behavior in this group. Let's all give the children a big round of applause."
2. The child leader continues with, "The major job everyone has this week is to make a play date with a new child. Agree on this person with your parent. Remember that you are to call this person for your out-of-group call to come up with games to play. This will be your only required out-of-group call."
3. Parent and child group leaders go around the room, and one by one make sure parent and child agree on a plan for whom to call to make the play date and what inside toy they are bringing next week.

Children's Friendship Training

Parent Handout—Session 8

Effective Ways to Resist Being Teased

1. Children will pick on others to tease chronically because they find it fun to watch their victim's reactions. Reactions that spur on perpetrators usually involve "losing one's cool" or not knowing what to do.

2. More effective strategies against perpetrators involve making teasing less fun for them but not getting them angry.

(a) Walking away may sometimes work,

(b) Telling the teacher or other authority figure tends not to work for children past first grade, since peers will tease them about this ("tattle tale").

(c) An effective strategy we have taught your child is to **make fun of the tease**. What they will be doing is making fun of the perpetrator's inability to tease well. This is different from teasing back: The child does not sink to the level of the perpetrator, and may gain sympathy from onlookers for this.

Examples:

Child response: That's so old it's got dust on it.

Child response: And your point is . . .

Child response: Talk to the hand 'cause the face ain't listening.

Child response: Whatever . . .

Child response: I fell off my dinosaur when I first heard that.

Child response: Can't you think of anything else to say?

Child response: So what?

Child response: Tell me when you get to the funny part.

Child response: Thanks for sharing.

Child response: [Exaggerated yawn, covering mouth, exaggerated stretching.]

Child response: Huh? Huh? Huh? [Exaggerated pretending to not hear the teasing.]

Child response: Boo hoo hoo [said flatly while hand is rubbing eye in exaggerated pretend crying.]

Child response: I don't get it.

Child response: Yeah, and . . .

The essential elements are:

Showing the tease does not bother the child (having an unconcerned attitude).

Having a series of short, humorous responses to successive teases.

Not sinking to the perpetrator's level by personal attacks on him.

Parent Assignments

1. Play date and phone call with a new child.

2. (Optional) You and your child may practice "making fun of the tease," if your child agrees.

Respect Toward Adults

Treatment Rationale

When a child's defiant or disruptive behavior gets him or her in trouble with a supervising adult, some parents may act in such a way as to further injure their child's reputation. This is not well documented in the research literature but has been observed in our clinical practice. The treatment hypothesis is that parents may be provided with more effective ways to view and handle the situation and children may be taught better responses after their behavior has drawn negative attention from an adult.

Research on Components of Disruption

17.1 Importance of Compliance With Adults

Roff et al. (1972) first identified a subgroup of rejected children who have difficulty with authority figures. Noncompliance to adult requests, a hallmark of oppositional defiant disorder, is also a good predictor of peer rejection (Hinshaw & Melnick, 1995; Milich & Landau, 1982).

Gresham, Noell, and Elliott (1996) presented evidence that a child's compliance with teachers as well as his or her relationships with peers enters into teachers' judgment of social competence.

It is unclear in this case whether teachers may be expressing a bias against children who don't obey their instructions or are accurately reflecting the views of peers that children who get into trouble with teachers are to be avoided (cf. Ritchey, 1981, cited in Foster, 1983).

Three studies support the contention that disruptive and defiant behavior toward adults directly influences peer evaluations: Dodge et al. (1990) found that behaviors that drew reprimands from the supervising adults were among a constellation of variables that identified those who quickly became rejected in a new peer group. Dodge et al. (1985) showed that the level of compliance with teacher norms discriminated rejected from accepted children. Frederick and Olmi (1994) presented evidence that disruption of the classroom brought about by a child with ADHD increases teacher negative behavior toward the whole class.

17.2 Defining Problems with Supervising Adults

It has been estimated that about 50% of children who meet criteria for oppositional defiant disorder (ODD) exhibit noncompliance to adults only at home (D. Cantwell, personal communication). More commonly, we have encountered rejected children who exhibit the behaviors not only with parents but also with other supervising adults.

The supervising adult may be the child's classroom teacher or a coach or supervisor of an after-school activity.

Many parents understand and attempt to respond to complaints from these adults. However, some parents respond to adult complaints by committing one or both of two significant errors. The first error is to avoid getting involved at all until it is too late and perhaps the adult threatens to expel the child from the activity. The second error is to hear and "believe" the child's account of conflict without checking with the complaining adult. It is likely that both of these errors result from a parent's lack of strategies for adequately dealing with the discomfort and embarrassment of these situations. When parents take either of these two dysfunctional approaches, the supervising adult typically feels unsupported and may take more drastic measures against both the child and the parent. Thus, part of the treatment focus should be on giving parents better alternatives to use when confronted by an adult complaining about their child.

Nelson and Roberts (2000) observed that the primary difference in elementary school children identified by teachers as disruptive relative to other students is their response to teacher intervention. Children identified as disruptive tended to persist after teacher intervention, whereas other students stopped. This suggests that intervention focus more on the persistence of disruptive behavior in the face of adult intervention.

17.3 Implications From Research and Clinical Practice

It is clear that child noncompliance with adult supervisors can have negative effects on peer relationships. Research suggests that instruction for children should focus on their response to an adult reprimands (rather than total cessation of offending behaviors). Effective parent responses to adult complaints can also help. Decreasing this conflict may have positive effects on the child's peer relationships and reputation.

How to Conduct the Session

Until Now

Children are continuing to have supervised play dates. Children who have been victimized have been taught a technique for handling teasing.

In This Session

Parents will give their reports of how the second supervised play date went. Parents will continue to need feedback on how to "fine tune" these play dates to increase their potential benefits. Some parents may have practiced "making fun of the tease" with their child as homework. Children and parents are given instruction on how to handle situations in which the child has conflict with an adult.

Parent Session Plan 9

Initial Gathering

Check child toys as they come in. Have parents hold toys that are in excluded categories.[1]

Homework Review

1. There are three homework assignments (not including inside toy) and not enough time to review all in depth.
2. Making fun of the tease: Ask if any child used it on a perpetrator, brother or sister, or practiced it with the parent (either a success or failure at making fun of the tease)? Sometimes parents will begin a discussion of their child's feelings about being teased. Cut this off, saying that this is counterproductive because it validates the teaser and focuses the child on the feelings rather than the comeback.

---

[1]Obsessions, trading cards, water pistols, anything that shoots projectiles, computer games, video games, books, arts and crafts, Magic cards, Dungeons & Dragons, monopoly. Chess or Mastermind allowed only if they checked with the group last week.

3. The out-of-group call: (a) Was the other child interested or excited by the call, and (b) did the children have things to talk about (in a two-way conversation)? If this call went well, it should have resulted in the play date.

4. Recount the second play date: (a) Was the parent there to supervise? (b) Did the parent have to intervene to enforce the good host rules? Did the child comply with the good host rules? This is the teaching function of this play date. (c) Did the child mind not having TV/video games (at this point the children are more willing to accept this): (d) Did parents try to get to know the other child's parents? (e) Compare the quality of play with the last play date—were both good or one better than the other? What was child's evaluation?

Clinical Examples of Homework Compliance

Second Play Date Was a Charm

A mother of a fourth-grade boy (who previously disobeyed the "no Nintendo rule" with his last guest) reported a successful play date this week. The guest was a different, better behaved boy. In addition (as a result of the noncompliance on the last play date), Nintendo was taken away for 2 days. This time, the boys played together very well. Parent and child began to see the value of limiting Nintendo, particularly during play dates.

Confident Comeback to Being Teased

The mother of a sixth-grade boy reported that he was teased with "Why don't you go home [pointing to the trash can]?" She said her child retorted confidently and sarcastically (with an amused expression on his face), "Funny" (while pointing to the perpetrator with both hands). The teasing stopped.

Making Fun of the Tease in Response to Harassment

The mother of a fourth-grade girl reported that her daughter tried "making fun of the tease" with a girl who was harassing her constantly. According to the mom, the perpetrator stopped. However, at end-of-session reunification mom and daughter compared notes. Her daughter said that the girl started harassing her again (but she hadn't responded by "making fun of the tease"). Without any input from the group leader, mom said, "You have to keep on doing it. We'll practice some more at home."

Potential Problems

Evading Play Date Supervision 1

The father of a sixth-grader said that his son would play with children in the neighborhood, but refused to have them in for a supervised play date. The group leader suggested that his son didn't want to be watched. The group leader asked if there was currently "junk food" in the house. Dad said "yes." The group leader suggested getting rid of all "junk food" in house and buying "junk food" that his son and guest could request solely before each play date. They could only have the desired treats while they played together inside.

Evading Play Date Supervision 2

The mother of a third-grade boy with Asperger's disorder said her son refused to have a play-date at his own house and would only go over to another child's house. The mom overheard him say that this was because he couldn't play video games at his own house while he could do so elsewhere. The group leader suggested that he not be allowed to go over to another child's house for a play date unless he had one at his own house first.

Deferring Reciprocated Play Dates

Several parents brought up that after good play dates at their house their child was subsequently invited to the guest's house. Parents were told to have all of the play dates at their house until they were sure that their child was following the rules of a good host. Parents asked for graceful ways to defer these invitations. Another parent in the group suggested that "we'll have to get the kids together sometime soon" can be a polite way of saying, "not right now."

Handling Being Turned Down for a Play Date

A mother of a third-grade boy said that her son had a good phone call with another boy. However, when she and the other boy's mom got on the phone, the other mother said they were busy that weekend. The mom asked the group leader if she should call her again. The group leader replied that it is customary for the mother who said "no" to initiate the next request. They should not keep trying in the face of rejections such as "no time right now."

Wrong Person in Charge of the Details

A fourth-grade boy made his out-of-group call and seemed to have a good phone call. When he asked for a play date, the other boy (not his parent) said he didn't have time. Without talking to either mom, the son ended the call. The parent group leader said the mom should remind her son before the call that *she* is the one to work out arrangements with the other mom. The next week, when her son called back and asked for another play date, the other boy agreed and the moms made the appointment.

Giving Up Too Easily During Continued Teasing

The mother of a fifth-grade boy reported that her son was being teased for being "gay" (a common tease used by perpetrators provoking preteen boys). She reported that her son used one of the comebacks but gave up after the first try because the perpetrator came back even harder. The mom verbalized her fear that some of the comebacks might encourage the perpetrator to tease her son even more. One of the dads suggested comebacks that emphasized a combination of scornful voice tone and smooth replies (e.g., "That's getting a little old," "I guess that's the best that you can do," "What else have you got?"). The mom laughed and took notes.

Homework Assignment

The goal for the last 5 weeks of the intervention is to have at least one play date per week. If the child has trouble with play dates, then these should take place *only* at the child's house. This may have to continue after Session 12 (the final group session), if necessary. Parents should also try to set up play dates with as many different children as possible right now, although they may continue to invite over children who had previously successful play dates (for "extra credit"). Inviting over different playmates each week will give parents and children more options in selecting potential best friendships to pursue. This is discussed more fully in Session 10 (see Chap. 18).

1. Parents are to continue to schedule play dates at their house and not let their child accept an invitation to another child's house unless they have had no "good host" rule infractions for at least three play dates in a row.
2. Have parent think of a new child for next week—they are to try a few different playmates before the class is over so their child will have a choice of who they want to develop friendships with based on actual experience.[2]
3. Next week the children are to bring in an *outside* toy that can be used in a team sport. Prohibitions apply as in the first six sessions.[3]

Parent Handout

The handout for this session is supposed to provide the few parents who take counterproductive approaches to adult complaints about their child with an alternative frame of reference. The handout is meant more as an initial exposure and perhaps to be used as later reference (cf. Frankel, 1996, Chap. 25). Only the parents who are currently involved with the issues covered by the

---

[2]*Best* is a new playmate never played with individually before (can be someone the child has known for a while but never invited over). *Next best* is someone they haven't invited over in a long while who used to be friends. *Third best* is someone they invite over rarely. *Fourth best* is another present good friend.

[3]*Dangerous/aggressive toys*—martial arts toys, Super Soakers, water balloons; *solitary/parallel play*—books, skateboards, toy guns; *too good a toy*—expensive toy that will upset the child if lost or damaged.

handout will have questions. The main point to this handout is that sometimes parents will "automatically" take the child's side (whether justified or not). This will always exacerbate the situation, make the complaining adult feel less supported, and provoke the adult to go to greater extremes.

1. Review parent handout, "Handling Adults Complaining About Your Child." (There is no group leader guide, as the handout is read without further explanation).

Clinical Example of Parent Enlisting the Aid of Her Child's Teacher

The mother of a fifth-grader with Asperger's disorder said that four other children would accuse her son of doing things he didn't do and get him in trouble with the teacher. The group leader asked, "How do you know he didn't do them?" She replied that she didn't. It was clear that the mom uncritically adopted her son's viewpoint without getting another side to the incidents. The mom could place a call to the teacher to get his or her perspective regarding the incidents. This approach might lead to the teacher watching the children more closely next time to see whether her son was in fact being unfairly blamed.

Child Session Plan 9

Homework Review

The group leader reviews children's play dates and attempts at "making fun of the tease." Expect that about half of the children will have something to report. The other half will benefit from hearing success stories and all will benefit from added rehearsal of "making fun of the tease" embedded in the homework review.

1. Briefly review the "slipping in" assignment.
2. *Review play date.* Ask who did play date homework and pick only children who did. Allow them to describe their play date only if it followed the rules. If not, cut them off and ask who did the homework assignment. Ask, "Did you call first to figure out what to do? What were things you decided to do? Did you do what you decided on the play date. Who got to pick the games? Did your guest have a good time? Did you have a good time?"
3. Ask, "Did anyone make fun of the tease?" Ask for details and correct children who applied it incorrectly by asking the group, "What would be a way to make fun of the tease?" Continue practicing this technique by having each child come up with one way of making fun of the tease and correcting errors. Don't allow any child to say what particular tease was used.

Clinical Example of Reviewing "Making Fun of the Tease" Homework Review

GL: Did anyone try to tease you last week?

Child: This kid was guarding me in basketball and making noises. That usually gets me upset. I ignored him.

GL: What happened next?

Child: Nothing, we just continued playing.

GL: So he didn't make you lose your concentration on the game! Well done!

Girl: A boy teased me. He called me names. I said, "well that's nice." He said another name and I said, "Whatever . . . "

GL: What happened next?

Girl: He walked away.

GL: That's great, so he saw he wasn't going to push your buttons. What if he called you another name, what else could you have said?

Girl: Talk to the hand 'cause the face ain't listening.

GL [laughing]: Good comeback!

Potential Problem

Reverting Back to Ineffective Strategy

One third-grade girl reported she was teased by another girl and replied "I don't like that," and "that's being mean." The group leader pointed out that those comebacks are exactly what the perpetrator wants to hear and asked other children in the group for comebacks. Several children replied with appropriate comebacks and the group leader had the girl repeat the ones she liked best.

Didactic

Few children admit that accusations are justified—so teaching them to deal with *unjustified* accusations should also make it easier for them to deal with justified accusations. Use a Socratic method only for the first point here (see Table 10.2).

1. Ask, "Why do adults sometimes unjustly accuse children?" and quickly state, "The child has a bad reputation." Have children say what can a child do to other kids that gives him or her a bad reputation (use these points as a template):
   Trying to get others in trouble.
   Saying things about others that they didn't do.
   Not following the rules at games.
   Taking other kids' things.
   Bossing other kids around.
   Laughing when someone is wrong.
2. Ask, "What can a kid do to an adult that gives him a bad reputation?":
   Rolling your eyes at adult.
   Smiling or ignoring adults when they accuse you.
   Calling an adult names, cursing, telling them you won't listen.
3. Demonstrate these all in one example and ask what will happen if children do this. (Answer: They will go to principal's office or get into more trouble.)
4. How to handle adults who are unjustly accusing you:
   Don't loose your cool, answer back, give dirty looks, smile at, ignore, or role your eyes at the adult. An adult won't listen as readily, even if you're right, if you are disrespectful.
   Do try to explain the situation to the adult *only once*. If this doesn't work, *stop talking and be quiet*, even if the adult is wrong. If you do this, the adult might listen to your explanation the next time. You might say "If it will keep me out of trouble then I'll . . . (cooperate with the adult)."

5. Practice how to answer with each child. Remind them to answer only once and then listen quietly. Warn them you will be unjustly accusing them in the remainder of the session.

Clinical Example of Presenting Reasons for Unjust Accusations

GL: What kind of things do kids do to give themselves a bad reputation with the teacher or with a coach? They roll their eyes, curse, don't listen or are disrespectful to the teacher. Maybe they tried to get the teacher in trouble with their parents and told lies. What happens if kids do these things: If you start yelling or cursing or kick a trash can?

Child: You go to principal's office or get into more trouble.

GL: That's right, you'll get busted for this and it won't matter what the original offense was.

Potential Problem

Trying to Evoke a Wider Discussion

A third-grade girl asks, "What if your friend is getting in trouble and you know who really did it, should you help your friend and tell?" The group leader says that we are only talking about if *you* are the one who is unjustly accused and avoids the wider discussion.

Homework Assignment

1. Practice making fun of the tease on child perpetrators (*not on the out-of-group call*).
2. Invite a new child over for a play date.
3. Next time—bring a game that can be used in an *outside team* sport: basketball, soccerball, Nerfball, Frisbee, handball, Vortex.

Real Play

The children should continue to show improvement on their good host behavior as they have had two play dates supervised by their parents.

1. Break up into guest and host and practice being a good host (as in Sessions 7 and 8). The group leader may go around to each dyad and ask whose idea it was to play the game they are playing. Praise hosts who followed the guest's suggestion.

2. Coaches walk among the playing dyads staying next to each pair long enough to get a sense of the action and then make a reasonably related but unjust accusation of one of the children. *Younger children*: Exaggerate the first two times you accuse, sound as insincere as possible, so they understand what's going on. *Older children*: Launch directly into an unjust accusation, because you will stun them with the first accusation and they will naturally be quiet. Praise them for doing this. Make sure that the child knows that each accusation was a "test" after their response.

Clinical Example of Unjust Accusation

GL [watching children playing cards, pointing to the child just took a turn]: You cheated! I saw you take a card from the bottom of the deck!

Child: [pauses, somewhat bewildered.]

GL: That's great! You handled that unjust accusation very well. You didn't argue, roll your eyes or ignore me. Terrific! Now remember, I was only testing you and you did well!

End-of-Session Reunification

1. "Today we worked on being respectful toward adults. We also worked on being a good host on a play date. I saw a lot of good host and respectful behavior in this group. Let's all give the children a big round of applause."

2. The child leader continues with, "The major job everyone has this week is to make a play date. Remember that you are to call this person for your out-of-group call and have a two-way conversation in order to come up with games to play."

3. Have each child name his or her play date candidate and outside toy (team sports) for next time in front of the child's parent.

Children's Friendship Training

Parent Handout—Session 9

Handling Adults Complaining About Your Child

Children who have friendship problems sometimes compound their problems by being disrespectful of supervising adults. Examples are arguing with the adult, rolling their eyes, laughing, or walking away, instead of listening to supervision. This also may hurt their reputation with peers. We are teaching your child to act respectfully when they are *unjustly* accused by an adult. Children are more apt to "buy into" handling being *unjustly* accused.

Rules for children to follow when accused by an adult (whether justified or not):

1. **Don't** ignore the adult, answer back, smile, give dirty looks or roll your eyes. An adult won't listen, even if you're right, if you are disrespectful.
2. **Do** try to explain the situation to the adult **only once.** If this doesn't work the first time you explain yourself, it won't work at all—Be **quiet.**

Rules for parents to follow to defuse the situation:

1. Get as much detail about the incident from your child as you can, before you determine if your intervention is needed. Always give the adult the benefit of the doubt. Don't say anything disrespectful about the other adult (you want to model respectful behavior toward this adult even if they were wrong).

If you decide to talk to the adult, then consider the following when making contact with the adult:

2. Be polite—check if you are talking to the adult at a good time for him or her.
3. Keep your cool, ask for the other adult's side of the issue, whether or not you think your child was at fault. Frequently, the other adult will have important information.
4. Express your concern about the issue and your availability to work together with the adult. This may defuse the issue, but if your child is at fault and continues his or her misbehavior, this won't last.
5. Have the other adult suggest what you both can do about this. If it is reasonable, then try it. If it works—great! (If it doesn't work, at least it was the other adult's suggestion.)

Parent Assignments for Next Session

1. Arrange one play date with a new child at your house as before.
2. Have your child select **an outside toy** that can be used in **team** sports.

   Good toys—basketball, soccerball, Nerfball, handball, Vortex, etc.

   Bad toys—martial arts toys, Super Soakers, books, skateboards, toy guns, expensive toys that will upset your child if lost.

PART III

CHAPTER

18

Managing Competition/ Gender Differences

Treatment Rationale

Sessions 8 through 12 help parents and children build a network of peers for more intimate relationships. The play-date homework assignments and parent supervision of play dates are central to this. The treatment hypothesis is that parents and children will need guidance in selecting peers and making choices for peer interaction. This guidance, given through feedback after each play-date homework assignment, will help parents embark on a productive long-term approach to their child's friendships.

The handouts during Sessions 9, 10, and 11 are intended to educate parents more broadly about peer relationships. The focus of parent Session 10 is on gender differences. This may be helpful because most children in these groups are male and mothers take the most active parent role in developing peer networks for them. This session may help mothers understand differences between how they approached peer relationships as children and how their sons typically do it. Mothers of girls may better understand their daughter's peer-group context.

Research on Gender Differences

The characteristics of cross-sex friendships were reviewed in Chapter 4, and levels of friendship for boys and girls were discussed in Chapter 7. This chapter focuses on other differences in friendship [patterns] between boys and girls.

18.1 Girl and Boy Subcultures

Beginning by about second grade, boys and girls tend to segregate themselves from one another and develop their own subcultures. Girls who are proficient in male activities (e.g., baseball) may continue to be accepted by both sexes. The sexes each have their own determinants of social status (Rogosch & Newcomb, 1989). Girls are more likely to attend to physical attractiveness, degree of amiability, or snobbery, while boys attend to the "neat-cool" dimension of each other's characteristics. Maccoby (1986) observed that boys' best friendships tend to share activity interests and physical skills, whereas girls' best friendships tend to share psychological interests.

18.2 Differences in Friendship Networks

Because girls' friendships tend to be more exclusive than boys' (Eder & Hallinan, 1978), it is no surprise that girls tend to play in smaller groups than boys, usually two or three (Maccoby, 1986), and have smaller peer networks than boys (Benenson, Apostoleris, & Parnass, 1998). Larger networks for boys have been observed as early as age 5 (cf. Daniels-Beirness, 1989). These studies are based mostly on observation of public behavior in school settings.

A *clique* is defined as a group of girls (usually four to five) who are close friends with each other and have regular interaction as a group. Many parents are aware of the clique phenomenon, which seems unique to girls' friendships and may manifest mostly in home situations. Girls can maintain interaction in larger groups when they form a clique (cf., Frankel, 1996). The clique of girls will often rebuff attempts by other girls to participate in their conversations or activities (this is also true in dyadic interactions).

Studies of stability of friendships over time find that boys seem to add to their collection of friends whereas girls seem to cull friends. Within a school year, girls had more exclusive dyadic friendships than boys, with initially triadic friendships changing to dyadic friendships as the school year progressed (Eder & Hallinan, 1978). Boys with many friends were more likely to make new friends, whereas girls with many friends were less likely to make new friends (cf. Daniels-Beirness, 1989). A long-term follow-through study by Berndt and Hoyle (1985) supported this pattern. Although boys and girls increased the number of friends throughout the school year and throughout elementary school, girls made fewer friends than boys and limited the size of their friendship networks more than boys.

18.3 Differences in Intensity of Relationship

Berndt and Hoyle (1985) characterized girls' friendships as more "intensive" than boys. Girls seemed more comfortable when they were with a single best friend (cf. Daniels-Beirness, 1989). When compared to boys, girls reported more positive support from friends (Crick & Grotpeter,

1996), knew more about their friend's behavior at school, and were more influenced by their very best friend (Berndt & Keefe, 1995). Boys' friends were more likely to know each other than girls' friends (Berndt & Hoyle, 1985), suggesting more diverse direct contact. Because both boys and girls seemed to be aware of most of their peer group's popularity, these authors hypothesized that boys knew this from direct interaction with other boys whereas girls knew this from keen interest and frequent discussions.

18.4 Implications From Research and Clinical Practice

Boys and girls segregate in public play, starting by second grade. They begin to focus on different aspects of social relationships. It is imperative that group process reflect this by promoting segregation of boys and girls in practice and homework components of the intervention. Although supporting existing cross-sex friendships, the intervention emphasizes development of same-sex friendships.

Research supports that boys are more open-ended both in terms of allowing others to join their play and in forming stable and ever-expanding friendships, whereas girls are more exclusive, reaching a limit to the number of friendships they maintain. This seems to imply that the prognosis for girls is not as good as that of boys for integration into their peer groups throughout the intervention. Over the course of running 90 treatment groups, we have integrated girls into our ongoing groups of boys (as separate subgroups). At first this was done with some trepidation. After analyzing the data, we found that comparison of pre- and posttreatment mean differences in outcome measures resulted in a nonsignificant trend for girls to do better than boys.

How to Conduct the Session

Until Now

Children are continuing to have supervised play dates. Parents and children are continuing to evaluate how different playmates behave and get along with their child on play dates.

In This Session

The most important work of this session is to help parents and children make sound choices in building the child's friendship network. After using good host rules on play dates, children are now ready to further integrate good sportsmanship within a competitive game.

Parent Session Plan 10

Initial Gathering

1. Check child toys as they come in. Have parents hold toys that are in excluded categories.[1]

Homework Review

1. There are two homework assignments (not including outside toy) and not enough time to review all in depth. Tell parents that you want them to focus on (a) the out-of-group call, which led up to (b) the play date.
2. Ask if any child used "making fun of the tease" on a perpetrator, brother or sister, or practiced it with a parent.
3. For the out-of-group call, (a) was the other child interested or excited by the call, and (b) did the children have things to talk about (in a two-way conversation)?
4. Recount the third play date: (a) Was a parent there to supervise? (b) Did the parent have to intervene to enforce the good host rules? Did the child comply with the rule? This is the teaching function of this play date. (c) Did the parent try to get to know the other child's parents?
5. Have parents compare the quality of play with the last play dates. What was their child's evaluation? You might find that play dates go well with one or two different children and go less well with one child. This latter play date may have had more bickering and perhaps the guest was harder to control. If this was the child's only play date, the child might choose to have the poorer behaving child over again out of desperation. But because he or she has a choice, chances are the child won't pick this guest again, and parents should not encourage him or her to do so.[2]

6. Tell parents that the development of a best friend is like true love. This also occurs with adult friendships: Everyone has his faults—good friends overlook each other's faults and smooth things over quickly. If there are too many faults to overlook, then people don't become best friends. A harmonious play date is a good example of how when children like each other sufficiently, they are more inclined to smooth things over rather than argue over trivial matters.

Clinical Examples of Homework Compliance

Good Taste in Children

The mother of a third-grade boy reported that of her son's three play dates, one was harder for her to supervise, with frequent bickering. The other two were easy. When she asked her son to consider how much he liked each child, he liked the bickering child least. The group leader pointed out that her son had good taste. If the bickering child was his only play date, he might have been desperate enough to invite him back.

Generalization to Another Child's Home

The mother of a sixth-grade girl reported that her daughter had an appointment to do homework together with another girl. After the homework was finished, it evolved into a play date. Her mother was able to watch this. She noted that her daughter continued to be a good host even though she was at the other child's house.

Potential Problems

Inattentiveness on Play Dates

The mother of a fifth-grade boy with ADHD reported that her son would start playing on his

---

[1] *Dangerous/aggressive toys*—martial arts toys, Super Soakers, water balloons; *solitary/parallel play*—books, skateboards; *too good a toy*—expensive ball that will upset the your child if lost.

[2] Friendship is a personal choice, based in part on comfort level with other children. Some children should not be friends, either because they have nothing in common, don't especially like each other, or in the case of children with antisocial interest, are bad for each other.

play dates and then wander off in the middle of the game. The group leader asked if he was taking medication. The mother said he was not currently. She noted that the stimulant he used to take seemed to help her son's social persistence. The mom agreed to consult with her physician in order to try medication before the next play-date.

Homework Assignment

1. The goal over the remaining sessions is to continue to have at least one play date per week. This is to help parents give children a "tune-up" on good host behavior. If their child has trouble with play dates, then these should take place only at their house. They should be reminded again that when they supervise the play dates they may have to step in one or two times to correct infractions of a rule of a good host. This should continue until there are no "good host" rule infractions for three play dates in a row. This may have to continue after Session 12, if necessary.
2. Parents should also try to set up play dates with as many different children as possible across these play dates. This is because children have different "chemistry" with each other. Think of a new child for next week.[3]

Parent Handout

Children have begun to make new friends and started to have successful play dates. Now is a good time for parents to be aware of sex differences in play and friendships in order to adjust their expectancies of what may happen. The handout contains only the essential information that parents might be able to use at this point. Group leaders should read the literature review section of this chapter (also review Chaps. 4 and 7) in order to be able provide answers to typical parent questions.

1. Tell parents that the children are being taught how to be a good winner. Many children in our classes have an inappropriate social goal—to win at all costs. Accepted children value continuing relationships over winning, and

that's what we hope to start changing in their children.
2. Review the parent handout, "Cultural Differences between Boys and Girls" [there is no group leader guide, as the handout is read without further explanation].

Child Session Plan 10

Homework Review

1. *Review play date.* Ask who did play-date homework and pick only children who did. Allow them to report their play date only if it followed the rules. If not, cut them off and ask who did the homework assignment. Questions to ask: Name one thing you did. What was your favorite part? Did you call first to figure out what to do? Who got to pick the games? Did your guest have a good time? Did you have a good time?
2. To the group as a whole, ask if anyone "made fun of the tease." Correct children who didn't do it properly by asking the group, "What would be a good way to make fun of the tease?" Briefly practice this technique by having each child come up with one way of "making fun of the tease" and correcting errors.
3. Ask if anyone was unjustly accused by an adult and review with the child how he or she handled it. Correct errors that the child made, if necessary.

Clinical Example of Homework Compliance

Unjustly Accused by Mom

A fifth-grade girl said her mom accused her of taking her ring. She said, "No, I didn't take it," and suggested her mom look in her bedroom again. Her mother subsequently found the ring in the bedroom. The child was praised for "keep-

---

[3]*Best* is a new playmate never played with individually before (can be someone the child has known for a while but never invited over). *Next best* is someone they haven't invited over in a long while that used to be friends. *Third best* is someone they invite over rarely. *Fourth best* is another present good friend.

ing her cool" and responding appropriately to being unjustly accused.

Didactic

Until now the focus has been on getting along with the other members of a team the child has slipped into. Now the focus shifts more broadly to everyone in the game. The "rules for a good winner" are presented using a Socratic method (see Table 10.1). The group leader keeps in mind the template for the rules in the session plan.

1. Quickly present the rules for being a good winner:
   (a) Praise or "high-five" your teammates.
   (b) Praise the other team for a good game or really trying.[4]
   (c) Pretend that winning was not important to you.
   (d) *Don't* laugh or tease the other team members—in the future you may be asking them to play with you.
2. You are to use tokens again in the real play portion. Remind children about tokens for deck play—tokens count as stars.

Clinical Example of Presenting Rules for a Good Winner

GL: How can you be a good winner?

Child: You shouldn't throw a big party if you've won.

Child: You could just say, "I won."

GL: You don't have to say it, everyone will know it. You can say, 'It was a great game."

Child: I usually say, "nice try."

Child: The coach usually makes us shake hands with everyone on the other side.

GL: Whose team might the "losers" be on next time?

Child: Maybe your team.

Homework Assignment

1. Invite a new child over for a play date.
2. Bring in outdoor team sport game.

Real Play

For the first time, the group leader lets the children choose their own games. The children are not generally ready to be team captains and choose team members. If you let them do this without structure, the better athletes will choose to be together against everyone else. This will make for an uneven match, angry feelings, and ultimately, chaos. Instead, the group leader chooses two teams approximately matched for size, speed, and ability. Some games are more ideal for teaching purposes than others. Tokens continue to help to promote good sportsmanship and keep the tone cooperative and positive (consult the game rules for this session for reminders on how to deliver tokens). The following is a general template for game play:

1. Allow children to pick their own games and spontaneously use joining techniques to join in other's games (rules for Magic Johnson basketball and soccer are provided again in case they pick these games).
   - Advise the children that games that involve a significant risk of embarrassing or injuring a peer will not be helpful in developing new friendships.[5]
   - Help them pick games in which the children control the flow of activities without any adult intervention (e.g., basketball, soccer, or volleyball).
   - Avoid waiting games like Capture the Flag and Prisoner, where the children are called out a couple at a time, as they offer less opportunity for giving compliments.
2. Have the children vote on the game they will play before heading out to the play deck. The children don't all have to play the same game, although no one is allowed to play by him/herself. Girls can choose a different game than boys.
3. The group leader chooses sides of approximately equal ability.

---

[4]The children who are on the other team today may be deciding if they want the child to play with them next time.

[5]Examples are "Warball" (a variation on the game "Dodgeball" that involves more aggressive throwing of the ball at members of the other team) and "Buns Up" (where part of the game involves a penalty whereby children have to bend over while their peers are allowed to hurl a ball at their buttocks).

4. Give out tokens for good sport/good winner behavior.
5. If play starts to get too rough, give "cool down" time to everyone, while explaining to the group that things were getting too rough and that they need to cool down and think about the rules.
6. At the end of play, count only the total number of group tokens, adding each child's tokens to the total. Have all the children count along. Avoid comparisons between children or pointing out who received the most tokens, as this will foster a counterproductive form of competition.
7. Ask children if they had a good time. Ask why they had a good time. (Answers: Because they made sure other children had a good time, everyone had an equal opportunity to shoot the ball, and no one was getting injured or intimidated by rough play.)

Clinical Examples of Children's Responses to Organizing Their Own Play

Spontaneous Organization of Play

Five second-grade boys decided to play basketball. The four second- and third-grade girls went to a different part of the play deck and organized a soccer game.

Spontaneous "Slipping In"

The children decided on two games: a Four Square handball game and a game of kickball. The children in Four Square saw the kickball game and all decided they wanted to play that game instead. The Four Square children slipped in appropriately (by waiting on the sidelines and then asking to join the side with fewer children).

Spontaneous Concern Over Injury

When one child fell and was (mildly) hurt, some of the children stopped playing to see if he was OK. They were given tokens for good sportsmanship.

Potential Problems

Breaking Old Habits 1

A sixth-grade boy in a basketball game charged aggressively up to the boy he was guarding, began flailing his arms, and then attempted to steal the ball from the other boy by wildly slapping at his arms, hands, and the basketball. The group leader gave him a prompt. He immediately stopped this behavior.

Breaking Old Habits 2

A fifth-grade boy with ADHD initially rebelled against the "no stealing" and "no rough contact" rules to a game of basketball. He loudly announced to the group "At my school we play Jungle Ball. We don't care if anyone gets hurt. That's just the way we play. I'm not going to play Sissy Ball." After reluctantly playing the game with the new set of rules, the boy admitted during debriefing that he had more fun in the less aggressive format.

End-of-Session Reunification

1. As soon as parents and children are reunited, the child group leader begins by praising the children (as a group) for what they did in this session. "Today we worked on being a good sport. I saw a lot of good sports in this group. Let's all give the children a big round of applause for their effort."
2. The child leader continues with, "The major job everyone has this week is to make a play date.
3. Have each child name his or her play date guest and outside toy (team sports) for next time, in front of the parent.

Children's Friendship Training

Parent Handout—Session 10

Cultural Differences Between Boys and Girls

GOAL: To allow parents to recognize different patterns in boy and girl friendships.

Beginning by about second grade, boys and girls tend to segregate themselves from one another and develop different cultures.

1. Some girls may cross this boundary by being proficient in male interests (e.g., baseball, football).
2. Some boys and girls may maintain close cross-sex friendships in private but are reluctant to play with each other in public.
3. Cross-sex friendships (as well as same-sex friendships) are more beneficial when friends treat each other as equals.

Studies watching how children play suggest that the following are most important for parents to know:

Among acquaintances:

1. Girls tend to level status among themselves, whereas boys' groups are more likely to have a specifically designated leader.
2. Girls tend to play in smaller groups (usually two or three) than boys.
3. Girls who are proficient in male activities (e.g., baseball) may continue to be accepted by both sexes. Well-liked boys tend to be accepted by both sexes.

Among close friends:

1. Some girls (but not all) form "cliques" with other girls, whereas boys have two levels of closer friends, "favored few" and "very best friends."
2. Girls' friendships tend to be more exclusive, with new friendships replacing, rather than adding to, old ones.
3. Boys' close friends tend to share activity interests and physical skills, whereas girls' close friends tend to share conversation.

Children's Friendship Training

Child Sessions 10 and 11

Rules for Magic Johnson Basketball

Gather Children

1. Tell children that tokens will be given to those who praise others or give "high-fives," follow any "rule of being a good sport" or "rule of being a good winner," or are considerate of others in any way.

Assign Sides

2. The group leader chooses sides of approximately equal ability.

Tell Game Rules

3. Rules of a regular basketball game are used, except the primary emphasis is on cooperative team play and the following behaviors earn prompts and time outs:
   - Stealing the ball or attempts thereof.
   - Aggressive physical contact (e.g., fouling others by slapping instead of just blocking or excessive, stifling defense that intimidates the other child).
   - Trying to keep score.
   - Excess celebration after a score.
   - The ball must be passed at least once prior to a goal being scored.

Start the Game, Monitor and Control Behavior

4. Children who "ball hog" excessively lose their opportunity to shoot any baskets (they are only allowed to rebound, dribble and pass the ball to others).

Core Instruction

5. Tokens are given for any behavior related to the rules of a good sport/winner. Do not give tokens for anything else, such as, eye contact or saying other person's name, as this will dilute the focus on good sportsmanship. How to give tokens:
   (a) Move in and out of play among the children, much as a basketball referee does.
   (b) Receiving a token should cause only a momentary disruption of the child's attention to the game.
   (c) Speak telegraphically to state why a child earned a specific token, while handing the child the token. Examples: "for being gentle just now," "for giving a 'high-five.'"
   (d) Withhold tokens if children look or ask for one after doing a desired behavior (but praise them for the behavior). Some children will begin "performing" in front of the coaches with the sole desire of obtaining the token and losing focus on the other aspects of the game being played.
   (e) If a child argues with you over not being given a token, give the child a prompt, followed by a time out if the arguing continues.

Debriefing at the End of Game

6. Count only the total number of group tokens, adding each child's tokens to the total. Have all the children count along. Avoid comparisons between children or pointing out who received the most tokens, as this will foster a counterproductive form of competition.

7. Ask children if they had a good time. Ask why they had a good time. (Answers: Because they made sure other children had a good time, everyone had an equal opportunity to shoot the ball, and no one was getting injured or intimidated by rough play.)

Children's Friendship Training

Child Sessions 10 and 11

Rules for Soccer

Gather Children

1. Gather children in two groups for two concurrent games (such as one small game of soccer and one game of basketball or handball).

Assign Sides

2. Assign two teams as evenly as possible, based on children's athletic talents and pick the first goalies (children seldom want to be goalie because he/she stays in one place).

Tell Game Rules

3. Do not keep score and direct children not to.
4. Children have to pass constantly between at least two children.
5. The following behaviors earn prompts and time outs: Ball hogging, trying to keep score, bumping, playing with physical aggression, kicking a ball directly into another child, diving at the ball recklessly, or excessive and inappropriate celebration after scoring.

Start the Game, Monitor and Control Behavior

6. Encourage each team to rotate goalies regularly and by themselves. If this doesn't happen spontaneously, do it for them.
7. If one player is left out of scoring goals, stop the game and ask the team members how they are going to work the child into the next goal.

Core Instruction

8. Tokens are given for any behavior related to the rules of a good sport/winner. Do not give tokens for anything else, such as, eye contact or saying the other person's name, as this will dilute the focus on good sportsmanship. How to give tokens:
   (a) Move in and out of play among the children, much as a basketball referee does.
   (b) Receiving a token should cause only a momentary disruption of the child's attention to the game.
   (c) Speak telegraphically to state why a child earned a specific token, while handing the child the token. Examples "for being gentle just now," "for giving a 'high-five.'"
   (d) Withhold tokens if children look or ask for one after doing a desired behavior (but praise them for the behavior). Some children will begin "performing" in front of the coaches with the sole desire of obtaining the token and losing focus on the other aspects of the game being played.
   (e) If a child argues with you over not being given a token, give the child a prompt, followed by a time out if the arguing continues.

Debriefing at the End of Game

9. Count only the total number of group tokens, adding each child's tokens to the total.
10. Have all the children count along. Avoid comparisons between children or pointing out who received the most tokens, as this will foster a counterproductive form of competition.
11. Ask children if they had a good time. Ask why they had a good time (Answers: Because they made sure other children had a good time, everyone had an equal opportunity to shoot the ball, and no one was getting injured or intimidated by rough play.)

PART III

CHAPTER

19

Avoiding Physical Fights

Treatment Rationale

The combination of peer rejection and aggression is a prognostic red flag for children. This combination occurs in a substantial minority of children enrolled in social skills programs. The treatment hypothesis is that parents and children may be provided with more effective ways to view the situation and how to obtain effective help. The material in this session provides parents with the foundation to intervene when their child gets into physical fights with peers. It also alerts children about the consequences of physical aggression and strategies for avoiding peers who get into fights.

19.1 Importance of Avoiding Conflict

Aggressive children are also quick to respond to provocation. Dodge, McCluskey, and Feldman (1985) reported that a child's response to provocation was one of the most problematic situations identified by teachers and clinicians. Bryant (1992) found that fourth- and sixth-grade children who were liked by peers were more likely to use a calm approach to resolve conflicts. In contrast, sociometrically rejected and controversial children were viewed as using an aggressive retaliation social goal more than were popular, neglected, and average children (cf. Chap. 13 for a review of social goals).

19.2 Definition and Sex Differences in Aggression

Aggression can be defined broadly as achieving goals in a coercive manner. Methods of coercion differ between the sexes. Boys use more physical confrontation whereas girls use more verbal confrontation in the form of "relational aggression" (cf. Chap. 9). Boys' conflicts are typically motivated by power assertion, whereas girls' conflicts involve the "he said/she said" dispute, "e.g., 'And Stephen said that you said that I was showin' off just because I had that blouse on'" (Hartup & Laursen, 1993, p. 56). Frankel (1996) distinguished between frequent fighters, who are nonselective in their targets and generally aggressive (cf. Patterson, 1986), versus bullies, who are very selective in targets and not generally aggressive (cf. Chap. 16; Olweus, 1993). Frequent fighters represent a portion of children who victimize others (Coie, Christopoulos, Terry, Dodge, & Lochman, 1989). When these boys' attempts at dominance are resisted, they continue to fight until the victim submits.

Grotpeter and Crick (1996) found that the prevalence of physical aggression in boys was matched by the prevalence of relational aggression in girls. The sequelae were also similar for both types of aggression: peer ratings of dislike, greater feelings of loneliness and depression. One difference between the types of aggression was that teachers were less able to detect relational

164

aggression than physical aggression (cf. French, 1990). Crick (1996) conducted a longer term study (over the course of a school year) for third through sixth graders. Crick found that the stability of relational aggression over 9 months for girls (r = .78) exceeded that for overt aggression for boys (r = .68) during the same period. Relational aggression at the beginning of the school year aided prediction of peer rejection for girls but not boys at the end of the year. Follow-up studies of physically aggressive, rejected boys have pointed to a poorer long-term adjustment. However, similar studies have yet to be done on relationally aggressive girls.

19.3 Comorbidity of Peer Rejection and Aggression

Aggressive behavior is highly predictive of rejection (Newcomb et al., 1993) and may precede it (Coie & Kupersmidt, 1983). Approximately 30% to 50% of rejected boys are also aggressive (Cillesson, van Ijzendoorn, Van Lieshout, & Hartup, 1992; Coie et al., 1989). Rejected boys who are also aggressive are also less likely to have best friends (Kupersmidt, DeRosier, & Patterson, 1995).

Coie et al. (1989) suggested that the aggression and peer rejection are generally additive in their adverse effects on longer term outcome. Bierman and Wargo (1995), in a 2-year follow-up study of 81 youths, 8 to 20 years old found that aggressive-rejected children were far more likely to experience negative behavioral and social outcomes than aggressive-nonrejected or nonaggressive-rejected children were. Wentzel and Asher (1995) reported that rejected children who are also aggressive are at higher risk for school drop-out and later criminality.

19.4 Developmental Trajectories of Children With Aggression

Aggression becomes a prognostic red flag by second or third grade. First graders who are ranked high on unprovoked aggression actually tend to be more popular. This is probably because frequency of aggression is confounded with frequency of interaction and aggression is more the norm among first-grade boys. This changes dramatically by third grade, where aggression is clearly not the norm.

Aggression among first graders is primarily in response to provocation (reactive aggression; cf. Chap. 6), whereas aggression among third graders is primarily unprovoked (Coie et al., 1989). According to Schwartz et al. (1997), rejected-aggressive third-grade boys escalate their aggression if resisted and continue to fight until the victim submits. Aggressive nonrejected boys don't tend to persist. Aggressive-rejected boys are twice as likely to form relationships with other high-conflict children as nonaggressive-rejected boys, with each boy disliking the other. These authors summarized the developmental changes as follows:

> As boys grow older, they begin to recognize when it makes sense to let some negative exchanges pass without comments or overt reaction. Rejected boys do not seem to keep pace with these changing norms for aggressive behavior. They continue to use direct aggression as a way of getting what they want. . . . While, on the surface of things, they may seem to be getting away with this inappropriate behavior, to the extent that other boys fail to reciprocate, they also pay a serious price for this social deviance. Other boys dislike them and increasingly avoid interacting with them . . . they become limited in their choice of relationships to boys who are much like themselves. (p. 233)

Patterson, DeBaryshe, and Ramsey (1989) described the results of their long-term follow-up research on a cohort of highly aggressive boys. Early concomitants of child conduct problems were poor parental discipline and inadequate parental monitoring of free time. Some of these children went on to be rejected by peers and experienced academic failure in middle childhood. In late childhood and adolescence this evolved into acceptance by a deviant peer group and delinquency. Clearly, moving children out of the rejected category and promoting association with friends who don't have antisocial interests can have a great impact on eventual outcome.

19.5 Research on Cognitive Bias and Aggression

One approach to treating aggressive behavior has been suggested by social cognitive studies. Early studies (cf. Dodge et al., 1986) identified aggressive children as having negatively biased social perceptions to ambiguous or accidental circumstances. For example, they attribute malevolent intent toward a peer brushing by and knocking over blocks with which they are building. Studies of fifth graders (Bell-Dolan, 1995), and third through sixth graders (Quiggle, Garber, Panak, & Dodge, 1992) demonstrate that this may not be a factor unique to aggressive children. Results showed that anxious children tended to misinterpret nonhostile situations as hostile more than children who were not anxious. The difference between these two populations was that the aggressive child was more likely to use an aggressive response and the anxious child was more likely to withdraw in response to ambiguous or negative cues from peers (Quiggle et al., 1992).

The negative cognitive bias of aggressive and anxious children may either cause their behavior or result from their realistic expectancies of social responses to their behavior (e.g., the effects of a negative reputation in the case of aggressive-rejected children; cf. Chap. 11). An important research question is wheather the biases decrease with successful peer experiences or whether they need to be specifically addressed during intervention. This research is currently in the planning stages.

19.6 Implications From Research and Clinical Practice

Aggression considerably worsens the prognosis for the rejected child and increases the probability that the child will exclusively associate with other aggressive children. These are friends of desperation, because the children do not rate these friendships positively. Parents can exacerbate this situation in two ways. First, they may encourage association with other aggressive children. Second, they may support their rejected child's misinterpretation of nonhostile acts as hostile. As parents begin to see positive changes in peer relations as a result of treatment, it may be helpful to instruct them on how to recognize and avoid this potential pitfall.

How to Conduct the Session

Until Now

Children are continuing to have supervised play dates with different guests. Parents and children are continuing to evaluate how different playmates behave and get along with their child on play dates.

In This Session

The most important work of this session is to help parents and children make sound choices in continuing to build the child's friendship network. Some children will be ready to accept invitations to other children's houses for play dates. Parents will be prepared for this event. The instructional focus (session handout) for parents turns to how to deal with their children's aggressive behavior. As reviewed in Chap. 3 and this chapter, only 30% of children with peer problems also have problems with aggression, so that this handout will only apply to a minority of parents.

Parent Session Plan 11

Initial Gathering

1. Check child toys as they come in. Have parents hold toys that are in excluded categories.[1]

Homework Review

1. There are two homework assignments (not including outside toy) and not enough time to review all in depth. Tell parents that you want them to focus on (a) the out-of-group call, which led up to (b) the play date.
2. For the out-of-group call: (a) Was the other child interested or excited by the call, and (b) did the children have things to talk about (in a two-way conversation)?

---

[1]*Dangerous/aggressive toys*—martial arts toys, Super Soakers, water balloons; *solitary/parallel play*—books, skateboards; *too good a toy*—expensive ball that will upset the child if lost.

3. Recount the fourth play date: (a) Was a parent there to supervise? (b) Did the parent have to intervene to enforce the good host rules? Did the child comply with the rule? Is this getting better? (c) Did the parent try to get to know the other child's parents? (d) Compare the four play dates with each other. What was the child's evaluation?

4. Remind parents that play dates are an important step to having a best friend. Best friends are the child's first exposure to "true love." Good best friends like each other enough to patch over minor differences and to be considerate of each other. They value being with each other more than having to play video games. They have little trouble coming up with things they both like to do and are autonomous in this respect during play dates.

Clinical Examples of Changes Brought About by Play-Date Homework Compliance

Going Outside of His Circle

The mother of a third grader reported that her son avoided meeting new children and tried to stick with his one good friend. She noted that because it was homework for the class, he asked four other boys on play dates that he wouldn't have were it not for the class. Her son got along very well with two of the boys and will be playing more with them in the future. The group leader suggested that this might take some pressure off the preexisting friendship. Her child will not be alone if his best friend is playing with other boys at recess that he doesn't like. He now has other friends to hang around with.

Children Don't Have to Be Friends

The mother of a third grade girl reported that she used to make her daughter get together with another girl, even though she didn't like this girl and they quickly ran out of things to do on play dates. After inviting over three other girls, she and her daughter realized that her daughter had better play dates with girls that they both liked.

Potential Problem
The Other Child Was Not a Good Host

Parents are concerned that when children have play dates at another child's house, they see that others may not follow good host rules. The group leader suggested the following guidelines: "When in our house we follow our rules but we can't force other people to do the right thing. When you're in somebody else's house you still have to try to be a good guest, even if the other child is not being a good host." The child does not have to accept invitations to a poor host's house.

Homework Assignment

Most parents will have arranged four or five play dates with different children. Parents who still have to intervene to enforce the rules of a good host should continue having play-dates only at their house. The remaining parents may be ready to accept play date invitations for their child to another child's house. Therefore, this is a good time to review what parents should do when accepting invitations for their child to play at another house (points 3 and 4):

1. Continue to schedule play dates. Think of a new child for next week.[2]
2. Tell parents, "If parents let their child accept an invitation to another child's house before they are ready, they may misbehave. Other parents will not usually tell you about his, they will just get busy the next time you want to invite their child over to your house and never invite you back. (Parents should feel free to do this with a guest that doesn't work out for their child.)"
3. If at least three play dates have gone well without any reminders to follow a good host rule, then parents can begin accepting invitations

---

[2]*Best* is a new playmate never played with individually before (can be someone the child has known for a while but never invited over). *Next best* is someone they haven't invited over in a long while who used to be friends. *Third best* is someone they invite over rarely. *Fourth best* is another present good friend.

for their child to another child's house. When they get the call, parents should check with their child (out of range of phone). They should accept only if their child wants it. If the child doesn't want it, the parent should make up an excuse for not arranging a play date (we're busy, we'll get back to you . . .). Sometimes children will change their minds about a playmate, so keep options open.

4. At the time of play date at another child's house: Parents should not just drop off and pick up, they should come in and chat with the other parent (especially at pick-up time). Out of the corner of their eye, they can watch their child playing and get to know the other parent a little bit to see how comfortable they are sending their child over.

5. Next week is graduation. We supply the pizza and drinks and parents supply desserts to make it more festive. Parent should either buy desserts—a little for everyone, or make, for example, brownies and cut up in little pieces so that everyone gets one. (a) Siblings have to stay in the parent room; (b) no friends and no pictures because of confidentiality. Session 12 will be 1½ hours long for graduation. Announce room and time changes.

6. Why a graduation party? Finality and sense of accomplishment for the children. Cite the "Wizard of Oz" effect, that the three characters did lots of difficult tasks but didn't feel any better about themselves until they each got a token of appreciation at the end.

Parent Handout

The first handout is essentially a debriefing script that parents can employ when their child gets into trouble at school for aggressive behavior. The child will invariably give a justification for his or her behavior (he or she was provoked) or a denial (he or she has been wrongly accused because the teacher likes to pick on him or her). This may apply even when the child attacked without provocation, has physically attacked another after a verbal provocation, or was finally caught by a teacher after a continuing pattern of attacks.

Parents can give conflicting messages by unconditional acceptance of the child's story. The handout addresses how parents can best respond to the child's version of the negative report from the teacher. Because the handout isn't concerned with "getting to the bottom of things," parents are usually silent when they listen to the presentation.

1. Review parent handout, "Decreasing Physical Fights between Your Child and Others" (no group leader guide). Some parents (usually dads) will take issue with the approach advocated in the handout and will advocate their child responding in an aggressive fashion. The group leader can raise issues such as "How do you know your child's account is accurate?" "What's the message you give when you encourage fighting back?" "How might hitting a bully backfire?"

2. Review second parent handout, "Graduation Party Handout" (no group leader guide). Address any changes in time and location.[3] The parents should handle any nonmainstream food restrictions. For instance, Orthodox Jewish participants can provide their own kosher foods. Children need to have a good time and not feel excluded (i.e., "My parents don't allow me to eat any of the things on the table"). Therefore, now is not the time for parents to enforce a sugar ban or to bring in "healthy foods" that none of the children will eat.

Child Session Plan 11

Homework Eeview

1. *Review play date*. Ask who did play-date homework and pick only children who did. Allow them to tell about their play date only if it followed the rules. If not, cut them off and ask who did the homework assignment. Questions to ask each child: Name one thing you did. What was your favorite part? Name something that didn't go so well. Did you call first to figure out what to do? What did you decide to do? Did you do what you decided on the phone? Who got to pick the games? Did your guest have a good time? Did you have a good time?

---

[3]Parents are to provide treats because they can do it better than group leaders can. It is also a standard social role for parents during their child's life transitions.

2. Ask if anyone was unjustly accused by an adult and review with the child how they handled it. Correct errors that they made, if necessary.

Didactic

The purpose of this didactic presentation is to set the tone for subsequent verbal exchange with peers and parents. The frame of reference adopted is that other children (labeled as "bullies" for ease of explanation and acceptance by the children) are aggressive and the aggressive acts get them in trouble. Aggressive children should be avoided (now that the children have alternatives due to having play dates with well-behaved children). Present the following *without* using a Socratic method:

1. Ask the children: What is a bully? What is the problem with being a bully? What happens when they are caught? What happens when they get older? Does anyone know a bully who gets good grades? Some kids aren't bullies but they like to dress and act like they are in a gang. What's wrong with that?
2. Ways to stay out of a fight:
   Avoid the bully, play somewhere else, don't talk to them.
   Get involved with other children who are playing—bullies like to pick on kids when they are by themselves.
   Play near an adult supervisor.
   Don't do anything to provoke the bully (teasing, making faces, tattling for silly things, etc.).
   Don't watch other children fighting or try to break it up—you may get in trouble.

Homework Assignment

1. Invite a new child over for a play date (no toy for next session).

Note: Announce that Session 12 will be 1½ hours long for graduation, and room and time changes, if applicable.

Tell the children that they will fill out some forms (pos/tests) and what the program will provide (the UCLA program provides pizza and drinks) and that their parents will provide the rest (treats and desserts). They will watch part of a video, which the program will provide. Some children may ask to bring their own choice of movies. The group leader should discourage this, as there may be inappropriate scenes (even in PG-rated movies).

Real Play

The real play portion of this session is identical to that of Session 10. The following is a general template for game play:

1. Allow children to pick their own games and spontaneously use "slipping in" techniques to join in other's games (rules for Magic Johnson basketball and Soccer are provided again in case they pick these games).
   (a) Advise the children that games that involve a significant risk of embarrassing or injuring a peer will not be helpful in developing new friendships.[4]
   (b) Help them pick games in which the children control the flow of activities without any adult intervention (e.g., basketball, soccer, or volleyball).
   (c) Avoid waiting games like Capture the Flag and Prisoner, where the children are called out a couple at a time, as they offer less opportunity for giving compliments.
2. Have the children vote on the game they will play before heading out to the play deck. The children don't all have to play the same game, although no one is allowed to play by him/herself. Girls can choose a different game than boys.
3. The group leader chooses sides of approximately equal ability.
4. Give out tokens for good sport/good winner behavior.
5. If play starts to get too rough, give "cool down" time to everyone, while explaining to the group that things were getting too rough and that they need to cool down and think about the rules.

[4]Examples are "War Ball" (a variation on the game "Dodge Ball" that involves more aggressive throwing of the ball at members of the other team) and "Buns Up" (where part of the game involves a penalty whereby children have to bend over while their peers are allowed to hurl a ball at their buttocks).

6. Count only the total number of group tokens, adding each child's tokens to the total. Have all the children count along. Avoid comparisons between children or pointing out who received the most tokens, as this will foster a counterproductive form of competition.

7. Ask children if they had a good time. Ask why they had a good time (Answers: because they made sure other children had a good time, everyone had an equal opportunity to shoot the ball, and no one was getting injured or intimidated by rough play).

End-of-Session Reunification

1. Announce, "Today we worked on being a good sport. I saw a lot of good sports in this group. Let's all give the children a big round of applause."

2. The child leader continues with, "The major job everyone has this week is to make a play date."

3. Go around the room, and one by one make sure parent and child agree on a plan for whom to call for the play date (no toy to be brought for next session).

Children's Friendship Training

Parent Handout—Session 11

Decreasing Physical Fights Between Your Child and Others

Long-term studies show that children who have difficulty with peers and also get into physical fights have a much worse outcome. The evidence is clear that physical fights must be discouraged.

1. Do not support fighting, even in self-defense (you never know that it was truly self defense).
2. Ask for your child's view of the incident—say nothing supportive (unless he or she states ways he or she tried to stay out of the fight).
3. Help your child figure out something better to do the next time the situation arises. "Fighting is never a good choice. What will you do the next time someone takes your ball?" Some things to try next time:

Provocation—Another child . . .	*Next time, you should first try to . . .*
Is playing with a toy he doesn't know is yours.	Tell him that it's yours.
Frequently takes away a ball or toy of yours.	Older children—show no reaction. Younger children—tell an adult.
Teases you.	Use the "make fun of the tease" technique.
Hits, pushes you.	Stay out of arm's reach. Hang around with other kids. Stay near the yard monitor.
Intrudes on group game.	Let the other kids handle it.

4. Attempt to secure a promise from your child to try this next time.
5. **Provide an immediate, brief consequence for fighting each time it occurs.**
   - Select a consequence you can enforce.
   - The consequence should be brief (grounding for a couple of hours on the day of the fight is better than grounding for longer periods).
   - The consequence should not be fun: no games, TV, pleasant conversation, team sport, scout meeting, and so on.
   - State the precise consequence before beginning it, for example, "I'm glad we came up with something better for you to try next time. But for now, I will have to ground you until 6:00 p.m. No TV or games until then."
6. After the consequence is over, do not discuss it further—"wipe the slate clean."
7. **If this is not effective—seek professional help.**

The most effective approach for this is parent training, in which you work one-on-one or in a group with a counselor, usually over no more than 6 to 12 sessions, designing and trying different approaches.

Children's Friendship Training

Graduation Party Assignment—Given on Session 11

Due on Session 12

Time:

The party will begin ½ hour before our regular start time.

Place:

_____

We supply:

Decorations, pizza, and drinks.

Parents supply:

Desserts to make it more festive. Parents can either purchase or make treats for the children. Parents are encouraged to bring "fun" desserts (such as cupcakes and donuts) that their children will perceive as a treat (and a reward for their hard work), rather than healthy (but generally less desirous) selections (such as celery sticks, fruit salad, diet cookies, fruit "roll ups," etc.).

Other guidelines:

1. Siblings may be brought but must stay in the parents' room until the graduation ceremony.
2. Due to concerns about confidentiality, no friends are allowed to attend and no photography is allowed.

Children's Friendship Training

Child Sessions 10 and 11

Rules for Magic Johnson Basketball

Gather Children

1. Tell children that tokens will be given to those who praise others or give "high-fives," follow any "rule of being a good sport" or "rule of being a good winner," or are considerate of others in any way.

Assign Sides

2. The group leader chooses sides of approximately equal ability.

Tell Game Rules

3. Rules of a regular basketball game are used, except the primary emphasis is on cooperative team play and the following behaviors earn prompts and time outs:
   - Stealing the ball or attempts at it.
   - Aggressive physical contact (e.g., fouling others by slapping instead of just blocking or excessive, stifling defense that intimidates the other child).
   - Trying to keep score.
   - Excess celebration after a score.
   - The ball must be passed at least once prior to a goal being scored.

Start the Game, Monitor and Control Behavior

4. Children who "ball hog" excessively lose their opportunity to shoot any baskets (they are only allowed to rebound, dribble and pass the ball to others).

Core Instruction

5. Tokens are given for any behavior related to the rules of a good sport/winner. Do not give tokens for anything else, such as, eye contact or saying other person's name, as this will dilute the focus on good sportsmanship. How to give tokens:
   (a) Move in and out of play among the children, much as a basketball referee does.
   (b) Receiving a token should cause only a momentary disruption of the child's attention to the game.
   (c) Speak telegraphically to state why a child earned a specific token, while handing the child the token. Examples: "for being gentle just now," "for giving a 'high-five'."
   (d) Withhold tokens if children look or ask for one after doing a desired behavior (but praise them for the behavior). Some children will begin "performing" in front of the coaches with the sole desire of obtaining the token and losing focus on the other aspects of the game being played.
   (e) If a child argues with you over not being given a token, give the child a prompt, followed by a time out if the arguing continues.

Debriefing at the End of Game

6. Count only the total number of group tokens, adding each child's tokens to the total. Have all the children count along. Avoid comparisons between children or pointing out who received the most tokens, as this will foster a counterproductive form of competition.

7. Ask children if they had a good time. Ask why they had a good time (Answers: Because they made sure other children had a good time, everyone had an equal opportunity to shoot the ball, and no one was getting injured or intimidated by rough play).

Children's Friendship Training

Child Sessions 10 and 11

Rules for Soccer

Gather Children

1. Gather children in two groups for two concurrent games (such as one small game of soccer and one game of basketball or handball).

Assign Sides

2. Assign two teams as evenly as possible, based on children's athletic talents, and pick the first goalies (children seldom want to be goalie because he or she stays in one place).

Tell Game Rules

3. Do not keep score and direct children not to.

4. Children have to pass constantly between at least two children.

5. The following behaviors earn prompts and time outs: ball hogging, trying to keep score, bumping, playing with physical aggression, kicking a ball directly into another child, diving at the ball recklessly, or excessive and inappropriate celebration after scoring.

Start the Game, Monitor and Control Behavior

6. Encourage each team to rotate goalies regularly and by themselves. If this doesn't happen spontaneously, do it for them.

7. If one player is left out of scoring goals, stop the game and ask the team members how they are going to work the child into the next goal.

Core Instruction

8. Tokens are given for any behavior related to the rules of a good sport/winner. Do not give tokens for anything else, such as, eye contact or saying other person's name, as this will dilute the focus on good sportsmanship. How to give tokens:

    (a) Move in and out of play among the children, much as a basketball referee does.

    (b) Receiving a token should cause only a momentary disruption of the child's attention to the game.

    (c) Speak telegraphically to state why a child earned a specific token, while handing the child the token. Examples: "for being gentle just now," "for giving a 'high-five.'"

    (d) Withhold tokens if children look or ask for one after doing a desired behavior (but praise them for the behavior). Some children will begin "performing" in front of the coaches with the sole desire of obtaining the token and losing focus on the other aspects of the game being played.

    (e) If a child argues with you over not being given a token, give the child a prompt, followed by a time out if the arguing continues.

Debriefing at the End of Game

9. Count only the total number of group tokens, adding each child's tokens to the total. Have all the children count along. Avoid comparisons between children or pointing out who received the most tokens, as this will foster a counterproductive form of competition.

10. Ask children if they had a good time. Ask why they had a good time. (Answers: because they made sure other children had a good time, everyone had an equal opportunity to shoot the ball, and no one was getting injured or intimidated by rough play.)

Graduation

Treatment Rationale

A formal graduation ceremony is an essential feature of time-limited group treatment. The instruction or treatment phase is over and the "life-application phase" begins. The treatment hypothesis is that urging parents to continue the types of play supervision initiated during treatment, having a final ceremony, and encouraging parents to check back for outcome feedback will facilitate maintenance of treatment gains.

Many parents feel that children need to be in adult-structured activities (Scouts and teams) in order to continue to promote their friendships. This alone isn't effective for the friendless child because he or she is likely to repeat the patterns of behaviors that impair relationships with peers. Parents need to be aware that the patterns they set up during treatment need to continue in order for their children to progress and that continuing supervised play dates are the most important activity to continue their child's progress.

20.1 Advantages and Disadvantages of Adult-Structured Activities

We define *adult-structured activities* as formalized activities in which the adults determine most of the play choices for children. Examples are karate classes, Little League baseball, Cub Scouts, and AYSO soccer. Ladd and Price (1987) found that 83% of parents of kindergartners involve their children in adult-structured activities. Parke & Bhavnagri (1989) reported that 78% of mothers report volunteering to help out at least occasionally in one such activity. They report an increase in participation in these activities with the age of the child, peaking among preadolescent children.

Ladd and Price (1987) and Bryant (1985) reported that involvement in adult-structured activities is not significantly related to social adjustment. Bryant (1989) found that social perspective taking was negatively linked to involvement in organizations such as Scouts and teams among children of unemployed mothers but positively linked among children of mothers who were employed full time.

Belka (1994) had the following criticisms of games that are organized and led by adults:

1. They are elitist—they favor highly skilled children. In an elimination game, the children who need to play the most are eliminated first.
2. There has been no evidence forthcoming that games burn up excess energy so that children learn better in academic subjects.
3. Many games emphasize standing, not participation and learning. Some games force children to wait up to 90% of the time on the sidelines.
4. In a typical game, children don't receive any direct instruction on the physical elements of the game.

In contrast to the negative aspects of adult-structured activities, Dishion, Andrews, and Crosby (1995) found that 73% of best friends in their study originally met children in school or some other structured activity (71% lived within three blocks of each other). They found that best friends who meet through school and organized activities are less at risk for problematic behavior than children who meet each other through unsupervised settings. Therefore, the most important social contributions from adult-structured activities occur immediately before and after the meetings (meeting new acquaintances and arranging play dates). Parents must not only maintain the adult-structured activities (because most of them depend on parent volunteers) and associated community networks, but must ensure that their children use them as a springboard to more intimate friendships (Parke & Bhavnagri, 1989).

Adult-structured activities have other indirect benefits. Hartup (1996) presented evidence that friends are most similar to each other in areas of high *reputational salience*. Areas high in *reputational salience* are more important in establishing a child's reputation among the peer group. One such area among boys is physical activity (Challman, 1932). In other words, boys who like physical activities tend to be friends with other boys who feel the same about physical activities (and similarly for boys who dislike physical activities). Athletically inclined boys would more easily meet each other through adult-structured sports, whereas boys who disdain sports might find each other through Scouts or classes.

20.2 Importance of Children Organizing Their Own Games

According to Devereux (1976), the adult-structured sports activity "is threatening to wipe out the spontaneous culture of free play and games among American children, and it is therefore robbing our children not just of their childish fun but also of some of their most valuable learning experiences" (p. 38).

Devereux reviewed observational studies in England and Israel that documented thousands of games and their variants that children played spontaneously, without adult supervision of any kind. He contended that adult interest in organizing games for children has resulted in a decline of this subculture. Children are spending more time on fewer sports, abandoning the variety that former generations had. He cited an interview study of Little Leaguers reporting that 84% of them said they spent half to most of their leisure time on baseball. "Through their participation in a wide variety of different game types, in which the various elements of skill, chance, and strategy are variously recombined in gradually increasing complexity, children find an opportunity to experiment with different success styles and gain experience in a variety of cognitive and emotional processes which cannot yet be learned in full-scale cultural participation" (Devereux, 1976, p. 41). The variety of games children used to know made it more likely for less coordinated children to find their "niche" in group activities.

In organizing and playing games with each other, children have to deal with the fact that some rules are necessary and they must formulate fair rules so the games are fun for everyone (cf., Hart, 1993). Children also

> learn how to get a game started and somehow keep it going, as long as the fun lasts. How to pace it. When to quit for a while to get a round of cookies or just sit under a tree for a bit. How to recognize the subtle boundaries indicating that the game is really over—not an easy thing, since there are no innings, no winners or losers—and slide over to some other activity. (Devereux, 1976, pp. 48–49)

Ceremonies before the play begins (e.g., choosing sides, establishing rules, setting boundaries) are essential features of children's organized games. For instance in handball, children will spend what seems to adults endless time on disallowing different shots that they have names for: no Americans (ball hits wall before ground), no waterfalls (ball hits at a high angle and glances off the wall), no babies (ball makes a very small bounce right next to the wall), no poppies (ball hits wall and the ground at the same time). After about ten minutes of this, they will finally start the game.

20.3 Implications for Clinical Practice

Clearly, some of the most important benefits derived from after-school sports are gained before and after the adult-structured portion takes place. Children and parents meet each other and arrange to get together for play dates. Aside from that, adults can offer structured practice to develop children's athletic skills. Organized sports are to be encouraged for these components. However, there are clear limits to the benefits of adult-structured activities. Such activities should not play a dominant role in a child's life, such that there is no time left for self-generated play activities and play dates, which contribute to more intimate friendships. This is a message that parents need to hear in order to resist the temptation to commit their child's time to these activities to the exclusion of play dates and spontaneous activities organized by their children.

How to Conduct the Session

Until Now

Children have learned new ways of entering a group, sustaining play with positive affect, being a good host, and resisting teasing. They have learned how to gather useful information about their playmates to better organize play.

In This Session

Parent support and follow-through with homework assignments were most important in generalization during the intervention and will be most important in maintenance. Important evaluative feedback has come from parents reporting on homework assignments. How children were performing in session was of secondary importance and often is not indicative of skills demonstrated at home and in the schoolyard. Parents must be reminded of the importance of what they have done with their children. In order for gains to continue, parents and children must continue to work together using the methods set up during treatment.

Parent Session Plan 12

Additional Materials for This Session

1. Diplomas should be printed on fancy paper with each child's name and signed by the group leaders.
2. Party decorations, plates, and cups should be in hand.
3. A separate table should be set up in the children's room on which to place the food and drinks.
4. A VCR and monitor with a supply of screened, age-appropriate tapes should be set up in the children's room. The children will vote for the videotape that they would most like to see.

Initial Gathering

1. Prior to arrival, Pizza should be ordered to arrive at the start of the session. Decorate the child session room in a festive manner consistent with graduation (i.e., "Happy Graduation" garlands, colored streamers, party plates and disposable tablecloths). An extra table should be set up for food and drinks.
2. Have parents and children assemble outside both rooms until the session start time.
3. Have parents drop children and treats off in the child session room on the way to the parents' room. Parents may also elect to bring food for the parent session.

Homework Review

1. There are two homework assignments and not enough time to review all in depth. Tell parents that you want them to focus on (a) the out-of-group call, which led up to (b) the play date.
2. Recount the fifth play date: Was the parent there to supervise? Did the parent have to intervene to enforce the good host rules? Did the child comply with the rule? Is this getting better? Did parents try to get to know the other child's parents?
3. Ask if there were any play dates at another child's house: Did parents check if their child

wanted the play date before arranging it? Did parents stop by to chat with the host's parents?

4. Emphasize that parents are to continue having and monitoring play dates. This class helped them to start doing this with the goal of continuing the progress indefinitely.
5. Many children are now ready for (a) play dates considerably longer than 1½ hours (if a shorter play date went well with the new child), and (b) repeated play dates with the same child.
6. For developing best friends, children should concentrate on two to four other children, seeing them each at least two or three times each month.

Posttreatment Assessment and Debriefing

Because the session plan will present typical outcomes from this program and suggestions for maintenance of treatment gains, any outcome measures filled out by parents should be completed before the handout is given. It is also beneficial to have parents reauthorize their permission to call the child's teacher for posttesting at this point.

1. Have parents fill out posttreatment assessment forms and consents for teacher posttreatment calls (optional).[1]
2. Tell parents the typical results of comparing pre- versus posttesting: (a) 90% of parents report some improvement on the SSRS (play dates going better and on the road to best friends); (b) only 20% of children report low self-esteem at first, and of these, 80% report higher self-esteem on posttest; (c) 70% of teachers report improvement at school (peer reputation and acceptance by classmates).
3. Two points about these results: First, they depend on parents and children coming to a minimum of nine sessions and attempting to do homework assignments. Second, there is no guarantee that any child will improve.
4. Reasons for posttreatment assessment forms: (a) a commitment to keeping things constant so as to assure consistently successful outcomes,[2] (b) giving parents feedback on their child, and (c) assessing any changes made in

the program, to ensure that the changes have improved the program.

Parent Handout

1. Review parent handout, "Where to Go From Here" (no Group leader guide).

Potential Problems

Do We Have to Keep Up These Play Dates for the Rest of Our Child's Life?

The answer is a resounding "yes," at least through middle school. Play dates are not only a way of initiating friendships but also a way of maintaining and strengthening more intimacy with peers. Continuing the family practice of play dates in the home will also allow parents to better monitor children when they reach adolescence.

What About Family Time?

Family time is important, but it is equally important that children develop good peer relationships and best friendships. Many families like to spend part of a weekend together. It is also important to reserve play-date time and to arrange the play dates by mid-week.

"Fix My Child" and Tell Me About It Later

Some parents still seem to expect that group leaders will "do their thing" and then tell parents about it after the fact. After the last session, they want to know what the group leader has learned about their child in sessions. They think that this feedback will be valuable, although usually feedback like this has little effect on child or parent

[1]Postteacher calls are collected on the basis of positive continuing consent. If parents don't give a signed release to get the teacher call on this session, then no call is made, even if parents consented before treatment started.
[2]The results of assessment of each group of 10 children should be inspected to see that at least 90% of parent reports improve and at least 50% of teacher reports improve. (Children with ADHD not prescribed stimulants and children with an autism spectrum disorder prescribed medication are not expected to do as well on teacher report.)

behavior. No feedback like this is given (only that the important feedback came from the parents reporting on homework at the beginning of each session).

End-of-Session Reunification

1. Child and parents come together to have a graduation ceremony.

Child Session Plan 12

Posttesting

Expect the children will come in excited and "revved up." We give them the self-esteem form to fill out first (usually taking about 10 minutes) and then start the party.

1. Coaches monitor that the children are conscientiously and independently filling out forms, quietly answering any questions the children have.
2. Remind the children who finish early to remain quiet until all children complete the forms. Praise children for doing this, saying things like, "I like how quiet you are," or "You're being very considerate of the children who are still working."
3. The consequence for misbehavior is to miss part of the party (in 1-minute increments of time out outside of the room). Give prompts as usual, but not a time out until the actual party.

Party

Have a supply of videotapes on hand to show. You can provide the group with three choices and have them vote. Good tapes should be entertaining (after all, they are supposed to have fun at a party), without inappropriate messages, violence, or adult themes. Group leaders should personally screen them before showing them. Prosocial messages are unfortunately rare in movies these days. The movies may be silly.

Some movies to consider (we endorse none):

Fourth graders and below: *Beethoven* (1992), *Richie Rich* (1994), *Free Willy* (1993), *Bad News Bears* (1976), *Honey, I Shrunk the Kids* (1989), *Mrs. Doubtfire* (1993), *Short Circuit* (1986).

Fourth graders and above: *Back to the Future* (1985), *Clueless* (1995), *Angels in the Outfield* (1994).

Children usually don't mind if the movie doesn't finish before the graduation ceremony begins. If a child protests, the child can rent the movie at the local video store.

1. Play the movie, allowing about 15 minutes at the end of the session for the graduation ceremony. Children go to the table to get treats as they want.

End-of-Session Reunification (Graduation)

1. Bring the parents (and siblings) in from their room. Siblings may be allowed to have treats from the child session room at this time.
2. The ceremony should only take about 5 minutes (otherwise the children will be quite bored) and should be moderately corny. Begin the graduation ceremony, instructing the children as to how to receive their "diplomas."
3. Coaches and group leaders applaud after each child is given a diploma. Parents always join in.
4. After the last child is awarded his or her diploma, the group leader should give parents a round of applause for their part in the process.

Children's Friendship Training

Parent Handout—Session 12

Where to Go From Here

GOAL: To maintain and expand upon any gains realized from the group. **Making and keeping friends is something your child needs to do himself or herself, but you should support his or her efforts.**

1. The most important contribution you can make to your child's social development is to encourage informal, one-on-one play dates with two or three different children (more than this is not better).

   (a) You should continue to make and monitor weekly play dates with your child in the manner you have done for the homework assignments.

   (b) You and your child must select these children together. They should be convenient for your child to meet with, while also being easy for you to manage in your home.

   (c) Avoid scheduling play dates with children with whom your child does not get along.

   (d) Always find things to praise about your child's behavior after the play date is over.

   (e) Schedule the length of the play date to help success. Always schedule for a shorter period than you feel your child will be able to handle. Always schedule a short (e.g., 1-hour) first play date.

   (f) Try to get to know the parents of children with whom your child plays well. Be sure to talk to them when they pick up their child. You may be able to make regular dates after several successful play dates with one child.

2. Your child need not be friends with the most popular children:

   (a) "Popular" does not necessarily mean they are "nice."

   (b) Setting sights too high is asking for rejection.

   (c) Very often less popular children are more easily approached, have greater availability for play dates making for easier scheduling, and they often make better friends.

3. Activities that are structured by adults (Scouts, sports, classes) have important benefits for children, when:

   (a) They emphasize good sportsmanship rather than winning or losing.

   (b) They help children develop athletic skills or expose them to new experiences.

   (c) They allow children to make new friends through informal periods (before and after each activity).

   (d) They are not so demanding of a child's time that he or she has no time for close friendships.

5. Continue to provide consequences every time your child gets into a physical fight. The frequency of physical fights should get lower. If it does not, and it continues to be a problem, seek professional help. Our program coordinator is available to make referrals. Contact person phone number:_____

References

Achenbach, T. M. (1991). *Integrative guide for the CBCL/ 4–18, YSR, and TRF profiles.* Burlington: University of Vermont Department of Psychiatry.

Afifi, A., & Clark V. (1984). *Computer aided multivariate analysis.* Toronto: Lifetime Learning.

Aho, S. (1998). The teaser and the teased pupils at school. *Scandanavian Journal of Educational Research, 42,* 309–318.

Altman, I., & Taylor, D. (1973). *Social penetration: The development of interpersonal relationships.* New York: Holt, Rinehart & Winston.

Asher, S. R. (1983). Social competence and peer status: Recent advances and future directions. *Child Development, 54,* 1427–1434.

Asher, S. R. (1990). *Recent advances in the study of peer rejection.* In S. R. Asher & J. D. Coie (Eds.), Peer rejection in childhood (pp. 3–14). Cambridge: Cambridge University Press.

Asher, K. A., & Hymel S. (1981). *Children's social competence in peer relations: Sociometric and behavioral assessment.* In J. D. Wine & M. D. Smye (Eds.), Social competence (pp. 125–157). New York: Guilford.

Asher, S. R., Markell, R. A., & Hymel, S. (1981). Identifying children at risk in peer relations: A critique of the rate-of-interaction approach to assessment. *Child Development, 52,* 1239–1245.

Asher, S. R., Singleton, L. C., Tinsley, B. R., & Hymel, S. (1979). A reliable sociometric measure for preschool children. *Developmental Psychology, 15,* 443–444.

Asher, S. R., & Wheeler, V. A. (1985). Children's loneliness: A comparison of rejected and neglected peer status. *Journal of Consulting & Clinical Psychology, 53,* 500–505.

Atkins, M. S., & Stoff, D. M. (1993). Instrumental and hostile aggression in childhood disruptive behavior disorders. *Journal of Abnormal Child Psychology, 21,* 165–178.

Austin, A. M. B., & Draper, D. C. (1984). Verbal interactions of popular and rejected children with their friends and nonfriends. *Child Study Journal, 15,* 309–323.

Azmitia, M., & Montgomery, R. (1993). Friendship, transactive dialogues, and the development of scientific reasoning. *Social Development, 2,* 202–221.

Bagwell, C. L., Newcomb, A. F., & Bukowski, W. M. (1998). Preadolescent friendship and peer rejection as predictors of adult adjustment. *Child Development, 69,* 140–153.

Barkley, R. A. (1990). *Attention-deficit hyperactivity disorder.* New York: Guilford Press.

Barkley, R. A. (1991). *ADHD clinic parent interview.* Unpublished assessment outline. University of Massachusetts, School of Medicine, Worcester.

Barth, R. (1979). Home-based reinforcement of social behavior: A review & analysis. *Review of Educational Research, 49,* 436–458.

Bauminger, N., & Kasari, C. (2000). Loneliness and friendship in high-functioning children with autism. *Child Development, 71,* 447–456.

Bearison, D. J., & Gass, S. T. (1979). Hypothetical and practical reasoning: Children's persuasive appeals in different social contexts. *Child Development, 50,* 901–903.

Beelman, A., Pfingsten, U., & Lösel, F. (1994). Effects of training social competence in children: A meta-analysis of recent evaluation studies. *Journal of Clinical Child Psychology, 23,* 260–271.

Belka, D. E. (1994). *Teaching children games*. Oxford, OH: Human Kinetics.

Bell-Dolan, D. J. (1995). Social cue interpretation of anxious children. *Journal of Clinical Child Psychology, 24*, 2–10.

Bell-Dolan, D. J., Foster, S. L., & Christopher, J. S. (1992). Children's reactions to participating in a peer relations study: An example of cost-effective assessment. *Child Study Journal, 22*, 137–156.

Bell-Dolan, D. J., Foster, S. L., & Christopher, J. S. (1995). Girls' peer relations and internalizing problems: Are socially neglected, rejected, and withdrawn girls at risk? *Journal of Clinical Child Psychology, 24*, 463–473.

Bell-Dolan, D. J., Foster, S. L., & Sikora, D. M. (1989). Effects of sociometric testing on children's behavior and loneliness at school. *Developmental Psychology, 25*, 306–311.

Benenson, J. F. (1990). Gender differences in social networks. *Journal of Early Adolescence, 10*, 472–495.

Benenson, J., Apostoleris, N., & Parnass, J. (1998). The organization of children's same-sex peer relationships. In W. M. Bukowski & A. H. Cillessen (Eds.), *Sociometry then and now: Building on six decades of measuring children's experiences with the peer group* (pp. 5–23). San Francisco: Jossey-Bass.

Berndt, T. J., & Hoyle, S. G. (1985). Stability and change in childhood and adolescent friendship. *Developmental Psychology, 21*, 1007–1015.

Berndt, T. J., & Keefe, K. (1995). Friends' influence on adolescents' adjustment in school. *Child Development, 66*, 1312–1329.

Bierderman, J., Munir, K., & Knee, D. (1987). Conduct and oppositional disorder in clinically referred children with attention deficit disorder: A controlled family study. *Journal of the Academy of Child and Adolescent Psychiatry, 26*, 724–727.

Bierman, K. L. (1986a). Process of change during social skills training with preadolescents and its relation to treatment outcome. *Child Development, 57*, 230–240.

Bierman, K. L. (1986b). The relationship between social aggression and peer rejection in middle childhood. In R. Prinz (Ed.), *Advances in behavioral assessment of children and families* (vol. 2, pp. 151–178). Greenwich, CT: JAI Press.

Bierman, K. L. (1989). Improving the peer relationships of rejected children. In B.B. Lahey & A.E. Kazdin (Eds.), *Advances in clinical child psychology* (vol. 12, pp. 53–85). New York: Plenum Press.

Bierman, K. L., & Furman, W. (1984). The effects of social skills training and peer involvement in the social adjustment of preadolescents. *Child Development, 55*, 151–162.

Bierman, K. L., & Smoot, D. L. (1991). Linking family characteristics with poor peer relations: The mediating role of conduct problems. *Journal of Abnormal Child Psychology, 19*, 341–356.

Bierman, K. L., Smoot, D. L., & Aumiller, K. (1993). Characteristics of aggressive-rejected, aggressive (non-rejected) and rejected (non-aggressive) boys. *Child Development, 64*, 139–151.

Bierman, K. L., & Wargo, J. B. (1995). Predicting the longitudinal course associated with aggressive-rejected, aggressive (nonrejected), and rejected (nonaggressive) status. *Development & Psychopathology, 7*, 669–682.

Bishop, J. A., & Inderbitzen, H. M. (1995). Peer acceptance and friendship: An investigation of their relation to self-esteem. *Journal of Early Adolescence, 15*, 476–489.

Black, B., & Hazen, N. L. (1990). Social status and patterns of communication in acquainted and unacquainted preschool children. *Developmental Psychology, 26*, 379–387.

Borja-Alvarez, T., Zarbatany, L., & Pepper, S. (1991). Contributions of male and female guests and hosts to peer group entry. *Child Development, 62*, 1079–1090.

Boulton, M. J. (1999). Concurrent and longitudinal relations between children's playground behavior and social preference, victimization, and bullying. *Child Development, 70*, 944–954.

Boulton, M. J., & Smith, P. K. (1994). Bully/victim problems in middle-school children: Stability, self-perceived competence, peer perceptions and peer acceptance. *British Journal of Developmental Psychology, 12*, 315–329.

Boulton, M. J., & Underwood, K. (1992). Bully/victim problems among middle school children. *British Journal of Educational Psychology, 62*, 73–87.

Brochin, H. A., & Wasik, B. H. (1992). Social problem solving among popular and unpopular children. *Journal of Abnormal Child Psychology, 20*, 377–391.

Brown, G. S., Bhrolchain, M. N., & Harris, T. (1975). Social class and psychiatric disturbance among women in an urban population. *Sociology, 9*, 223–254.

Bryant, B. K. (1985). The neighborhood walk: Sources of support in middle childhood. *Monographs of the Society for Research in Child Development, 50* (3, serial no. 210).

Bryant, B. K. (1989). The need for support in relation to the need for autonomy. In D. Belle (Ed.), *Children's social networks and social supports* (pp. 332–351). New York: Wiley.

Bryant, B. K. (1992). Conflict resolution strategies in relation to children's peer relations. *Journal of Applied Developmental Psychology, 13*, 35–50.

Bryant, B. K., & DeMorris, K. A. (1992). Beyond parent-child relationships: Potential links between family environments and peer relations. In R. D. Parke & G. W. Ladd (Eds.), *Family–peer relationships: Modes of linkages* (pp. 159–189). Hillsdale, NJ: Lawrence Erlbaum Associates.

Budd, K. S. (1985). Parents as mediators in the social skills training of children. In L. L'Abate & M. A. Milan (Eds.), *Handbook of social skills training and research* (pp. 245–262). New York: Wiley.

Buhrmester, D. (1990). Intimacy of friendship, interpersonal competence, and adjustment during preadolescence and adolescence. *Child Development*, *61*, 1101–1111.

Buhrmester, D., & Furman, W. (1987). The development of companionship and intimacy. *Child Development*, *58*, 1101–1113.

Buhrmester, D., Camparo, L., Christensen, A., & Gonzalez, L. S. (1992). Mothers and fathers interacting in dyads and triads with normal and hyperactive sons. *Developmental Psychology*, *28*, 500–509.

Bukowski, W. M., Gauze, C., Hoza, B., & Newcomb, A. F. (1993). Differences and consistency between same-sex and other-sex peer relationships during early adolescence. *Developmental Psychology*, *29*, 255–263.

Bukowski, W. M., & Hoza, B. (1989). Popularity and friendships. Issues in theory, measurement and outcome. In T. J. Berndt & G. W. Ladd (Eds.), *Peer relationships in child development* (pp. 15–45). New York: Wiley.

Bukowski, W. M., & Newcomb, A. F. (1985). Variability in peer group perceptions: Support for the "controversial" sociometric classification group. *Developmental Psychology*, *21*, 1032–1038.

Bukowski, W. M., Pizzamiglio, M. T., Newcomb, A. F., & Hoza, B. (1996). Popularity as an affordance for friendship: The link between group and dyadic experience. *Social Development*, *5*, 189–202.

Burleson, B. R. (1985). Communication skills and childhood peer relationships: An overview. In M. McLaughlin (Ed.), *Communication yearbook* (Vol. 9, pp. 143–180) London: Sage.

Cairns, R. B., Perrin, J. E., & Cairns, B. D. (1985). Social cognition in early adolescence: Affiliative patterns. *Journal of Early Adolescence*, *5*, 339–355.

Carlson, C. L., Lahey, B. B., Frame, C. L., Walker, J., & Hynd, G. W. (1987). Sociometric status of clinically referred children with attention deficit disorders with and without hyperactivity. *Journal of Abnormal Child Psychology*, *15*, 537–547.

Carter, D. B., & McCloskey, L. A. (1984). Peers and the maintenance of sex-typed behavior: The development of children's conceptions of cross-gender behavior in their peers. *Social Cognition*, *2*, 294–314.

Cash, T. F. (1995). Developmental teasing about physical appearance: Retrospective descriptions and relationships with body image. *Social Behavior & Personality*, *23*, 123–129.

Chambless, D. L. (1996). In defense of dissemination of empirircally supported psychological interventions. *Clinical Psychology: Science and Practice*, *3*, 230–235.

Challman, R. (1932). Factors influencing friendships among preschool children. *Child Development*, *3*, 146–158.

Chennault, M. (1967). Improving the social acceptance of unpopular educable mentally retarded pupils in special classes. *American Journal of Mental Deficiency*, *72*, 455–458.

Cillesson, A. H., van Ijzendoorn, H. W., Van Lieshout, C. F., & Hartup, W. W. (1992). Heterogeneity among peer rejected boys: Subtypes and stabilities. *Child Development*, *63*, 893–905.

Cochran M., & Davila V. (1992). Societal influences on children's peer relations. In R. D. Parke & G. W. Ladd (Eds.), *Family–peer relationships: Modes of linkages* (pp. 191–212). Hillsdale, NJ: Lawrence Erlbaum Associates.

Coie, J. D., Christopoulos, C., Terry, R., Dodge, K. A., & Lochman, J. E. (1989). Types of aggressive relationships, peer rejection, and developmental consequences. In B. H. Schneider, G. Attili, J. Nadel, & R. P. Weissberg (Eds.), *Social competence in developmental perspective* (pp. 223–237). Boston: Kluwer Academic.

Coie, J. D., & Dodge, K. A. (1983). Continuities and changes in children's social status: A five year longitudinal study. *Merrill-Palmer Quarterly*, *29*, 261–282.

Coie, J. D., Dodge, K. A., & Copoletti, H. (1982). Dimensions and types of social status: A cross-age perspective. *Developmental Psychology*, *18*, 557–570.

Coie, J. D., Dodge, K. A., & Kupersmidt, J. B. (1990). Peer group behavior and social status. In S. R. Asher & J. D. Coie (Eds.), *Peer rejection in childhood* (pp. 17–59). New York: Cambridge University Press.

Coie, J. D., & Kupersmidt, J. B. (1983). A behavioral analysis of emerging social status. *Child Development*, *54*, 1400–1416.

Conoley, J. C., & Conoley, C. W. (1983). A comparison of techniques to effect sociometric status: A small step toward primary prevention in the classroom? *Journal of School Psychology*, *21*, 41–47.

Corsaro, W. A. (1981). Friendship in the nursery school: Social organization in a peer environment. In S. R. Asher & J. M. Gottman (Eds.), *The development of children's friendships* (pp. 207–241). New York: Cambridge University Press.

Cousins, L. S., & Weiss, G. (1993). Parent training

and social skills training for children with attention-deficit hyperactivity disorder: How can they be combined for greater effectiveness? *Canadian Journal of Psychiatry, 38*, 449–457.

Cowen, E. L., Pederson, A., Babigan, H., Izzo, L. D., & Trost, M. A. (1973). Long-term follow-up of early detected vulnerable children. *Journal of Consulting and Clinical Psychology, 41*, 438–446.

Crick, N. R. (1995). Relational aggression: The role of intent attributions, feelings of distress, and provocation type. *Development and Psychopathology, 7*, 313–322.

Crick, N. R. (1996). The role of overt aggression, relational aggression, and pro-social behavior in the prediction of children's future social adjustment. *Child Development, 67*, 2217–2327.

Crick, N. R., & Grotpeter, J. K. (1995). Relational aggression, gender, and social-psychological adjustment. *Child Development, 66*, 710–722.

Crick, N. R, & Grotpeter, J. K. (1996). Children's treatment by peers: Victims of relational and overt aggression. *Development and Psychopathology, 8*, 367–380.

Crick, N. R., & Ladd, G. W. (1990). Children's perceptions of the outcomes of social strategies: Do the ends justify being mean? *Developmental Psychology, 26*, 612–620.

Damon, W. (1977). *The social world of the child.* San Francisco: Jossey-Bass.

Daniels-Beirness, T. (1989). Measuring peer status in boys and girls: A Problem of apples and oranges? In B. H. Schneider, G. Attili, J. Nadel, & R. P. Weissberg (Eds.), *Social competence in developmental perspective* (pp. 107–120). Boston: Kluwer.

Devereux, E. C. (1976). Backyard versus Little League baseball: The impoverishment of children's games. In D. M. Landers (Ed.), *Social problems in athletics* (pp. 37–56). Chicago: University of Illinois Press.

Dishion, T. J. (1990). The family ecology of boys' peer relations in middle childhood. *Child Development, 61*, 874–892.

Dishion, T. J., Andrews, D. W., & Crosby, L. (1995). Anti-social boys and their friends in early adolescents: Relationship characteristics, quality, and interactional process. *Child Development, 66*, 139–151.

Dishion, T. J., Capaldi, D., Spracklen, K. M., & Li, F. (1995). Peer ecology of male adolescent drug use. *Development & Psychopathology, 7*, 803–824.

Dishion, T. J., French, D. C., & Patterson, G. R. (1995). The development and ecology of antisocial behavior. In, D. Cicchetti & D. J. Cohen (Eds.), *Developmental psychopathology* (vol. 2, pp. 421–471). New York: Wiley.

Dodge, K. A. (1983). Behavioral antecedents of peer social rejection and isolation. *Child Development, 54*, 1386–1399.

Dodge, K. A. (1985). Attributional biases in aggressive children. In P. D. Kendall (Ed.), *Advances in cognitive-behavioral research and therapy* (vol. 4, pp. 73–110). Orlando, FL: Academic Press.

Dodge, K. A., & Coie, J. D. (1987). Social information-processing factors in reactive and proactive aggression in children's peer groups. *Journal of Personality and Social Psychology, 53*, 1146–1158.

Dodge, K. A., Coie, J. D., & Brakke, N. P. (1983). Behavioral patterns of socially rejected and neglected preadolescents: The roles of social approach and aggression. *Journal of Abnormal Child Psychology, 10*, 389–410.

Dodge, K. A., Coie, J. D., Pettit, G. S., & Price, J. M. (1990). Peer status and aggression in boys' groups: Developmental and contextual analysis. *Child Development, 61*, 1289–1309.

Dodge, K. A., McClaskey, C. L., & Feldman, E. (1985). Situational approach to the assessment of social competence in children. *Journal of Consulting and Clinical Psychology, 53*, 344–353.

Dodge, K. A., Pettit, G. S., McClaskey, C. L., & Brown, M. M. (1986). Social competence in children. *Monographs of the Society for Research in Child Development, 51*, (2, serial no. 213).

Dodge, K. A., Schlundt, D. C., Schocken, I., & Delugach, J. D. (1983). Social competence and children's sociometric status: The role of peer group entry strategies. *Merrill-Palmer Quarterly, 29*, 309–336.

Doyle, A., Connolly, J. K., & Rivest, L. (1980). The effect of playmate familiarity on the social interactions of young children. *Child Development, 51*, 217–223.

Doyle, A. B., Markiewicz, D., & Hardy, C. (1994). Mothers' and children's friendships: Intergenerational associations. *Journal of Social and Interpersonal Relationships, 11*, 363–377.

Eder, G., & Hallinan, M. T. (1978). Sex differences in children's friendships. *American Sociological Review, 43*, 237–250.

Ehlers, S., Gillberg, C., & Wing, L. (1999). A screening questionnaire for Asperger syndrome and other high-functioning autism spectrum disorders in school age children. *Journal of Autism and Developmental Disorders, 29*, 129–141.

Eifert, G. H., Schulte, D., Zvolensky, M. J., Lejuez, C. W., & Lau, A. W. (1997). Manualized behavior therapy: Merits and challenges. *Behavior Therapy, 28*, 499–509.

Epstein, J. L. (1983). Selection of friends in differently organized schools and classrooms. In J. L. Epstein

& N. L. Karweit (Eds.), *Friends in school* (pp. 73–92). San Diego: Academic Press.

Erdley, C. A., & Asher, S. R. (1996). Children's social goals and self-efficacy perceptions as influences on their responses to ambiguous provocation. *Child Development, 67,* 1329–1344.

Erwin, P. (1993). *Friendships and peer relations in children.* New York: Wiley.

Erwin P. G. (1994). Effectiveness of social skills training with children: A meta-analytic study. *Counseling Psychology Quarterly, 7,* 305–310.

Evers-Pasquale, W. (1978). The peer preference test as a measure of reward value: Item analysis, cross-validation, concurrent validation, and replication. *Journal of Abnormal Child Psychology, 6,* 175–188.

Feldman, E., & Dodge, K. A. (1987). Social information processing and sociometric status: Sex, age, and situational effects. *Journal of Abnormal Child Psychology, 15,* 211–227.

Finnie, V., & Russell, A. (1988). Preschool children's social status and their mothers' behavior and knowledge in the supervisory role. *Developmental Psychology, 24,* 789–801.

Fonzi, A., Schneider, B. H., Tani, F., & Tomada, G. (1997). Predicting children's friendship status from their dyadic interaction in structured situations of potential conflict. *Child Development, 68,* 496–506.

Foster, S. (1983), Critical elements in the development of children's social skills. In R. Ellis & D. Whitington (Eds.), *New directions in social skills training* (pp. 229–265). New York: Methuen.

Frankel, F. (1996). *Good friends are hard to find: Help your child find, make, and keep friends.* Los Angeles: Perspective.

Frankel, F. (2002a). *Sources of friendships for mothers of children with and without peer problems.* In preparation.

Frankel, F. (2002b). *Measuring the quality of play dates.* In preparation

Frankel, F. (in press). Parent-assisted children's friendship training. In T. Hibbs (Ed.), *Psychosocial treatments for child and adolescent disorders: Empirically based approaches* (2nd ed.). Washington, DC: American Psychological Association.

Frankel, F., Cantwell, D. P., & Myatt R. (1996). Helping ostracized children: Social skills training and parent support for socially rejected children. In E. D. Hibbs & P. S. Jensen (Eds.), *Psychosocial treatments for child and adolescent disorders: Empirically based approaches* (pp. 591–617). Washington, DC: American Psychological Association.

Frankel, F., & Erhardt, D. (2001). *Social skills training for medicated ADHD Children.* Washington: National Institute of Mental Health grant R01 MH92628.

Frankel, F., & Feinberg, D. T. (2002). Social problems associated with ADHD vs. ODD in children referred for friendship problems. *Child Psychiatry and Human Development,* in press.

Frankel, F., & Myatt, R. (2002). Parent-assisted friendship training for children with autism spectrum disorders: Effects of psychotropic medication. Submitted for publication.

Frankel, F., Myatt R., & Cantwell, D. P. (1995). Training outpatient boys to conform with the social ecology of popular peers: Effects on parent and teacher ratings. *Journal of Clinical Child Psychology, 24,* 300–310.

Frankel, F., Myatt, R., Cantwell, D. P., & Feinberg, D. T. (1997a). Use of child behavior checklist and *DSM–III–R* diagnosis in predicting outcome of children's social skills training. *Journal of Behavior Therapy and Experimental Psychiatry, 28,* 149–161.

Frankel, F., Myatt, R, Cantwell, D. P., & Feinberg, D. T. (1997b). Parent-assisted children's social skills training: Effects on children with and without attention-deficit hyperactivity disorder. *Journal of the Academy of Child & Adolescent Psychiatry, 36,* 1056–1064.

Frankel, F., & Simmons, J. Q. (1992). Parent behavioral training: Why and when some parents drop out. *Journal of Clinical Child Psychology, 21,* 322–330.

Frederick, B. P., & Olmi, D. J. (1994). Children with attention-deficit/hyperactivity disorder: A review of the literature on social skills deficits. *School Psychology Review, 31,* 288–296.

French, D. C. (1988). Heterogeneity of peer-rejected boys: Aggressive and non aggressive subtypes. *Child Development, 59,* 976–985.

French, D. C. (1990). Heterogeneity of peer-rejected girls. *Child Development, 61,* 2028–2031.

Furman, W. (1985). What's the point? Issues in the selection of treatment objectives. In B. H. Schneider, K. H. Rubin, & J. E. Ledingham (Eds.), *Children's peer relations: Issues in assessment and intervention* (pp. 41–54). New York: Springer-Verlag.

Furman, W. (1987). Acquaintanceship in middle childhood. *Developmental Psychology, 23,* 563–570.

Furman, W., Rahe, D. F., & Hartup, W. W. (1979). Rehabilitation of socially withdrawn preschool children through mixed-age and same-age socialization. *Child Development, 50,* 915–922.

Garvey, C. (1984). *Children's talk.* Cambridge, MA: Harvard University Press.

Gelb, R., & Jacobson, J. L. (1988). Popular and unpopular children's interactions during cooperative and competitive peer group activities. *Journal of Abnormal Child Psychology, 16,* 247–261.

George, T. P., & Hartmann, D. P. (1996). Friendship

networks of unpopular, average, and popular children. *Child Development, 67,* 2301–2316.

Getz, J. A., Goldman, J. A., & Corsini, D. A. (1984). Interpersonal problem-solving in preschool children: A comparison of assessment procedures using two-dimensional versus three-dimensional stimuli. *Journal of Applied Developmental Psychology, 5,* 293–304.

Glow, R. A., & Glow, P. H. (1980). Peer and self-rating: Children's perception of behavior relevant to hyperkinetic impulse disorder. *Journal of Abnormal Child Psychology, 8,* 397–404.

Goodwin, S. E., & Mahoney, M. J. (1975). Modification of aggression through modeling: An experimental probe. *Journal of Behavior Therapy & Experimental Psychiatry, 6,* 200–202.

Gottman, J. M. (1977). Toward a definition of social isolation in children. *Child Development, 48,* 513–517.

Gottman, J. M. (1983). How children become friends. *Monographs of the Society for Research in Child Development, 48* (serial no. 201).

Gottman, J. M. (1986). The world of coordinated play: Same- and cross-sex friendship in young children. In J. M. Gottman & J. G. Parker (Eds.), *Conversations of friends: Speculations on affective development* (pp. 139-191). New York: Cambridge University Press.

Gottman, J. M., Gonso, J., & Rasmussen, B. (1975). Social interaction, social competence and friendship in children. *Child Development, 46,* 709–718.

Gottman, J. M., & Parkhurst, J. T. (1980). A developmental theory of friendship and acquaintanceship processes. In W. A. Collins (Ed.), *Development of cognition, affect and social relationships* (Minnesota Symposium on Child Psychology, vol. 13, pp. 197–253). Hillsdale, NJ: Lawrence Erlbaum Associates.

Grenell, M. M., Glass, C. R., & Katz, K. S. (1987). Hyperactive children and peer interaction: Knowledge and performance of social skills. *Journal of Abnormal Child Psychology, 15,* 1–13.

Gresham, F. M. (1982). Social interactions as predictors of children's likability and friendship patterns: A multiple regression analysis. *Journal of Behavioral Assessment, 4,* 39–54.

Gresham, F. M., & Elliott, S. N. (1990). *Social skills rating system: Manual.* Circle Pines, MN: American Guidance Service.

Gresham, F. M., & Nagle, R. J. (1980). Social skills training with children: Responsiveness to modeling and coaching as a function of peer orientation. *Journal of Consulting and Clinical Psychology, 48,* 718–729.

Gresham, F. M., Noell, G. H., & Elliott, S. N. (1996). Teachers as judges of social competence: A conditional probability analysis. *School Psychology Review, 25,* 108–117.

Gresham, F. M., & Stuart, D. (1992). Stability of sociometric assessment: Implications for uses as selection and outcome measures in social skills training. *Journal of School Psychology, 30,* 223–231.

Grotpeter, J. K., & Crick, N. R. (1996). Relational aggression, overt aggression, and friendship. *Child Development, 67,* 2328–2338.

Hallinan, M. T. (1980). Patterns on cliquing among youth. In H. C. Foot, A. J. Chapman & J. R. Smith (Eds.), *Friendship and social relations in children* (pp. 321–343). New York: Wiley.

Harrist, A. W., Zaia, A. F., Bates, J. E., Dodge, K. A., & Pettit, G. S. (1997). Subtypes of social withdrawal in early childhood: Sociometric status and social-cognitive differences across four years. *Child Development, 68,* 278–294.

Hart, C. H. (1993). *Children on playgrounds.* Albany: State University of New York Press.

Harter, S. (1982). The perceived competence scale for children. *Child Development, 53,* 87-97.

Hartup, W. W. (1983). Peer relations. In E. M. Hetherington (Ed.), P. H. Mussen (Series Ed.), *Handbook of child psychology: Socialization, personality and social development* (vol. 4, pp. 103–196). New York: Wiley.

Hartup, W. W. (1993). Adolescents and their friends. In B. Laursen (Ed.), *Close friendship in adolescence: New directions for child development* (pp. 3–22). San Francisco: Jossey-Bass.

Hartup, W. W. (1996). The company they keep: Friendships and their developmental significance. *Child Development, 67,* 1–13.

Hartup, W. W., Glazer, J. A., & Charlesworth, R. (1967). Peer reinforcement and sociometric status. *Child Development, 38,* 1017–1024.

Hartup, W. W., & Laursen, B. (1993). Conflict and context in peer relations. In C. H. Hart (Ed.), *Children on Playgrounds* (pp. 44–84). Albany, NY: State University of New York Press.

Hepler, J. B., & Rose, S. F. (1988). Evaluation of a multi-component group approach for improving social skills of elementary school children. *Journal of Social Service Research, 11,* 1–18.

Hibbs, E. D., Clarke, G., Hechtman, L., Abikoff, H., Greenhill, L., & Jensen, P. (1997). Manual development for the treatment of child and adolescent disorders. *Psychopharmacology Bulletin, 33,* 619–629.

Hinshaw, S. P., & Melnick, S. M. (1995). Peer relationships in boys with attention deficit hyperactivity disorder with and without comorbid aggression. *Developmental Psychopathology, 7,* 627–647.

Hodges, E. V. E., Boivin, M., Vitaro, F., & Bukowski, W. M. (1999). The power of friendship: Protection against an escalating cycle of peer victimization. *Developmental Psychology, 35,* 94–101.

Hodges, E. V. E., Malone, M. J., & Perry, D. G. (1997). Individual risk and social risk as interacting determinants of victimization in the peer group. *Developmental Psychology, 33,* 1032–1039.

Hodges, E. V. E., & Perry, D. G. (1999). Personal and interpersonal antecedents and consequences of victimization by peers. *Journal of Personality & Social Psychology, 76,* 677–685.

Homel, R., Burns, A., & Goodnow, J. (1987). Parental social networks and child development. *Journal of Social and Personal Relationships, 4,* 159–177.

Howes, C. (1988). Same- and cross-sex friends: Implications for interaction and social skills. *Early Childhood Research Quarterly, 3*(1), 21–37.

Howes, C. (1990). Social status and friendship from kindergarten to third grade. *Journal of Applied Developmental Psychology, 11,* 321–330.

Hughes, H. M. (1984). Measures of self-concept and self-esteem for children age 3–12 years: A review and recommendations. *Clinical Psychology Review, 4,* 657–692.

Hupp, S. D. A., & Reitman, D. (1999). Improving sports skills and sportsmanship in children diagnosed with attention-deficit/hyperactivity disorder. *Child & Family Behavior Therapy, 21,* 35–51.

Hymel, S. (1986). Interpretations of peer behavior: Affective bias in childhood and adolescence. *Child Development, 57,* 431–445.

Hymel, S., Rubin, K. H., Rowden, L., & LeMare, L. (1990). Children's peer relationships: Longitudinal prediction of internalizing and externalizing problems from middle to late childhood. *Child Development, 61,* 2004–2021.

Jensen, P. S., Martin, D., & Cantwell, D. P. (1997). Comorbidity in ADHD: Implications for research, practice and *DSM–V. Journal of the Academy of Child & Adolescent Psychiatry, 36,* 1065–1079.

Jeske, P. J. (1985). Piers-Harris Children's Self-Concept Scale. In J.V. Mitchell, Jr. (Ed.), *Ninth Mental measurements yearbook* (Vol. 1, pp. 1169–1170). Lincoln: University of Nebraska, Buros Institute of Mental Measurement.

Johnston, C., Pelham, W. E., & Murphy, H. A. (1985). Peer relationships in ADHD and normal children: A developmental analysis of peer and teacher ratings. *Journal of Abnormal Child Psychology, 13,* 89–100.

Johnstone, B., Frame, C. L., & Bouman, D. (1992). Physical attractiveness and athletic and academic ability in controversial-aggressive and rejected-aggressive children. *Journal of Social & Clinical Psychology, 11,* 71–79.

Kavale K. A., Mathur S. R., Forness S. R., Rutherford,

R. B., & Quinn, M. M. (1996). Effectiveness of social skills training for students with behavior disorders: A meta-analysis. In T. Scruggs & M. Mastropieri (Eds.), *Advances in learning and behavioral disabilities* (vol. 11, pp. 1–26). Greenwich, CT: JAI Press.

Kazdin, A. E., Esveldt-Dawson, K., French, N. H., & Unis, A. S. (1987). Problem-solving skills training and relationship therapy in the treatment of antisocial child behavior. *Journal of Consulting & Clinical Psychology, 55,* 76–85.

Kehle, T. J., Clark, E., Jenson, W. R., & Wampold, B. E. (1986). Effectiveness of self-observation with behavior disordered elementary school children. *School Psychology Review, 15,* 289–295.

Keltner, D., Young, R. C., Heerey, E. A., Oemig, C., & Monarch, N. D. (1998). Teasing in hierarchical and intimate relations. *Journal of Personality & Social Psychology, 75,* 1231–1247.

Kennedy, J. (1992). Relationship of maternal beliefs and child-rearing strategies to social competence in preschool children. *Child Study Journal, 22,* 39–55.

Kim, O. H. (1999). Language characteristics and social skills of children with attention deficit hyperactivity disorder. *Dissertation Abstracts International Section A: Humanities &Social Sciences, 60*(5-A), 1513.

Kochenderfer, B. J., & Ladd, G. W. (1997). Victimized children's responses to peers' aggression: Behaviors associated with reduced versus continued victimization. *Development & Psychopathology, 9,* 59–73.

Kovacs, D. M., Parker, J. G., & Hoffman, L. W. (1996). Behavioral, affective, and social correlates of involvement in cross-sex friendship in elementary school. *Child Development, 67,* 2269–2286.

Kupersmidt, J. B., DeRosier, M. E., & Patterson, C. J. (1995). Similarity as the basis for children's friendships: The roles of sociometric status, aggressive and withdrawn behavior. *Journal of Social and Personal Relationships, 12,* 439–452.

Kupersmidt, J. B., Griesler, DeRosier, M. E., Patterson, C. J., & Davis, P. W. (1995). Childhood aggression and peer relations in the context of family and neighborhood factors. *Child Development, 66,* 360–375.

Ladd, G. W. (1981). Effectiveness of a social learning method for enhancing children's social interaction and peer acceptance. *Child Development, 52,* 171–178.

Ladd, G. W. (1983). Social networks of popular, average and rejected children in school. *Merrill-Palmer Quarterly, 29,* 283–307.

Ladd, G. W. (1992). Themes and theories: Perspectives on processes in family-peer relationships. In

R. D. Parke & G. W. Ladd (Eds.), *Family–peer relationships: Modes of linkages* (pp. 3–34). Hillsdale, NJ: Lawrence Erlbaum Associates.

Ladd G. A., & Asher S. R. (1985), Social skill training and children's peer relations. In. L. L'Abate & M. A. Milan (Eds.), *Handbook of social skills training and research* (pp. 219–244). New York: Wiley.

Ladd, G. W., & Emerson, E. S. (1984). Shared knowledge in children's friendships. *Developmental Psychology, 20,* 932–940.

Ladd, G. W., & Golter, B. S. (1988). Parents' management of preschoolers peer relations: Is it related to children's social competence? *Developmental Psychology, 24,* 109–117.

Ladd, G. W., & Hart, C. H. (1992). Creating informal play opportunities: Are parents' and preschoolers' initiations related to children's competence with peers? *Developmental Psychology, 28,* 1179–1187.

Ladd, G. W., Hart, C. H., Wadsworth, E. M., & Golter, B. S. (1988). Preschoolers peer networks in nonschool settings: Relationships to family characteristics and school adjustment. In S. Salzinger, J. Antobus, & M. Hammer (Eds.), *Social network of children, adolescents, and college students* (pp. 61–92). Hillsdale, NJ: Erlbaum.

Ladd, G. W., LeSieur, K., & Profilet, S. (1993). Direct parental influences on young children's peer relations. In S. W. Duck (Ed.), *Understanding relationship processes 2: Learning about relationships* (pp. 152–183). London: Sage.

Ladd, G. W., & Mize, J. (1983). A cognitive-social learning model of social skill training. *Psychological Bulletin, 90,* 127–157.

Ladd, G. W., & Price, J. M. (1987). Predicting children's social and school adjustment following the transition from preschool to kindergarten. *Child Development, 58,* 1168–1189.

Ladd, G. W., & Price, J. M. (1993). Playstyles of peer-accepted and peer-rejected children on the playground. In C. H. Hart (Ed.), *Children on playgrounds* (pp. 130–161). Albany: State University of New York Press.

Ladd, G. W., Profilet, S. M., & Hart, C. H. (1992). Parents' management of children's peer relations: Facilitating and supervising children's activities in the peer culture. In R. D. Parke & G. W. Ladd (Eds.), *Family–peer relationships: Modes of linkages* (pp. 215–253). Hillsdale, NJ: Lawrence Erlbaum.

La Greca, A. M. (1981). Peer acceptance: The correspondence between children's sociometric scores and teachers' ratings of peer interactions. *Journal of Abnormal Child Psychology, 9,* 167–178.

La Greca, A. M. (1993). Social skills training with children: Where do we go from here? *Journal of Clinical Child Psychology, 22,* 288–298.

Landau, S., & Milich, R. (1988). Social communication patterns of attention-deficit-disordered boys. *Journal of Abnormal Child Psychology, 16,* 69–81.

Landau, S., & Moore, L. (1991). Social skill deficits in children with attention-deficit hyperactivity disorder. *School Psychology Review, 20,* 235–251.

Langlois, J. H., & Downs, A. C. (1979). Peer relations as a function of physical attractiveness. *Child Development, 50,* 409–418.

Ledingham, J. E., & Younger, A. (1985). The influence of the evaluator on assessments of children's social skills. In B. H. Schneider, K. H. Rubin, & J. E. Ledingham (Eds.), *Children's peer relations: Issues in assessment and intervention* (pp. 111–121). New York: Springer-Verlag.

Ledingham, J. E., Younger, A., Schwartzman, A., & Bergeron, G. (1982). Agreement among teacher, peer and self-ratings of children's aggression, withdrawal and likability. *Journal of Abnormal Child Psychology, 10,* 363–372.

Lilly, M. S. (1971). Improving social acceptance of low sociometric status, low achieving students. *Exceptional Children, 37,* 341–347.

Lochman, J. E., Wayland, K. K., & White, K. J. (1993). Social goals: Relationship to adolescent adjustment and to social problem solving. *Journal of Abnormal Child Psychology, 21,* 135–151.

Lochman, J. E., & Wells, K. C. (1996). A social-cognitive intervention with aggressive children: Prevention effects and contextual implementation issues. In D. P. Ray & R. J. McMahon (Eds.), *Preventing childhood disorders, substance abuse, and delinquency* (pp. 111–143). Thousand Oaks, CA: Sage.

Lustig, J. L., Wolchik, S. A., & Braver, S. L. (1992). Social support in chumships and adjustment in children of divorce. *American Journal of Community Psychology, 20,* 393–399.

Maccoby, E. E. (1986). Social groupings in childhood: Their relationship to prosocial and antisocial behavior in boys and girls. In D. Olweus, J. Block, & M. Radke-Yarrow (Eds.), *Development of antisocial and prosocial behavior: Research, theories and issues* (pp. 263–284). New York: Academic Press.

Maccoby, E. E., & Jacklin, C. N. (1987). Gender segregation in childhood. In H. W. Reese (Ed.), *Advances in child development and behavior* (pp. 239–288). New York: Academic Press.

MacDonald, C. D., & Cohen, R. (1995). Children's awareness of which peers like them and which peers dislike them. *Social Development, 4,* 182–193.

Malik, N. M., & Furman, W. (1993). Practitioner Review: Problems in children's peer relations: What can the clinician do? *Journal of Child Psychology & Psychiatry, 34,* 1303–1326.

Markell, R. A., & Asher, S. R. (1984). Children's interactions in dyads: Interpersonal influence and sociometric status. *Child Development, 55,* 1412–1424.

Marriage, K. J., Gordon, V., & Brand, L. (1995). A social skills group for boys with Asperger's syndrome. *Australian and New Zealand Journal of Psychiatry, 29,* 58–62.

Matthys, W., Cuperus, J. M., & Van Engeland, H. (1999). Deficient social problem-solving in boys with ODD/CD, with ADHD, and with both disorders. *Journal of the Academy of Child & Adolescent Psychiatry, 38,* 311–321.

McFall, R. (1982). A review and reformulation of the concept of social skills. *Behavioral Assessment, 4,* 1–33.

McGuire, K. D., & Weisz, J. R. (1982). Social cognition and behavior correlates of preadolescent chumship. *Child Development, 53,* 1478–1484.

Melnick, S. M., & Hinshaw, S. P. (1996). What they want and what they get: The social goals of boys with ADHD and comparison boys. *Journal of Abnormal Child Psychology, 24,* 169–185.

Mesibov, G. B. (1984). Social skills training with verbal autistic adolescents and adults: A program model. *Journal of Autism and Developmental Disorders, 14,* 395–404.

Michelson, L., Foster, S. L., & Ritchey, W. L. (1977). Social skills assessment of children. In B. Lahey & A. Kazdin (Eds.), *Advances in clinical child psychology* (vol. 4, pp. 119–165). New York: Plenum.

Middleton, M. B., & Cartledge, G. (1995). The effects of social skills instruction and parental involvement on the aggressive behaviors of African American males. *Behavior Modification, 19,* 192–210.

Milich, R., & Dodge, K. A. (1984). Social information processing in child psychiatric populations. *Journal of Abnormal Child Psychology, 12,* 471–490.

Milich, R., & Landau, S. (1982). Socialization and peer relations in hyperactive children. In K. D. Gadow & I. Bialer (Eds.), *Advances in learning and behavioral disabilities: A research annual* (vol. 1, pp. 283–339). Greenwich, CT: JAI Press.

Miller, P. M., & Ingham, J. G. (1976). Friends, confidants, and symptoms. *Social Psychiatry, 11,* 51–58.

Mize, J., Pettit, G. S., & Brown, E. G. (1995). Mothers' supervision of their children's peer play: Relations with beliefs, perceptions, and knowledge. *Developmental Psychology, 31,* 311–321.

Nangle, D. W., Erdley, C. A., & Gold, J. A. (1996). A reflection of the popularity construct: The importance of who likes or dislikes a child. *Behavior Therapy, 27,* 337–352.

Nelson, J., & Aboud, F. E. (1985). The resolution of social conflict between friends. *Child Development, 56,* 1009–1017.

Nelson, J. R., & Roberts, M. L. (2000). Ongoing reciprocal teacher-student interactions involving disruptive behaviors in general education classrooms. *Journal of Emotional & Behavioral Disorders, 8,* 27–37.

Newcomb, A. F., & Bukowski, W. M. (1984). A longitudinal study of the utility of social preference and social impact sociometric classification schemes. *Child Development, 55,* 1434–1447.

Newcomb, A. F., Bukowski, W. M., & Pattee, L. (1993). Children's peer relations: A meta-analytic review of popular, rejected, neglected, controversial, and average sociometric status. *Psychological Bulletin, 113,* 99–128.

Newson, J., & Newson, E. (1976). *Seven years old in the home environment.* New York: John Wiley & Sons.

Oden, S. (1986). Developing social skills instruction for peer interaction and relationships. In G. Cartledge & J. F. Milburn (Eds.), *Teaching social skills to children: Innovative approaches* (2nd ed., pp. 187–218). New York: Pergamon Press.

Oden, S., & Asher, S. R. (1977). Coaching children in social skills for friendship making. *Child Development, 48,* 495–506.

Olweus, D. (1993). Bullies on the playground: The role of victimization. In C. H. Hart (Ed.), *Children on playgrounds* (pp. 45–128). Albany: State University of New York Press.

Ozonoff, S., & Miller, J. N. (1995). Teaching theory of mind: A new approach to social skills training for individuals with autism. *Journal of Autism and Developmental Disorders, 25,* 415–433.

Parke, R. D., & Bhavnagri, N. P. (1989). Parents as managers of children's peer friendships. In D. Belle (Ed.), *Children's social networks and social supports* (pp. 241–259). New York: Wiley.

Parke, R. D., MacDonald, A. B., & Bhavnagri, N. (1988). The role of the family in the development of peer relationships. In R. D. Peters & R. J. McMahon (Eds.), *Social learning and systems approaches to marriage and the family* (pp. 17–44). New York: Brunner/Mazel.

Parke, R. D., O'Neil, R., Spitzer, S., Isley, S., Welsh, M., Wang, S., Lee, J., Strand, C., & Cupp, R. (1997). A longitudinal assessment of sociometric stability and the behavioral correlates of children's social acceptance. *Merrill-Palmer Quarterly, 43,* 635–662.

Parker, J. G., & Asher, S. R. (1993). Friendship and friendship quality in middle childhood: Links with peer group acceptance and feelings of loneliness and social dissatisfaction. *Developmental Psychology, 29,* 611–621.

Parker, J. G., & Seal, J. (1996). Forming, losing, renewing, and replacing friendships: Applying temporal parameters to the assessment of children's friendship experiences. *Child Development, 67,* 2248–2268.

Parkhurst, J. T., & Hopmeyer, A. (1998). Sociometric popularity and peer-perceived popularity: Two distinct dimensions of peer status. *Journal of Early Adolescence, 18,* 125–144.

Patterson, C. J., Kupersmidt, J. B., & Greisler, P. C. (1990). Children's perceptions of self and of relationships with others as a function of sociometric status. *Child Development, 61,* 1335–1349.

Patterson, G. R. (1986). Performance models for antisocial boys. *American Psychologist, 41,* 432-444.

Patterson, G. R., DeBaryshe, B. D., & Ramsey, E. (1989). A developmental perspective on antisocial behavior. *American Psychologist, 44,* 329–335.

Patterson, G. R., Dishion, T., & Banks, L. (1984). Family interaction: A process model of deviancy training. *Aggressive Behavior, 10,* 253–267.

Peevers, B. H., & Secord, P. F. (1973). Developmental changes in attributions of descriptive concepts to persons. *Journal of Personality and Social Psychology, 27,* 120–128.

Pekarik, E., Prinz, R., Liebert, D., Weintraub, S., & Neil, J. (1976). The Pupil Evaluation Inventory: A sociometric technique for assessing children's social behavior. *Journal of Abnormal Child Psychology, 4,* 83–97.

Pelham, W. E., & Bender, M. E. (1982). Peer relationships in hyperactive children: Description and treatment. *Advances in Learning and Behavioral Disabilities, 1,* 365–436.

Pelham, W. E., Sturges, J., Hoza, J., Schmidt, C., Bijlsma, J. J., Milich, R., & Moorer, S. (1987). Sustained release and standard methylphenidate effects on cognitive and social behavior in children with attention deficit disorder. *Pediatrics, 80,* 491–501.

Perry, D. G., Kusel, S. J., & Perry, L. C. (1988). Victims of aggression. *Developmental Psychology, 24,* 807–814.

Perry, D. G., Perry, L. C., & Rasmussen, P. (1986). Cognitive social learning mediators of aggression. *Child Development, 57,* 700–711.

Perry, D. G., Williard, J. C., & Perry, L. C. (1990). Peer perceptions of the consequences that victimized children provide aggressors. *Child Development, 61,* 1310–1325.

Pettit, G. S., Bates, J. E., Dodge, K. A., & Meece, D. W. (1999). The impact of after-school peer contact on early adolescent externalizing problems is moderated by parental monitoring, perceived neighborhood safety, and prior adjustment. *Child Development, 70,* 768–778.

Pfiffner, L. J., & McBurnett, K. (1997). Social skills training with parent generalization: Treatment effects for children with attention deficit disorder. *Journal of Consulting & Clinical Psychology, 65,* 749–757.

Phillips, C. A., Rolls, S., Rouse, A., & Griffiths, M. D. (1995). Home video game playing in schoolchildren: A study of incidence and patterns of play. *Journal of Adolescence, 18,* 687–691.

Piers, E. V. (1984). *Piers-Harris Children's Self-Concept Scale–Rrevised manual.* Los Angeles: Western Psychological Services.

Pope, A. W., Bierman, K. L., & Mumma, G. H. (1989). Relations between hyperactive and aggressive behavior and peer relations at three elementary grade levels. *Journal of Abnormal Child Psychology, 17,* 253–267.

Possell, L. E., Kehle, T. J., Mcloughlin, C. S., & Bray, M. A. (1999). Self-modeling as an intervention to reduce disruptive classroom behavior. *Cognitive & Behavioral Practice, 6,* 99–105.

Poulin, F., Cilessen, A., Hubbard, J., Coie, J., Dodge, K., & Schwartz, D. (1997). Children's friends and behavioral similarity. *Social Development, 6,* 224–226.

Powell, T. H., Salzberg, C. L., Rule, S., Levy, S., & Itzkowitz, J. S. (1983). Teaching mentally retarded children to play with their siblings using parents as trainers. *Education and Treatment of Children, 6,* 343–362.

Prinstein, M. J., & La Greca, A. M. (1999). Links between mothers' and children's social competence and associations with maternal adjustment. *Journal of Clinical Child Psychology, 28,* 197–210.

Prinz, R. J., Blechman, E., & Dumas, J. E. (1994). An evaluation of peer coping-skills training for childhood aggression. *Journal of Clinical Child Psychology, 23,* 193–203.

Putallaz, M. (1983). Predicting children's sociometric status from their behavior. *Child Development, 54,* 1417–1426.

Putallaz, M. (1987). Maternal behavior and children's sociometric status. *Child Development, 58,* 324–340.

Putallaz, M., & Gottman, J. M. (1981). An interactional model of children's entry into peer groups. *Child Development, 52,* 986–994.

Quiggle, N. L., Garber, J., Panak, W. F., & Dodge, K. A. (1992). Social information processing in aggressive and depressed children. *Child Development, 63,* 1305–1320.

Ray, G. E., Cohen, R., Secrist, M. E., & Duncan, M. K. (1997). Relating aggressive and victimization behaviors to children's sociometric status and friendships. *Journal of Social & Personal Relationships, 14,* 95–108.

Renshaw, P. D., & Asher, S. R. (1983). Children's goals and strategies for social interaction. *Merrill-Palmer Quarterly, 29,* 353–374.

Renshaw, P. D., & Brown, P. J. (1993). Loneliness in middle childhood: Concurrent and longitudinal predictors. *Child Development, 64*, 1271–1284.

Rican, P. (1995). Sociometric status of the school bullies and their victims. *Studia Psychologica, 37*, 357–364.

Roff, M., Sells, B., & Golden, M. (1972). *Social adjustment and personality development in children*. Minneapolis: University of Minnesota Press.

Rogosch, F. A., & Newcomb, A. F. (1989). Children's perceptions of peer reputations and their social reputations among peers. *Child Development, 60*, 597–610.

Rose, A. J., & Asher, S. R. (1999). Children's goals and strategies in response to conflicts within a friendship. *Developmental Psychology, 35*, 69–79.

Ross, A. O. (1992). *The sense of self: Research and theory*. New York: Springer.

Rubin, K. H. (1982). Nonsocial play in prechoolers: Necessary evil? *Child Development, 53*, 651–657.

Rubin, K. H., Stewart, S. L., & Coplan, R. J. (1995). Social withdrawal in childhood. In T. H. Ollendick & R. J. Prinz (Eds.), *Advances in clinical child psychology* (vol. 17, pp. 157–196). New York: Plenum.

Rubin, Z., & Sloman, J. (1984). How parents influence their children's friendships. In M. Lewis (Ed.), *Beyond the dyad* (pp. 223–250). New York: Plenum Press.

Rucker, C. N., & Vincenzo, F. M. (1970). Maintaining social acceptance gains made by mentally retarded children. *Exceptional Children, 36*, 679–680.

Russell, A., & Finnie, V. (1990). Preschool children's social status and maternal instructions to assist group entry. *Developmental Psychology, 26*, 603–611.

Rutter, M., & Garmezy, N. (1983). Developmental psychopathology. In E. M. Hetherington (Ed.), P. H. Mussen (Series, Ed.), *Handbook of child psychology: Socialization, personality and social development* (vol. 4, pp. 775–911). New York: Wiley.

Sabongui, A. G., Bukowski, W. M., & Newcomb, A. F. (1998). The peer ecology of popularity: The network embeddedness of a child's friend predicts the child's subsequent popularity. In W. M. Bukowski & A. H. Cillessen (Eds.), *Sociometry then and now: Building on six decades of measuring children's experiences with the peer group* (pp. 83–91). San Francisco: Jossey-Bass.

Sakamoto, A. (1994). Video game use and the development of sociocognitive abilities in children: Three surveys of elementary school students. *Journal of Applied Social Psychology, 24*, 21–42.

Salmivalli, C., & Nieminen, E. (2002). Proactive and reactive aggression among school bullies, victims, and bully-victims. *Aggressive Behavior, 28*, 30–44.

Scambler, D. J., Harris, M. J., & Milich, R. (1998). Sticks and stones: Evaluations of responses to childhood teasing. *Social Development, 7*, 234–249.

Schutte, N. S., Malouff, J. M., Post-Gorden, J. C., & Rodasta, A. L. (1988). Effects of playing video games on children's aggressive and other behaviors. *Journal of Applied Social Psychology, 18*, 454–460.

Schwartz, D., Dodge, K. A., Pettit, G. S., & Bates, J. E. (1997). The early socialization of aggressive victims of bullying. *Child Development, 68*, 665–675.

Serbin, L. A., Marchessault, K., McAffer, V., Peters, P., & Schwartzman, A. E. (1993). Patterns of social behavior in 9- to 11-year-old girls and boys: Relation to teacher perceptions and to peer ratings of aggression, withdrawal and likability. In C. H. Hart (Ed.), *Children on playgrounds* (pp. 162–183.). Albany: State University of New York Press.

Shantz, D. W. (1986). Conflict, aggression and peer status: An observational study. *Child Development, 57*, 1322–1332.

Sheridan, S. M., Dee, C. C., Morgan, J. C., McCormick, M. E., & Walker, D. (1996). A multimethod intervention for social skills deficits in children with ADHD and their parents. *School Psychology Review, 25*, 57–76.

Shure, M. B., & Spivak, G. (1978). *Problem-solving techniques in childrearing*. San Francisco: Jossey-Bass.

Singleton, L. C., & Asher, S. R. (1977). Peer preferences and social interaction among third-grade children in an integrated school district. *Journal of Educational Psychology, 69*, 330–336.

Spivack, G., & Shure, M. B. (1974). *Social adjustment of young children: A congitive approach to solving real-life problems*. San Francisco: Jossey-Bass.

Steinberg, L. (1986). Latchkey children and susceptibility to peer pressure: An ecological analysis. *Developmental Psychology, 22*, 433–439.

Stormshak, E. A., Bierman, K. L., Bruschi, C., Dodge, K. A., Coie, J. D., & the Conduct Problems Prevention Group. (1999). The relation between behavior problems and peer preference in different classroom contexts. *Child Development, 70*, 169–182.

Swanson, J. M. (1992). *School-based assessments and interventions for ADD students*. Irvine, CA: K. C. Publishing.

Tassi, F., & Schneider, B. H. (1997). Task-oriented versus other-referenced competition: Differential implications for children's peer relations. *Journal of Applied Social Psychology, 27*, 1557–1580.

Taylor, A. R., & Asher, S. R. (1984). Children's goals and social competence: Individual differences in a game-playing context. In T. Field, J. L. Roopnarine, & M. Segal (Eds.), *Friendships in normal and handicapped children* (pp. 53–78). Norwood, NJ: Ablex.

Teeter, P. A. (1991). Attention deficit hyperactivity

disorder: A psychoeducational paradigm. *School Psychology Review, 20,* 266–280.

Tiffen, K., & Spence, S. H. (1986). Responsiveness of isolated versus rejected children to social skills training. *Journal of Child Psychology and Psychiatry, 27,* 343–355.

Tremblay, R. E., LeBlanc, M., & Schwartzman, A. E. (1988). The predictive power of first-grade peer and teacher ratings of behavior: Sex differences in antisocial behavior and personality at adolescence. *Journal of Abnormal Child Psychology, 16,* 571–583.

Tryon, A. S. & Keane, S. P. (1991). Popular and aggressive boys' initial social interaction patterns in cooperative and competitive settings. *Journal of Abnormal Child Psychology, 19,* 395–406.

Underwood, M. K., Kupersmidt, J. B., & Coie, J. D. (1996). Childhood peer sociometric status and aggression as predictors of adolescent childbearing. *Journal of Research on Adolescence, 6* , 201–223.

van Schie, E. G. M., & Wiegman, O. (1997). Children and videogames: Leisure activities, aggression, social integration, and school performance. *Journal of Applied Social Psychology, 27,* 1175–1194.

Vitaro, F., Tremblay, R. E., Kerr, M., Pagani, L., & Bukowski, W. M. (1997). Disruptiveness, friends' characteristics, and delinquency in early adolescence: A test of two competing models of development. *Child Development, 68,* 676–689.

Warm, T. R. (1997). The role of teasing in development and vice versa. *Journal of Developmental &*
Behavioral Pediatrics, 18, 97–101.

Wasserstein, S. B., & La Greca, A. M. (1996). Can peer support buffer against behavioral consequences of parental discord? *Journal of Clinical Child Psychology, 25,* 177–182.

Weisz, J. R., & Weisz, B. (1990). The impact of methodological factors on child psychotherapy outcome research. *Journal of Abnormal Child Psychology, 18,* 639–670.

Wentzel, K. R., & Asher, S. R. (1995). The academic lives of neglected, rejected, popular, and controversial children. *Child Development, 66,* 754–763.

Whalen, C. K., & Henker, B. (1985). The social worlds of hyperactive (ADHD) children. *Clinical Psychology Review, 5,* 1–32.

Wilson, G. T. (1996). Manual-based treatments: The clinical application of research findings. *Behaviour Research and Therapy, 34,* 295–315.

Zarbatany, L., Hartmann, D. P., & Rankin, D. B. (1990). The psychological functions of preadolescent peer activities. *Child Development, 61,* 1067–1080.

Zarbatany, L., McDougall, P., & Hymel, S. (2000). Gender-differentiated experience in the peer culture: Links to intimacy in preadolescence. *Social Development, 9,* 62–79.

Zentall, S. S. (1989). Self-control training with hyperactive and impulsive children. In J. N. Hughes & R.J. Hall (Eds.), *Cognitive-behavioral psychology in the schools* (p. 305–346). New York: Guilford.

Index